THE MYSTERY OF X-5

The Mystery of X-5

Lieutenant H. Henty-Creer's
Attack on the *Tirpitz*

by

FRANK WALKER
AND
PAMELA MELLOR

Foreword by
Vice Admiral Sir Arthur Hezlet
KBE, CB, DSO, DSC, DL

WILLIAM KIMBER · LONDON

First published in 1988 by
WILLIAM KIMBER & CO. LIMITED
100 Jermyn Street, London SW1Y 6EE

Parts I and III, © Pamela Mellor, 1988
Part II, Chapter 1 and 2, © Pamela Mellor, 1988
Part II, Chapter 3, © Frank Walker, 1988
Part IV, © Frank Walker, 1988

ISBN 0-7183-0628-7

Photoset in North Wales by
Derek Doyle & Associates Mold, Clwyd
and printed and bound in Great Britain by
Adlard and Son Limited
Dorking, Surrey, and Letchworth, Hertfordshire

For all who took part in the Tirpitz attack,
especially the four valiant men
who lost their lives in X-5

Frank Walker

For Gerard
who has been steadfast
through all difficulties

Pam

Contents

List of Illustrations

List of Maps

Foreword

by
Vice Admiral Sir Arthur Hezlet, KBE, CB, DSO, DSC, DL

It all now seems a very long time ago, but this book, especially the parts written by Henty himself, bring it all back vividly to me. I first met Henty at the Kyles of Bute Hydropathic Hotel which had just been taken over as the training base for this very brave enterprise. I was only a few years older than he was but of very different background and experience. I was a regular naval officer and already an experienced operational submarine captain sent to train volunteers to man the X-craft. However Henty and I got on well at once. I found him to be head and shoulders above his colleagues of the first training class. He was a delightful personality with a marvellous sense of humour while inside him burned a fire and determination to succeed. One would never have realised his limited education. I would have taken him for a university graduate rather than someone who had left school at thirteen. We got on together almost as equals and when the time came to select the operational X-craft captains from amongst the trainees, I had no hesitation whatever in recommending Henty as by far the best of the RNVR officers.

The book touches upon the strategic priority that the 'powers that be' put upon Operation Source, as the attack on the *Tirpitz* was called. The daily pressure by signal, letter and telephone put on Commander Ingram to mount the attack in March 1943 and to get a move on, was intense. My duties were not only training but to advise on operational matters too. To us fell much of the responsibility for developing the towing of X-craft by large submarines and the methods of attack. The accident to *X-3* was the final blow and the operation had to be put off until the autumn. I then left the X-craft business and went back to command an operational submarine.

I was, of course, pleased when my submarine was selected to tow an X-craft to North Norway and more so when I found out that we were to tow *X-5* with Henty in command. When we met again he had been promoted to lieutenant and he was, I thought, slightly

11

quieter with a greater air of responsibility. I was, of course very busy on the week-long voyage to the north and in the crowded wardroom of my submarine we had little time to talk. I had no doubt, however, that the fire within him burned as fiercely as ever and was now joined with an efficiency and experience which seemed bound to succeed. When I finally said goodbye to him and wished him luck just before slipping X-5, he seemed almost in a hurry to be gone and to get on with it. It never seemed to occur to either of us that we might never meet again.

Of what happened in the attack, at the time, I had no information. All I knew was that X-5 did not return and that we finally had to go home without her. Indeed it was not until after the war that I read the details in the despatches. The determination and courage of the Henty-Creer family to try and find the truth fill me with admiration.

The awarding or withholding of decorations and medals will always be bedevilled with controversy. Clearly the authorities try to do this difficult business as impartially and fairly as possible. Nevertheless for Henty to be merely 'mentioned in despatches' for his outstanding services to his country on this occasion and in which he made the supreme sacrifice, leaves one incredulous. The dilemma of the Admiralty and the rules and regulations which clouded the subsequent decisions have been fairly quoted in the book. Personally I agree with the Flag Officer (Submarines) original recommendation that Henty, Place and Cameron should all receive the highest decoration. This was right for these outstandingly brave men and I think it was a great pity that this recommendation was ever altered. I hope this book will be accepted not only as an interesting contribution to the history of this operation but as drawing attention to this previously little known naval hero.

Bovagh House
Aghadowey
Co. Londonderry
Northern Ireland

Prologue

This book is dedicated to Henty Henty-Creer and his crew of the miniature submarine *X-5* which, with her sister ships *X-6* and *X-7*, attacked the giant German battleship *Tirpitz* in Kaafjord in the far north of Norway on 22nd September 1943. Her crew consisted of:

Lieutenant Henty Henty-Creer, RNVR – Commanding Officer
Sub-Lieutenant D.J. Malcolm, RNVR – First Lieutenant
Sub-Lieutenant T.J. Nelson, RNVR – Diving Officer
Engineroom Articifer R.J. Mortiboys, RN – Engineer

The captains of *X-6* and *X-7* survived the war to tell their stories and both were awarded the VC. Henty and his crew did not survive and therefore had no tale to tell. Some were Mentioned in Despatches.

Many firmly believe that *X-5* not only reached her target but successfully laid her charges under the stern of *Tirpitz* and that her charges played a large part in crippling the giant ship. Some people may say, 'Why try and prove this? It happened over forty years ago and so many unsung heroes lost their lives in the war.' The answer lies in the sworn statements made shortly after the war by eye witnesses which give good evidence of *X-5*'s success but never received any official acknowledgement.

This book is an attempt to show that Henty and his crew in *Platypus* – officially *X-5* – did in fact all or more than could have been expected of them and that they fully deserved an honoured place in history. It describes Henty's background, what motivated him, a description of the attack, evidence of events and recent actions to try and locate any remains of *X-5*, and, in conclusion, ideas as to what may really have happened.

Acknowledgements

I wish to record my gratitude to Mr Ken Hudspeth, DSC and two bars, for his invaluable and untiring help in analysing the attack on *Tirpitz* and in providing technical background on the intricacies of X-craft, which he knew so well and commanded with such distinction; to Rear Admiral Godfrey Place, VC, CB, DSC, for his cooperation; to Dr Guenther Sachsse, German Ministry of Defence explosives expert, to Emeritus Professor of Chemistry at Newcastle University, Geoffrey Curthoys, and to the Materials Research Laboratories of the Australian Department of Defence for their advice on explosives; to the staff of the German Military Archives at Freiburg, and the Public Record Office and the Admiralty in London; to the ever-efficient Frau Ines Hoffmann-Schaeffer, of the Information Branch of the Australian Embassy, Bonn, for helping me as willingly after my retirement as she did when she was on my staff, and to Lieutenant-Colonel Gerard Mellor and his wife Pamela for assisting my research and making available their family documents and correspondence.

F.B. Walker

My grateful thanks for their help and forebearance to William Kimber, Oliver Colman, Amy Myers and Clifford Cobb.

In addition, I would like to add my thanks to Desmond Wetton (*Daily Telegraph* Naval Correspondent) who put me on the road to Kaafjord, and to John Owen (*Daily Telegraph*) for good reporting.

Pamela Mellor

Introduction

by
Pamela Mellor

In November 1834 a small ship called the *Thistle* put in to a strange bay at the bottom of the world to found a faraway settlement that in time was to become the state of Victoria, Australia. The leaders of this party were Edward and Stephen, sons of Thomas Henty.

Thomas Henty was a famous breeder of Merino sheep from whose flocks were developed the foundation of the Australian wool industry. History was made.

One hundred years later another small craft called *Platypus* put into a strange bay at the top of the world. The captain of this boat was also a Henty, a direct descendant of one of those Henty brothers who had founded that settlement in Victoria. This time, however, the mission was one of destruction, no less than that of the most powerful battleship the world had ever seen. Germany's pride – the *Tirpitz*.

Whereas the Henty brothers of 1834 have become an integral part of the history of Australia and their actions feted every year at the scene of their triumph, Portland, the deed of their 1943 descendant at Kaafjord in Northern Lappland has been written off and forgotten by his superiors, the Royal Navy, even though other participants in the action were highly decorated and their names recorded for posterity.

Thomas Henty, father of Stephen, came from a long-established Sussex family, who had farmed there for many generations. Thomas was the leading breeder in England of the Merino sheep. He was barred from many competitions so that some others could have a chance! He had exported some of his breeding stock to Macarthur, who had found them a great success and this connection led in due course to the ultimate wealth of Australia through the wool trade. Eventually he decided to emigrate to Australia himself.

In 1829 Thomas chartered the ship *Caroline* in which he sent out an advance party of some of his sons, forty servants and farm labourers, breeding stock (not only his Merinos but also bloodstock from which derived the famous Egremont strain) together with supplies and farm implements, etc., The latter included a plough which was to turn the first sod in Victoria (and which today can be seen in a museum in Portland, Victoria).

Thomas had been assigned 80,000 acres in a new colony being formed on the Swan River. The family did not think it altogether suitable when they saw it, the sheep died and did not take to the countryside. They eventually settled at Launceston in Tasmania, from where they sent out various search parties to find better land. This they found in unexplored land at Portland and formed their settlement there in 1834, two years before Bateman formed his settlement at Melbourne.

Henty's maternal grandmother came from the Cobham family whose history goes back many hundreds of years. They came from Northern Kent and amongst other places built Cooling Castle in Kent and Caister Castle in Norfolk.

As the fifteenth century began, the then Lord Cobham, also known as Sir John Oldcastle, was a personal friend of King Henry V, whose brother Humphrey married a Cobham heiress.

Lord Cobham was the leader of the Lollards, a breakaway religious movement. He finished up at the stake. Some say he was roasted to death over a slow fire. A plaque was for some years outside St Giles Church, London commemorating this. In somewhat different guise, he is believed to have been the model for Shakespeare's Sir John Falstaff. (The present Cobham title belongs to a later creation and had no connection with the Cobhams of this story.)

Henty was born in Sydney, Australia, in March 1920. His father Reginald came from a seafaring family originating from the Isle of Man. He and his twin brother, Bertie, both joined the navy at an early age; indeed they were two of the first officers commissioned in the then newly formed Royal Australian Navy. They were renowned for their initiative and boisterous behaviour. Soon after Henty's birth his father was appointed captain of the training ship *Tingara*, anchored in Sydney harbour. This ship had originally been built for the luxury passenger trade under sail between England and Australia. It was somewhat unique as a naval ship in that the captain's quarters included quarters for his family. Thus Henty was introduced to naval life at a very early age.

Henty's mother came from a well known early Australian

pioneering family. Her grandfather, Richmond Henty, was the eldest son of Stephen Henty, one of the Henty brothers who founded the settlement at Portland Bay in 1834 and who thus became one of the founding fathers of the State of Victoria. The centenary of their settlement was celebrated in 1934 and was attended by HRH the Duke of Gloucester.

Richmond himself was the first white baby to be born in Portland and thus the first white baby to be born in what was to become the state of Victoria.

Henty was tall, very slim with blue eyes and copper hair. As a boy he went to Gibbs' Preparatory School but, from the age of fourteen he had to go out and earn his living. At school he made many friends and wrote to the father of one of them in the hope of getting a job. He was no less than Alexander Korda, the mogul of the British film industry. Korda was very impressed by the boy's initiative and gave him a job straight away, although it was not on the acting side which Henty had hankered for.

At this time the family lived in Sidmouth, Devon, and Henty was left to look after himself for some time, staying at an hotel in South Kensington in which the family had made their headquarters during travels. His day started at 6 a.m. and he worked so hard and proved so popular that he quickly gained promotion.

In 1940 he was sent to Canada as a director of photography for the filming of *49th Parallel*. He had been offered exemption which he did not want. By now the war was a year old and Henty was desperate to get into the fighting. As soon as he returned to England he promptly joined the Navy as an AB in Special Service. Eventually he was sent to King Alfred for officer training.

In spite of the fact that he had left school at the age of thirteen, he passed out third of his course of 100. He was therefore given the choice of what branch he wished to join. Above all he wanted to be his own master and was therefore keen on MTBs. However, having read about Japanese miniature submarines, to miniature submarines he went.

At Barrow-on-Furness he watched the building of these experimental craft together with constant modifications to suit new ideas and the idiosyncrasies of their individual future commanders. Henty was the first to give his submarine a name, choosing *Platypus* as being a water animal which laid eggs. Then, with their craft they went up to Scotland to do their training. During this period Henty wrote his experiences. These are recorded in *Wavy Navy Occasions*.

PART ONE

Wavy Navy Occasions

The Autobiography of
Lieutenant Henty Henty-Creer

'To souls like these, in mutual friendship joined, Heaven dares entrust the cause of human kind.'

Addison 'The Campaign'

I

My First Ship

What a lot of colour can be crammed into one's first twenty years! The palette of my life has been so richly daubed, that the few black and grey lumps, added in the last few years, make a fine foil for all the gay and brilliant hues that a kind fate squeezed out with lavish hand, over a long period.

I was christened in the wardroom of a destroyer commanded by my father, but my earliest memories take me back to a naval training ship, which swung at anchor a few hundred yards from shore in one of the loveliest bays of Sydney Harbour.

That fine old ship *Tingara*, formerly named *Sabroan*, dated from 1866, was the largest composite ship ever built. She was 2,000 odd tons, 317 feet in length, with a forty foot beam and was of solid teak. She carried in her heyday, an acre of canvas, and must have been a lovely sight running with the best of those early clippers to Sydney and Melbourne, in seventy to eighty days. Her passenger accommodation was unequalled and our quarters were certainly spacious and luxurious. When the Navy took her over she was shorn of much of her beauty and spent the rest of her days as a training ship, only leaving her buoy in Rose Bay for a yearly refit at Cockatoo Island dry dock – and then ignominiously in tow.

My mother's drawing room – the old saloon – had half a dozen square ports, from which we had a continually changing view of the bay, according to wind and tide. All the windows in our quarters were squared ports from which we could see and hear all the boat work of the young trainees – some three hundred all told. At five I could lower a boat with the best of them, even though the craft I practised on, was a boot of my father's – with the laces for stays and the key of the nursery for davits. I knew every order and every bosun's pipe.

At sunset when the bugle went and the white ensign was furled for the night, we meticulously stood to attention at the salute – facing aft, no matter where we were on board, or what game we were engaged on. Not until the last notes had died away were activities resumed as if no break had occurred. Hats off to Naval training where routine becomes as automatic as breathing!

From the sternwalk we could often see the rival sixteen footers with their enormous spread of canvas, tearing across the harbour, their wet crews hanging precariously over the gunwale. Admiral Dumaresq was fond of this sport and I little thought then when watching his craft racing my father's, that one day his range finder at HMS King Alfred, would give me some complicated moments.

When our birthdays occurred, the first lieutenant 'dressed ship'. Flags were hung from stem to stern and the motor boat plied to and fro from the jetty bringing on board our young guests, their mothers and nurses.

The ship and my father, to us a distinguished figure in his naval uniform and brass hat, had faded out of the picture by the time I had grown too big for the smart little sailor suit made on board for me by the ship's tailor. Our bulldog, by the way, also wore a sailor suit and had general service ribbons up, but his differed from mine in that there was no back to his trousers!

My mother had unusual views on education and the upbringing of the young. And fortunately for us – she believed in travel for children. She had divorced my father. We saw more of the world in our first decade than most people see in a lifetime and we learned geography in a very pleasant way.

II

Youth's Odyssey

When I was seven we went to Fiji and spent a carefree year with a godmother, who had leased a few hundred acres from the Government and was engaged in a variety of agricultural projects.

To catch our next boat overseas, we made a three-day journey

from Suva in a filthy little twenty-five ton coaster, boasting only two
cabins, both of which were occupied on our first night by an
incredible assortment of nationalities, so that we were obliged to
sleep on deck amidst crates of fowls, tethered live stock, heaps of
copra and other very pungent items. To get to the lavatory and wash
basin – there was no bath – we had to go through the ladies' cabin.
We found this a very unpleasant arrangement, for the four bunks
seemed full of prostrate women and babies, and even the floor was
crowded with sleeping forms, and we had to pick our way very
carefully to avoid them.

We stopped at little settlements and lonely out-posts, off the
tracks of the big steamers, every few hours to take off weird cargoes.
At one place, too shallow at low tide for our small craft, the skipper
tossed overboard a parcel of mail in a kerosene tin wrapped in
waterproof. We watched it drift with the current to the water's edge
where a lonely figure, silhouetted against the fringe of mangroves,
stood waiting. We could see no habitation but were told by the
skipper that the place was called Londoni and that two men and one
woman had lived like hermits there for years, never speaking to each
other, their only link with the outside world our little tub.

New Caledonia and Malaya came next: a year in the heart of the
peninsula, on a rubber plantation, where life was made exciting by a
dashing young uncle who had a penchant for racing cars and fancy
dress dances, and a genius for arranging treats for the young, and
our nursery was presided over by a fat Chinese amah of marvellous
imperturbility.

Ceylon, and months on a tea estate with another uncle and a
grandmother – where life was rather more formal, with a Tamil
butler who watched over us suspiciously. But here, too, we found
plenty to interest us on long walks. There were twenty miles of road
on the estate, with tea growing on the hillsides and rubber on the
lowlands.

After a short time in England, Denmark and Belgium gave us
some happy times. Then my mother took a map, shut her eyes,
twirled a pencil three times and where the point landed we went: to
Montreux, Switzerland, for the year that was to polish me up for
entry to Dartmouth.

Then just as the Naval College loomed nearer, our life suddenly
became a muddle. England went off the gold standard and crashing
on that came the Malayan tin slump which swept away a goodly
portion of our income. Just about that time too the 'axe' began to

fall heavily in Naval circles. These events had a strong bearing on my life, for my mother, on the advice of a famous old admiral, decided against a Naval career for me, saying there would be no future for me there.

We returned to England, where I went to Gibbs' school, we then went down to Devon to lick our financial wounds and mark time till the markets improved. Those markets were not to rise till long after I had got myself a job, at the age of fourteen, in a film studio owned by Alexander Korda, the father of one of my school friends, and by that time I was well launched on my film career, and thought I could see a clear path to fame and fortune as a film magnate, so I did not shed tears over Dartmouth as I might have done had I been at a loose end.

This charming Hungarian – Alexander Korda – was about to put British films on the map and I was lucky to be taken under his kindly wing, and to get in on the ground floor before the big studios at Denham were built. London Film Productions was in its infancy then and operating from Elstree, the atmosphere was like a great family party.

I started on the lowest rung and worked hard. For the first few months I lived in the shabby old Naval and Military Hotel in South Kensington. I had to leave for work after a very early breakfast, scrounged by the night porter – a temperamental egg and stale bread – and got back at night almost too tired to eat. More often than not, dinner was 'off' and I tumbled straight into bed – very lonely and forlorn.

I did not enjoy those 'bachelor' few months before my mother came back to London, although Mr Korda (later Sir Alexander) was wonderfully kind to me. On Sundays, when not working, I spent the day in his Hampstead home.

A ski-ing holiday in the Austrian Tyrol with his son Peter made a happy break from a strenuous job. For there were no eight hour days in the career I had chosen and working on such films as *As You Like It*, for which Elizabeth Bergner had a habit of arriving at the studio about mid-day and working through the night, was very trying for everybody. Holidays were few and far between and life was often a dreary treadmill.

III

49th Parallel to the Arctic Circle

In the years that followed I climbed slowly up the film ladder having a finger in most of the big productions, my eye always on my goal – to become a director.

Korda's imagination and financial wizardry brought well deserved fame to Denham. To the big studios, which covered twenty-eight acres, came great continental directors, world-famous stars of film and stage, great actors, actresses, musicians, artists, technicians and craftsmen. And in those early days as Korda's protégé I was introduced to all the great ones. I met H.G. Wells, J.M. Barrie, Baroness Orczy, and Paderewski, to mention only a few. It was an enormous swirling world of many nationalities.

I was fascinated by this fantastic world of make-believe – the mixture of art and artifice which is the essence of film-making. I saw commonplace faces given allure and beauty by the cameraman; I saw great actors and actresses moved by the director like puppets across the stage, 'cabined and confined' by the exacting tape measure; I saw great forests and palatial palaces grow overnight.

I watched René Clair, Zoltan Korda, Michael Powell, Joseph Sternberg, Emeric Pressberger, Feyder and a host of others at work directing and writing. I worked with Hal Rosson, Lee Garmes, Harry Stradling, Georges Perinal, Freddy Young and other great cameramen, always absorbing film technique. These few years with the camera would be invaluable when my day came to direct.

In the winter of 1939 I went over to France on an army film to get French sets and shots of the British and French dispositions and the rumours I heard everywhere gave me furiously to think. We moved, too, among the French regiments whose utter lack of enthusiasm for the task ahead was deeply shocking to us all; even in the cafés the very atmosphere reeked of Gallic indifference and shoulder-shrugging.

As soon as my part in the army film was finished, I volunteered for the Navy, but on the very evening I had passed my medical, Michael Powell persuaded me to join his *49th Parallel* expedition which the Ministry of Information was sponsoring. As it was considered a film of national importance, leave was granted for three months. A year was to pass before I was free to join up.

The outfit did 16,000 miles in three months travelling along the 49th parallel over vast tracts of country from Montreal to the Rockies, then up north to Churchill on the shores of Hudson's Bay, where our little expedition ship had been chartered to take us across Ungava Bay and down the Labrador coast to the Bay of Islands, Newfoundland. It was a wonderful trip and a great finish to one chapter of my life.

Men in all these outposts were hard-bitten and fine. It was refreshing to talk to real people whose talk was not centred on money and ambition of some sort or another, but on their struggles to maintain their hold on these places where only real fighters could survive.

During our tour there had been many trials and tribulations for everyone, and some plane sequences on Lake Dubonnet had almost ended in casualties. At Cornerbrook, Newfoundland, we had enough adventures with the synthetic submarine to fill half a dozen chapters. This craft, designed by our art director David Rawnsley and built in Halifax, Nova Scotia, had been transported by train and ship to the Bay of Islands, where it was to be finally blown up. I little thought then, that a year or so later I should be playing about in British waters with a real submarine.

IV

Arrival at 'The Nest' and Bellbottoms

My last few minutes as a free citizen ticked away on Lowestoft platform. Behind the iron gates I could see the stocky figure of a chief petty officer whose small escort party in gaiters flanked him impressively. At last I was through the barrier with my old leather suitcase, with its heavy incrustations of foreign labels, and I stopped in front of the group and asked the way to the Naval barracks.

'Blimey!' said the Chief and winked at the others. 'Just you come along with me ... Hey! You, Jack! Take his case ... Ah yes ... Nice day, ain't it?'

The people waiting at the bus stop seemed extraordinarily interested in me. The four seamen in my escort stopped the crowd getting into the bus and I was ushered in first. By now it was obvious to me the Navy was out for enjoyment. All the passengers kept turning round and whispering to each other and eyeing me.

'You don't seem to get many recruits here, Chief?'

'Oh yes, indeed. We get our share. You ain't the first by any measure of means.'

I did not realise that everyone thought I was a captured deserter being taken back to barracks and that my escort was playing up to them.

The bus climbed a sloping road above the sea and stopped at a guarded gateway. This time I had to carry my own bag, but still my escort hung close. Crowds of sailors were coming out and they too watched me with a quite uncomfortable interest, as we went down to a large pre-war theatre.

I found myself in a one-time dressing room, with a couple of Scottish fishermen in rough mended suits and heavy jerseys, and a large black man from Cardiff, who seemed bemused and dazed by his surroundings. We were a strange quartet and we eyed each other with interest.

The young fisherlad, a tough little kiltie with a weather-beaten cap perched on the back of his head, and a fag in one corner of his expansive mouth, looked like one of the Dead-End Kids. His elderly companion was a study in reserved nervousness as he stood looking out through the little window on the crowded 'cells' opposite. He puffed at a stained clay pipe which soon filled the small place with a heavy pall of smoke.

For a long half hour we waited, and I tried to make contact, but could feel a subtle barrier between us, which was rather disconcerting. For years I had been rubbing shoulders with all sorts of men – 'chippies', 'sparks', scene shifters, plasterers, moulders and fitters, all staunch trade unionists – and had got on well with all of them, but these three were of another world. They had been 'down to the sea in ships' for most of their lives and they were rugged and tough. I, unfortunately, had never looked 'tough' and have always been cursed by a look of extreme youth.

The door suddenly swung open and a petty officer stood facing us. His looks filled us with speculation, as he flicked a keen knife glance at each of us, and as suddenly left. We had shot up off our bench, all rather keen on making a good impression, and we felt deflated after his silent, jack-in-the-box entrance and exit.

'My, oh my!' said the black man. 'Diss place about gives me the jitters.'

The elderly fisherman tossed his head and laughed, 'Never mind, Sam. Ut's us what's fighting this war. Them's lost without us!'

'Ah hope so, sah ... Ah hopes you is right!' The room was hot and beads of perspiration fell down his nervous face which he wiped agitatedly with a red rag.

The door flew open and we saw a commander standing in the corridor, flanked by several lesser lights. The fierce expression through his glasses was that of a much tried man. 'Open that window, petty officer.' An old fellow who had the air of our studio commissionaire gave us an appraising look as he jumped to obey.

'What's your name?' the commander asked the black man.

'Ma name, sah?'

'Yes, that's what I said.'

'Well, sah, somes calls me Frankling J. McPherson. Ah, er – '

'Yes, that's all right. What did you do?'

'Ah was a fireman in – '

'You mean a stoker?'

'No, sah! Ah means a fireman!'

'You put coal into a ship's furnace, didn't you?' severely corrected the great man.

'Yes, sah ... Dat's what ah been trying to tell you!'

'Next!' said the commander, now slightly ruffled.

Together came the reply, 'Fishin', sir.'

'Aberdeen?'

'Aye. That was it, sir.'

'Long?'

'All me life,' said the elderly one. The Dead-End Kid drew himself up to his full five feet: 'Since I was eight, sir.'

The commander turned to me: 'I suppose *you*,' he said with withering scorn, 'have come from Rex House?'

'Yes, sir.' I had been put down for Special Operations.

'One of those bloody bright yachtsmen they keep sending me.

Last week a fellow told me he had sailed across the North Sea! I suppose you have too. Well, let me inform you that there are bloody great cart tracks across the North Sea, so you can bloody well forget about that!' and out he went.

Of the colourful quartet, I suppose I was the most depressed. Volunteers from Rex House certainly were not popular here!

We followed the cheerful petty officer across the stage and found ourselves in a queue for a billet, where I ultimately collected my chit and received orders to report next morning at nine o'clock.

The sunshine seemed very good when I got outside past the main gates. The crowd of little urchins with their box carts who fought to carry my suitcase, seemed of another world and I began to thaw once more as we went up the hill to the bus stop. Life was certainly showing me new facets.

The thoughts of my film career and my exemption which I had thrown up so blithely the day before suddenly came back. What a fool I had been to throw freedom away so casually. The bus conductor must have sensed my feelings:

'Just joined the Nest?'

'Yes, I have.'

'Aye, well, it's tough at first they say. But you won't be long there, lad!'

My God! I thought. I hope not!

This was a seaport and my civilian clothes made me feel uncomfortably conspicuous. I hoped I would soon have my outfit.

At last I found the number of my billet and with it the usual crowd of little children clustering round the gate watching curiously as I stood waiting for the answer to my knock. There was a rustle of paper being picked up off the floor inside – a sound I could not interpret then but one I was to grow accustomed to in the months that followed. Then the door was opened by a little woman in a bright red jersey and soiled apron who looked up at me with surprise as I handed over the billeting chit. This she took and burst out laughing. 'Come in, come in and make yourself at home.'

I followed her to a little room flooded in light and smelling horribly of furniture polish, where three men sat at a meal; one was in his shirt sleeves, one in a singlet and the third in full sailor's kit. They all paused in their eating to sum me up.

'Blimey, mates, wot 'ave we 'ere?' said one.

'Nah then, lads, just you wake yourselves up and make room for a new chum!' the woman ordered and hustled off to get my whack –

some thick bread and margarine and a mug of tea.

I sat down to this unattractive meal and there was a silence broken at last by the high-pitched voice of the hostess: 'Just joined 'e 'as too, what do you know about that?'

A little pinched-faced fellow took a hefty bite out of his slice of bread. 'Blimey, mum, there's a fool born every minute.'

'Couldn't you keep out?' came from the one in shirt sleeves. My retort, 'I didn't wan't to,' seemed to flatten them. 'Coo-er ... You ain't going to tell us you *volunteered*?'

'Yes! Why not?'

The three took quick gulps of tea. I suspected they were pulling my leg and watched them warily.

'Blimey! Were you in trouble or something?' I shook my head. 'What about you fellows?' I asked.

'Us? We was conscripted.'

'Yes, that was as 'ow *we* come in.'

'Bloody cryin' shame I calls it,' said the third. And they watched me with wonder.

The quiet one in the singlet went on brooding.

After we had eaten, the woman beckoned me. 'Well, I'll show you your bed. Bit crowded I must confess, but there's a war on, you know!'

I followed her up the stairs to a little dark back room almost filled by a large double bed. Between the bed and the wall was a camp stretcher and under the window a chair that had lost its seat. A door led out into an even smaller room and one could just squeeze through this thoroughfare from the top of the stairs, past a small chest of drawers.

Large religious pictures were on the walls which were covered with a dark grey paper from which most of the flowers had faded. 'It will be a bit crowded tonight,' the little woman remarked as she drew the blackout curtains.

'That's all right, I don't mind sharing the room with someone else,' I said, knowing I should have to make the best of things and subconsciously patting myself on the back.

She looked at me in amazement and I saw I had dropped a brick. 'There's *four* in this room, you know.'

'Well, I'm sorry,' I said firmly, 'but we had better settle this right away. I don't mind sharing a *room*, but I'm not sharing a bed with anyone. I never have done and I don't intend to start now ... war or no war!'

She took it coolly. 'That's all right, I don't expect Fred will mind. *You* take the little bed.' Then confidentially, 'I know 'as 'ow you feel ... and I'm not saying I blame you! Some of them is dirt and that's the gospel truth.'

The arrival of the soap box boys with my rather expensive luggage had its effect, for she helped me in with it, saying in rather apologetic tones: 'I'm sorry about the room ... best I can do. You see I'm billeted for six in this house!'

Not bad business for her – a tiny house of three small bedrooms, for eight people; and one of them, the best one – kept for herself and her husband.

The room was warm and I felt ready for bed. The lad finished his shirts, the woman her washing up. I asked if I could have a wash. 'If you get your towel, I'll wash out this sink for you.'

So that was it! The sink stared at me with its face old and spotted, its wrinkles of grease and lathers of soap. The filthy water with un-savoury scraps of food was gurgling down the plughole. All my senses recoiled. In the days that followed, that sink saw some hefty morning scuffles, for we all shaved over the pots and pans, and often over last night's dirty dishes. There were five of us, and humour in the early morning was salty.

I turned in early hoping the others would be a peaceful lot, but at about eleven, the stairs creaked with noisy footsteps and the high-pitched voice of the woman followed them up; one was drunk. In a second or two a sailor stood in my doorway.

'Who's this bloody sod in my bed?' he asked truculently.

I expected trouble and sat up. He looked at me furiously, then his mood changed swiftly and with a magnificent wave of his hand, he said benevolently: 'It's all right, mate ... it's yours ... You keep it.' And passed into the next room to the double bed. The other two came up and then turned in, in their underclothes. I wondered where the 'Tom Cat' would shake down when he came off the tiles. Soon after the lights went out and a sour voice said in the darkness: 'And for Christ's sake don't stick your bloody knees in my stomach tonight!'

My bed was lumpy and I could not sleep. There were no sheets and the blankets were thin. The pillows smelled. I pushed them on the floor and used my overcoat instead.

The day dawned noisily to the raucous shouts of the woman below. Soon a general mêlée for the sink absorbed the attentions of the household. I dressed rather leisurely for I had been told not to report till after nine.

During breakfast – a tiny bit of bacon on a piece of bread – a tall Yorkshireman came in from a very prolonged week-end leave and everyone chorused, 'Hello Yorkie!' in surprised unison. He was a happy-faced fellow and laughed at their fears. He had been 'adrift' before and knew the ropes. His cheery bonhomie and 'What ho, mate,' in greeting me, was very pleasant to a novice and I was glad that he immediately took me under his wing.

Breakfast over we followed the others down the little cinder path through the back gate. 'No one's supposed to use the front door,' Yorkie advised as we walked beside the railway lines behind that row of squalid little houses. To the base a mile away.

Yorkie seemed to know everybody and by the time we got to the lower gate, there must have been a dozen fellows around me. He put me wise to many things. It was a good idea to get a crowd of fellows around you as soon as possible, he told me. If they liked you they would stand by your interests and you never knew when they would come in handy. Each one watched the drafting notices for his cobbers, and as soon as a name appeared they would meet if possible in the pub for a 'last one'.

I went back to the room I had been in yesterday, passing through the crowded hall up across the stage. There was a lot of gold braid and my passage was eyed with interest. Half way across a voice called out, 'Hey you – what do you want?' And I turned to a lieutenant-commander.

'I'm joining up, sir.'

He seemed a bit surprised: 'Oh, really? ... I see ... well, er, good luck,' and turned hastily away.

The little room was packed. New faces were sandwiched in and the smoke hung like a cloud. I felt more confident now and took a little more interest in my fellow 'sheep' looking so very self-conscious in their civvies amongst the mass of uniforms. This showed in the way they pulled at their fags and the overstrained little jokes. After half an hour we went backstage and out to a long block out-house, where we stood about outside in a ragged line. Men passed with rifles and fixed bayonets, with semaphore flags, with blankets – these were on draft – with wheel barrows, with pails and scrubbers. Men went through the mystery door and men came out.

We stood and waited. An hour went by before our turn came. The air was hot and sweaty – the smell of the unwashed herd, filled the little room where we were ordered to take off everything but our pants.

The training ship *Tingara* to which Henty-Creer's father (inset: Commander Reginald Creer) was appointed Captain soon after Henty's birth

(*Left*) Henty and his sister Deirdre aboard the *Moldavia*. (*Right*) Henty as a boy

Henty (seated right) on the set of *Knight Without Armour*

Standing in bare feet, we had another long spell of waiting. A black man was ahead of me and at last went in through the curtains but the doctor had not put in an appearance. Two sick bay attendants stamped our cards after an argument with our guide, and we dressed again.

'These are for the eye test, sir!' said a sick bay petty officer. When the doctor came:

'Already had their medical, have they?'

'Yes, all correct sir.'

The black man went in. The doctor was now sitting at his desk and watched him reading the letters on the board at the far end of the room, then called him over. 'Now Sam, read out those numbers,' and he flicked over the small pages of a multi-coloured spotted number sheet. Sam was quiet, his face stubborn, his expression 'shut in'.

'You speak English?' asked the doctor.

'I is an Englishman, sir,' the black man answered proudly. 'I is from Cardiff.'

'Well, call out the figures.'

Sam could read, but he was colour-blind. 'You ain't trying to fool me, is you, sah?' he asked in a worried voice.

'No, Sam, that's all right – you will be a stoker. All right?'

'You means a fireman?'

'Yes – all the same – stoker, fireman!'

Then the form was handed over.

'Right oh, chum, sign here – next one – come on, Jack, you're in the Andrew now, shake it up. Shake it up.'

'All right, all right, don't bloody well shout at me,' said an elderly fisherman behind.

Behind the counter, banter stopped and they eyed him with the critical glance of the service towards civilians. I wondered later how much of his kit they robbed him of to get even with his sturdy independence.

We went through another door rather like mass produced goods on a conveyor belt, and into a small caged-off structure on one side of the large hall where two sailors took my canvas kit bag, up-ending it on the floor. While one made up my name in black letters, the other relieved me of my civilian clothing.

An amazing process, this change-over into a new world. The two sailors went to great lengths to make me a 'tiddly sailor' as they called it, and I watched with horror as they attacked my jacket with a jack knife to lower the front and then bent my cap to a 'proper shape'. I felt rather like a sardine, but they would not let me get a bigger suit.

'Better 'ave it close fitting, see? ... You know what the girls like!'

They worked on my cap ribbon and made a 'tiddly' bow over the left ear. 'Mind yew – it's only for them what 'as crossed the line, see? ... but I expect you'll get away with it!'

I learnt afterwards that I should have 'dropped them half-a-crown' for their interest – but I was too much occupied with my transformation into a blue jacket to think of such things as tipping. When I at last left that wire cage and floundered into the crowded hall, a little group who had evidently been watching the programme through the mesh, surrounded me.

'Do you want to sell your civvies, mate?' 'No need to keep them things, Jack!'

I shook my head: – 'Nothing doing,' and they fell away to besiege the next one out.

'Cor! Bloody toff too! – blimey, 'e could'ave *given* them things away.'

Someone else came up. 'How are you fixed, mate?'

'Fixed?'

'Yus, how's the doh-ray-me?'

'Cash?'

'Yus, that's it, chum –'

'Oh, I'm all right!'

'Well if you was kind of short, see? ... Just let me know, and – '

'Oh no – but thank's very much.'

Struck by this friendliness I watched him resume his seat on a pile of kit bags amongst a crowd of fellows. They too, watched me with speculative interest, and soon one of their group detached himself and came over to me. 'Couldn't lend me half a dollar, mate?'

'Sorry, mate – not me.'

'Well, I was just thinking like ... '

Then a hand fell on my shoulder and there was Yorkie to extricate me from further importunities.

'Off, mate. You are talking to a cobber of mine!' he said. I thought for a second that sparks were about to fly. They eyed each other and if looks could kill, they both would have had the Last Post played for them.

'Don't you tell me to bugger off!'

'See you outside, mate!' said Yorkie and the man melted away into the mob.

We were given paybooks; we filled in forms; we made our dependent relative allotment. We signed our 'next of kin' paper. The Wrens were patient.

The machine wheels turned slowly. The sheep shepherded at each stage, moved in jerks from hut to hut until we found our section outside the gate once more – a strange band of race and colour, of deep water seamen, butchers, plumbers – and 'nautical actors'!

V

Little Wooden Faces

My uniform was tight and gave me an extraordinary feeling of nakedness in the cold wind and the early spring sunshine. The street was still comparatively empty and I was lucky enough to get a bus down through the town and over the bridge.

People no longer showed interest in me. I was now one more shape lost in the mighty flock in a town that was tired of sailors.

My little band was in one corner of the hall. Soon the bugle blew and we were chased out and somehow found ourselves on the 'lawn' where a squad was being drilled.

'New lot?'

'Yes, sir. Just joined, sir,' said the petty officer.

'I see.' The commander stood out in front and looked us over. Complete silence reigned. He paced up and down, then looked at his watch. 'Any seamen in this lot?' he asked hopefully.

The petty officer was at hand. 'Two, sir.'

'My God!' There was a long pause. Then as if struck by a brain wave, he once more looked us over. 'Well, I expect we will be able to make something out of them!' he said optimistically. 'Carry on, petty officer!'

It slowly dawned on even the most simple during those few minutes of his impersonal surveying that we were so many numbers, little wooden faces in blue. For two days we marched and counter-marched, from nine till twelve-thirty and from two-thirty till four-thirty. We marched until blisters and the sick bay had taken its toll of our class of some thirty of us. Then we spent Saturday morning listening to a gas lecture. 'Just to round your first week off, like,' our instructor said with a smile.

We marched and the six mile daily walk got some of us down. On Saturday afternoon we made for the baths. After five days' marching men certainly needed baths. The place was packed, and with a meek old sailor much in need of a wash, we spent an hour of that day waiting our turn. Hotels were banned and Salvation Army hostels had their queues. I was beginning to despair, when the air raid sirens again blared their ghoulish notes, emptying the baths in splendid time. I, and those used to the London blitzes, availed ourselves of the raid.

VI

On Draft

Yorkie's pals were now my pals who brought me the good news. 'On draft, mate!' they said as they passed me in the street. Yes, sure enough, I found my name on the list – after only one week. I was lucky. Life was good. All my fears of being lost were forgotten, and I and three other SS men piled happily into a lorry to be raced to the local station.

There were a dozen of us in the carriage, but the most amazing was a happy smiling fellow of about twenty-five, who seemed to be having a lot of trouble with his immediate associates. He held a model frigate and was much taken up protecting it from the lurching mob as we swayed along. He was unshaven with his cap on the back of his head, and said little to the 'cracks' that were passed.

One persistent little cockney on draft to the north of Scotland was hot on the scent. 'What are you doing with that, chum?'

'I made it.'

'Blimey, what for?'

'It's a hobby of mine.' His deep pleasant voice drew many imitators.

Others took up the call. 'Do you hear that, mates? It's a hobby!' 'Well I'll be stuffed! Fancy wasting time on a thing like that!'

'Ain't you got nothing better to do?' asked another.

'But I like doing this!'

'Got a girl, chum?'

'Yes I have, I … '

'Well gor blimey, mate, does she sit around and watch you?'

'Of course she does; she likes models too!'

'Blimey, yes, I can see that! She's got one all right.'

This effort was very much appreciated and the hunt was up. There were muffled remarks: 'The fellow's dippy … he's soft!'

A very refined copyist from the East End joined in: 'I say, old boy – are you *erctually* taking your ship to sea with you?' he drawled.

'Yes, why not?'

'What for? Where're you going to put it?'

'Oh, I'll find a spot … Can always tow it you know!'

'Yes, it's a fine sailor you know!'

'Now see here, chum, you're not on the bloody Round Pond now!'

But luckily at that point we rolled into the station yard and piled out.

That boat had a most amazing journey. At every change we made, groups of sailors gathered round. Its owner – he also was Special Service and his name was St Davids – was coming with us. At Liverpool Street station policemen stared, troops turned. Even the Railway Transport Officer, who packed us into a coach across London to Waterloo, could not resist a quiet dig. 'You won't need that where you're going, Jack. Better send it home!' But St Davids only smiled and his soft brown eyes looked on with never a thought that anything was amiss. We helped him with his gear, and as we passed through a London that was recovering from the Saturday night blitz, the model was passed from hand to hand. It was a lovely little craft.

But things were not going well at Waterloo. Saturday's night blitz had been quite effective and people were queueing up from the bridge to the station entrance for buses. Fire-engine hoses were out in long snake like lines, and the acrid smell of wet burning wood filled the heavy, hot atmosphere. We sat in the bus and waited while officialdom did its best to sort things out. If we had not been so frightfully keen, we could have 'gone adrift', have availed ourselves of the muddle, as some did, one saying, 'Things like this don't happen every day, mates – I'm off to see my wife!'

Finally we managed to get into the guards van for Portsmouth. It had been an awful ride through bombed and still burning London, but with that model frigate and all the attention it earned, it became memorable.

At eight-thirty we arrived and waited for a bus to take us to our new base and by nine-thirty were dumped with our kit bags on a long straight road.

We walked down the road feeling fed up and very tired. The bags grew heavier with every yard and when at last, in the darkness, we reached the small sand-bagged gates of HMS T – , we were ready for bed.

The petty officer entered our names in a book and sent a fellow off to get us some tins of corned beef. We were hungry and supperless and very new. We drew hammocks and two blankets each from a very bad-tempered store-keeper, who had turned in early and resented having now to go across to his long low brick building and open up. The blue police lights were on, casting a dull glow on the many sleeping forms in their hammocks.

'Don't make too much noise, you fellows,' said the petty officer, and left us to sort out our bedding. We had never lashed a hammock before or seen the operation and it was no picnic, but luckily for us some fellows with late passes arrived, and after enjoying our struggling efforts and our mistakes for awhile came to our help.

HMS T –

In spite of the trials and tribulations of the first night we were in high spirits when morning came.

Here in this very hush-hush base we felt we were near the heart of things that mattered to us – that we had joined a company of fellows with the same ideals, the same zest for adventure, the same keen desire to get at the enemy in the shortest possible time, and at the closest possible quarters; all Special Service men specially selected for raiding craft; all volunteers.

We were from every walk of life and every British dominion – a wonderful mixture, with small ship men predominating and a goodly sprinkling of yachtsmen who had helped with their boats at Dunkirk. Our imaginations rioted in rosy dreams of derring-do. We were pleased with ourselves and our lot, and cock-a-hoop with our prospects.

Our fall to earth was sudden and hard, and came early that first morning.

At eight a.m. Walthews, St Davids and I found ourselves at the wrong end of a long line of men. We had eaten breakfast on a spotless, wooden table and had helped wash up afterwards. The whistle blew, and in a wild rush with late-comers, we faced a baggy-eyed petty officer whose badges proved Whale Island was his spiritual home. With practised eye he spotted us at once, and came across. 'New, eh?' His look implied that there was not much doubt about it, and with a fearful, 'Party – Shun!' the game commenced. By the time our turn came to meet the officer even the 'Heads and Baths' party had left and we were alone.

'Rather a crowd this morning,' observed the officer.

'New arrivals, sir.'

'Ah. I see. Well, give them something to do will you?' And off he went back to the ward room.

We spent our first working hours emptying out the large bins of highly scented pig swills. It was not a romantic job, not even a heroic one – just unpleasant muck-carrying. St Davids stuck out his tongue a little further than usual, a habit of his in more troubled moments and Walthew grimly bit his upper lip. Someone tipped us off that there would be Divisions at nine o'clock and as we had only one uniform each the cleaning up of our own persons for inspection, very necessary after our unsavoury job, was only just finished in time.

After short prayers and the men had marched away again, we once more found ourselves alone on that bit of yellow gravel and we asked each other whether our papers could have been lost. I had been told at Rex House that I should have a commission in a very short time and the other three had been given much the same impression; we had all known, too, friends who had been given their gold stripes in a day or so and some who had not even gone through the formality of the blue jacket stage, but been sent straight to King Alfred. We began to wonder where we were, and what had gone wrong, but we were not given much time even for wondering.

The petty officer advanced on us with determination, and a little red-headed RNVR lieutenant looked in our direction and also came across. Who were we? Ah, yes. New arrivals.

We were told that courses were being given for promotion to petty officer's rank and asked if we would like to go in for the examination in three days' time.

When we suggested that we could just as well wait for the commission that had been talked about so much at Rex House, he looked aghast. In a broad Scottish accent he went to some length to explain the present White Paper system. We were told that at least three months' sea-time was necessary nowadays and some very strong 'recommends' before we even met a preliminary board, and he ended up with a short admonition that in any case it was not for us to *ask*, but to wait till we were 'spotted'.

I wondered what sort of film agent he would make. Rather flattened by all this, we followed him dejectedly into a little out building that served as a class room, where a Scots petty officer was lecturing on charts. Sitting in the background we mulled over our position and wondered where our case had been mishandled.

During 'stand easy' we tackled the petty officer, who was even more shaken by our viewpoint than the lieutenant had been, and very earnestly assured us that it would very likely take a year to get before a board.

We now realised that the system had tightened up considerably since those early days and roundly cursed the misinformers whose hackneyed phrases had lured us to dreams of quick promotion.

By the end of the first week we caught on to the dodgers and their little tricks. It made a vast difference to the day and outlook if one started off with emptying pig swills and galley garbage or spent the first duty hour before Divisions merely picking up cigarette ends lying on the gravel path that led to the quarter deck – a small lawn beside the officers' block. The two tasks were at the opposite ends of the duty lists, and while the former meant hard work, the latter was merely a question of strategy, of looking busy before the prowling eyes of authority, and was relatively cleaner.

There were other jobs of course. The 'heads and baths' was quite messy; the petty officers' breakfast 'washing up and sweep down' entailed an hour under the irritable eye of the president of that mess, and the canteen had to be scrubbed out, as also the class room, but there was no doubt that the cigarette party was quite the least trying, and one to be angled for.

VII

Boat Work: A Night of Fireworks

The days went by quickly and were full of interest. We were taken out on 'landings' which were little more than sunny picnics.

The flotilla of eight boats with a training class divided up, and complete even to a football, would sally off into the Solent in a surge of white foam at eighteen knots, to carry out flotilla manoeuvres. Each boat had a primus stove, and the stew was well doused down at lunch time with a bottle of beer. These classes were fun after the normal classroom and parade ground stuff and fellows were always in the best of spirits. Competition was keen between each boat and we found ourselves up against other lads who were now completing their six weeks course as raiding craft petty officers. The nights were cold, but the stars twinkled down as we splashed into the various beaches – sometimes with troops aboard and at others merely to give men practice at night work. We enjoyed ourselves, and an undercurrent of excitement seemed to run through it all. Our first disappointment over the boats – which were so small and fragile – passed when we realised that they were at that time the best the Navy had.

The grand climax came when, on the Friday of the second week, volunteers to act as seamen to the regular crews were called for, for a full scale manoeuvre.

We left the river early in line ahead, the leading boat with its spoonshaped bows pushing a wave of sparkling water that turned into a roll, disturbing the calm waters of the Solent as if a squadron of aircraft had taxied along it. With their green canopies and camouflaged deck mounting above the light grey hull, they made a pretty sight as they sped along through the foam, each boat keeping smoothly in the wake and several lengths astern of its leader.

The little white ensigns on which the large white numbers stood sharply out, flapped gaily on each stern. They were freshly painted and polished and put up a good show, we felt, as we passed destroyers and the boom defence, to the open sea.

All eyes kept a look out into the blue heavens for anything that might be a 'jerry' for with eight-ply hulls, we were rather conscious of such things and kept our Lewis guns at the ready. Firing them from the shoulder would probably have availed little – but their presence gave us confidence.

After a couple of hours we splashed into a south coast harbour, turning smartly together to port, straight for the steeply shelving pebble beach, where the Royal Marines were watching in platoons near a wired-off beach tea room, now flanked by great anti-tank stakes of concrete. The new Marines thoroughly enjoyed these exercises and envied us, with remarks about, 'Lucky old Navy – no bleeding marching!'

The roar of the boats died down as they went slowly into the peaceful harbour and tied up at a wartime jetty. Red tabs and gold braid dispersed and we were allowed a few hours off.

We went into the conscripts' training base and had afternoon tea, then back aboard for a primus supper. The evening mist came in cold and damp and we turned in early under our oilskins on the wooden seats that ran down the boat on either side, hoping to snatch a little sleep before 'zero hour' and the exercises of the night.

By ten the mist had become almost a fog and the cold was intense. Some had curled up inside the forward bulkhead and were soon asleep on the odds and ends kept there, with a fender for a pillow. I dozed off to the gentle lapping of water on the hulls and woke to the mounting roar of engines at eleven-thirty. It was a strange sound – the starting up of boat after boat. A quiet stretch of water that only a few minutes before had been almost dead, suddenly sprang to life. Not a light showed in the inky blackness; the stars were hidden by cloud. The 'swish-swish' of a barge approaching, followed by the low, heavy roar of its engines as it drew abeam, then passing softly away into the dim beyond, was the only sound.

The slower class of boats, armoured and packed with men, seemed to scrape past us by a very narrow margin. We were to be the last flotilla to leave this starting base and by midnight we were alone but very much awake. Eight boats had been slowly humming for some minutes and as the leader's voice rang through the blackness, we let go and went up harbour to the Marines' beach.

They were waiting – still in threes – up on the steeply sloping beach. A searchlight shining from the tea room, flickered across the shining tin hats and played on the water as we came in. The mist blanketed the boats whose position was betrayed by the silhouetted figures of the seamen standing in the bows. These fellows seemed to be 'walking' on the low layer of mist that hung heavily about five feet off the water obscuring the boats they handled.

The moon broke through soon afterwards making it all much easier. We soon saw that we were not alone; tanks were still being loaded into those great square barges and orders from loud speakers gave boats their starting times.

We embarked our men, glad to be off that dangerous beach before someone rammed us. Such accidents had already occurred and several unlucky boats were lying broadside on – out of circulation.

Out in the open we ran into slight head seas, and then ran down the coast for half an hour. Two red lights just visible marked the safe area in which to land on the heavily mined beach. We were careful to stop well opposite, and to lie some two miles off waiting for zero hour.

Several fellows were very seasick, and this did not do the others much good. In the very confined space and rather tense atmosphere, one could not help the feeling of nausea which tense excitement sometimes brings – my inside felt miserable.

Then suddenly a machine gun blazed off with 'tracers', and the whole beach woke up with a monstrous crescendo of 'defensive' gun fire. The sky overhead was filled with flares – red, green and white signals – and starlike clusters of floating fire. Search-lights came on and fanned out across the sea, showing up dozens of assorted craft in flotilla groups all waiting to go in at their appointed time.

Well up the beach, the first wave of tanks appeared to be climbing up a promenade. We lay in two groups of four boats, but soon scattered when another lot came straight for us, speeding shorewards.

Reforming into a slow moving circle, we too at last moved in. Distance at sea is very deceptive to the untrained, and that beach, as we moved in at eighteen knots, seemed a hell of a way off, but at last we were in the area where the overhead fireworks floated into the water.

From line ahead we suddenly changed, and keeping formation abreast, got to within five hundred yards before those fearful lights swept across our bows. A groan went up from the boat as the light lingered on us – 'That's done it,' said an officer. 'We're sunk.'

We were very depressed and those last few hundred yards seemed a waste of time. The light held us fast in its powerful beam and all round us shore guns dropped flares which hissed as they hit the water, and then were gone.

We made a beautiful landing. The crouching Marines on either side leapt off over the bows, into the waves we churned up, and were off over the beach wire as small land mines went off round us.

There was a little too much 'realism' for me and I was glad when it was over. We passed through the boom in the dawn and were in our river again for breakfast. Some turned in just as they were, in their boats, for it was captain's rounds ashore; the others landed and found quiet hideouts for a few hours. We were very tired but sleep was 'out of bounds'. We could have the morning off but there must be no hammock slinging.

At lunch time the captain read out a congratulatory note from the general in charge of operations ashore. We were the only flotilla to land on time and our captain was delighted, as he embroidered awhile on the subject of punctuality. But his face fell a little when he read out the numbers of boats 'sunk' – only one had got into the beach undetected!

We went into lunch grimly conscious of the hazards of the future and not a little put out.

At one o'clock the BBC blandly announced a description of the night's operations which was quite shocking to us all. We heard our eight frail ply-wood boats – 'so different from the rest' further described as 'low grey menacing shapes racing for the shore at colossal speed in perfect formation, their decks packed with the crouching figures of the Royal Marines who leapt ashore and charged the beach defences; and how as they did so, those perfectly handled boats sped out to sea again, untouched, victorious. His peroration ended with a few well chosen words on the great Naval tradition of our island, and his pride in being an Englishman.

This form of radio line-shooting was rather disgusting to us at the time. The mess broke into an uproar. 'Silly bastard – don't you know we were sunk?' yelled a young, overtired seaman.

'Someone ought to *shoot* sods like that!' said an irritated petty officer. 'Making the nation over confident. That's what that stuff does.'

VIII

Dartmouth with Crossed Anchors

July was hot and the river Dart glittered through the trees as the train sped slowly round the heavily timbered cutting towards our destination – and my first ship. I was rather surprised at the suddenness of this draft. Only a few hours before I had been working out in mid-stream, between intermittent showers of rain, helping to camouflage one of the raiding craft, when a messenger panted out to me, to report to the commander at once. Full of fears as to what my 'crime' had been, I hurried back along the half mile path and found the Master-at-arms mustering 'defaulters and request men'.

'Get to the head of the line and don't forget to stand to attention when commander comes in!' he ordered severely.

'What's it all about?' I asked anxiously.

'You are going to be promoted. Come and see me afterwards. You're on draft.'

The officers filed in and stood in the class room in a smart line behind a green baize-topped table, now cleared of paraphernalia. They looked grim and the long line of defaulters even more solemn.

'You takes a pace forward – turns right, then three paces forward and stand to attention,' whispered the Master-at-arms. 'Aye, and don't forget to salute when the commander finishes with you!'

I reassured him on that point and he smiled benignly, taking his stand to one side of the table.

It began to rain again. Long minutes seemed to pass. My thoughts carried me back to the time when I was a scout at my prep school. The whole set-up was the same, only now, older men were playing the game and I was in blue jacket's rig.

There was a movement amongst the officers and a nervous cough from the Master-at-arms followed by a loud, 'Request men and defaulters! Shun!'

The commander took up his stand and looked down at the book beside him. Without taking his eyes off this book and still bending over the table, I was duly 'rated up' and told to put up my petty officer's badge. It was over in a flash and I stood in the rain once more. I might have been a mechanical toy receiving a new label – so can some men reduce an occasion.

But standing there listening outside I was given the other side of the picture; a stoker petty officer guilty of some misdemeanour, was reduced to stoker in the twinkling of an eye with a delightful flow of nautical 'ticking off'!

I retired to the regulating office in quest of news – before I too could be recalled and demoted! It was quite shattering to be shown the ease at which one could fall and I wondered how long my 'hooks' would stay up.

On the train I sat beside an ERA from Birmingham – a mechanic in peacetime – with a thin red face and sharp long nose. He had been a bit surly at first when I was put in charge of our draft of two – my youthful appearance again. But now, after hours of travelling together through those rolling hills and along the rocky shore of the West Country, he had become himself once more, and even agreed to sell me one of his petty officer badges. I could now 'put up my hooks' before my new shipmates met me.

We caught the ferry to the Dartmouth side and then a boat up river. The great college and the host of little boats manned by the happy young Naval cadets looked very peaceful. But the corvettes and mine-sweepers and the small silver balloons, flying high above the great protecting hills that seemed to make the river safe from air attack, were a constant warning of ever present danger in a world at war.

In a bend of the river was our parent ship, with a long line of raiding craft moored up to the buoys between her and the shore, and around us sailed the diminutive future leaders of the Royal Navy.

A month passed and I was slowly absorbed into the flotilla. It was an amazing process, this settling down of a very mixed lot of fellows from every walk of life. They were all now petty officers and it was interesting to watch the reactions of a mess composed mainly of regulars, to our small body of hostilities only men. Among the latter were a Fleet Street reporter, a member of the Corn Exchange, a London policeman, a leather merchant, a professional racing cyclist and last but not least, one time conductor of opera – one Michael Scott, a charming fellow and my very good friend, who not many moons later was to find himself, with two stripes up, in charge of a flotilla in the Middle East, where he was eventually joined by one of the sub-lieutenants under whom he served as coxswain here.

The month spent waiting in the River Dart for our own parent ship to carry us away passed quickly with daily manoeuvres, and on occasional jaunts for tea and Devonshire cream up the river to Totnes.

Our day always started with a scramble across the fifty yards of water that separated the trot of boats from the ship, and then there was a strenuous spell of cleaning up after seagulls had been chased away; the engines would purr into a mighty roar, and after an hour or so our officers would appear and we would slip down river, past the boom and out to sea.

We had our swim from the stern of the ship, we sailed, we sunbathed, and at night we spent our money in Torquay. Life was altogether most amusing. It was an easy existence – almost too easy, and after we had learnt to put a boat on a beach, in all conditions of wind and sea, life began to take a routine shape and a certain amount of restlessness crept in.

One day towards the end of July our own parent ship, after days of idle rumour, suddenly appeared at the entrance. It was a great moment. We put on the usual show and went down river, in line ahead, to meet her.

The *Prince Philip* had the lines of a destroyer and was very impressive after the 'Old Tub'. But we were not at all pleased with the quarters we had been allotted. There were twenty petty officers in the ship's company and twenty-four in our flotilla and to hear that we were all to be crowded in a small space like sardines brought immediate protests from both sides.

The space was officially supposed to hold forty men – to judge by hammock slinging arrangements. This might look well on paper, but when forty-two men assembled there was hardly room to move. Some refused to draw hammocks and enterprisingly went exploring into the troop flats down below, not yet, of course, inhabited. Soon a whisper was passed round which sent us all down to inspect the sergeants' mess where we were disgruntled over the contrast between the splendid provision made for troops and the shockingly cramped quarters allocated to us. Looking at the large bunks with fine spring mattresses which lined the wall, we felt that Naval hospitality had gone too far! The ship had just been commissioned; now was our chance to look after our own yardarms – and we took it. When we had comfortably settled our baggage in, we felt much more pleased with life.

Next day our shake-down cruise began, and we followed our parent ship in flotilla formation out past the boom at some fifteen knots. A signal was hoisted and in two groups of four boats we deployed to port and starboard and ran alongside, only a few feet separating each boat as she steamed on. The hooks on the large metal blocks were open ones, but we were hoisted aboard in good time without damage to hands. After we secured for sea we went down for lunch.

Low cloud and dull light kept ack-ack on the quivive, and so we were not very surprised when, in the middle of eating our rice pudding, there was a sudden rattle of gunfire. Paint and iron shavings fell onto our plates and almost at the same moment the alarm bell sounded. We dived for the swing doors and made for our precious, freshly painted boats to inspect the damage.

The port side ones were in a sorry state. Cannon shells from two Messerschmitt 109s had gone through from hull to hull and out into the deck houses. My heart turned over when I looked at the boat over which we had toiled with such care, and with appropriate words I cursed the Hun. She was in an awful mess. Even my oilskins, which I had stowed in a tight roll, were now just a mass of dark dust and torn scraps, and the petrol tanks had been holed.

I climbed through the bulkhead with a wooden plug, but the hole was close to the after section and I could not get a hammer near it. While I wrestled with the wretched plug, petrol spurted over everything. Suddenly an extraordinary feeling of well-being surged through me and quite inconsequently I decided to have a talk with Hugh, our signalman. By the time I had struggled through to him I found with great amazement that I could neither stand up nor control my speech – I was drunk with petrol fumes and had to be hastily transported to sick bay for first aid. It was a wonderful feeling at the time but the hangover was atrocious.

For the next four days, running down the English Channel and then up the Irish sea, we worked steadily, helping the flotilla carpenter, a small bird-like creature from Cornwall, to get out the petrol tank, a job that was considerably protracted by his bouts of sickness and the heavy roll of the ship.

We worked till ten on those soft summer nights, patching up the boat with copper tingles, hoping to get her into the water with the rest when manoeuvres started.

The outer isles were lovely and gaunt with that forlorn look that is peculiar to these Scottish Isles. We lay in the lee of one of them in a

(*Left*) Henty and Sarah, a photograph taken in Hyde Park. (*Right*) Taken in Baffin Land where a German submarine was to be blown up during the filming of *49th Parallel*

Henty on his last film assignment, *49th Parallel* in Canada

Henty Henty-Creer

glassy calm, with clear blue sky overhead and over to the east the purple distance of the mainland. We manoeuvred for days in all weathers. There were night landings on strange beaches, lowering and hoisting evolutions at speed, 'action-stations' and all the rest.

They were not happy days for me. I did not like my ill-tempered sub-lieutenant with his foolish petty tantrums, his lack of restraint and humour; his very presence was blighting, and in some queer way prevented the simplest routine from working smoothly.

The little crew of our boat consisted of this very serious, very humourless VR sub-lieutenant, an engineer petty officer, one able seaman and myself. The young sub had an effect on us that was at times quite startling.

Hugh Bainbridge, our engineer petty, was a Norfolk man, a good friend and mainstay through many trials and tribulations. However the noxious sub left soon after and the ship was once more happy.

About this time a new chief cook arrived and became immediately popular, following, as he did, a very inefficient little hunchback whose culinary efforts had been as warped as his body. The new man was a tall well-built, middle-aged Jew, who after serving his time in the Navy, had made a name for himself in a famous London hotel. Then, as he put it: 'I couldn't go on when I knew how you poor serving gentiles were suffering!' He returned to the Navy as a chief petty officer cook, and was truly magnificent. The galley was spring-cleaned and food once more became a definite rendezvous with one's inner man and not a test of the little fellow's endurance.

Whilst we were having our mid-day meal the new cook would stand in the doorway and call, 'Now you yellow-bellied bastards – what's wrong with my food today?' The chorus of fearful abuse, which always followed as he sat down to be very carefully waited on by our two messmen, would send him into roars of laughter. He had a robust wit.

Our boat carried on for several weeks without an officer, then a buzz again began to filter through the ship that we were off 'to do a job'. Whether it was to be Norway or France did not worry anyone – spirits soared. Other ships had done their stuff; now it was our turn and we felt we had waited quite long enough.

IX

Abandon Ship

Liverpool seemed empty when we got off the train in the dawn. August was drawing to a close and the streets were wet with an early morning shower that made the skeletons of bombed buildings glisten ghostlike in that half light between the routine quiet abdication of the moon, and the determined sunrise.

We were returning to our flotilla from the four days' leave that had so suddenly been given to us. The walk down the long road that runs parallel with the river past the wreckage of commercial monuments which now looked grey and dead – almost like a Wellsian dream – was broken only by the long figure of a lonely policeman sheltering in a bombed doorway, his glistening cape quietly swaying in the breeze. The great burnt out warehouses made a sombre background for the war stained shipping and wet grey hulks. HMS *Prince Philip* looked small beside the big ships but the raiding craft gave a welcome pattern of colour to the drab scene.

Once up the gangway from the empty street it was as if we had stepped into a busy market. Civilian workmen were leaving and as they passed our unusual raiding craft they made many comments. 'Smart-looking life-boats, Jack.'

We sailed at noon. Dockers waved. Knowing little boys stood pointing. 'Coo, look at 'em! New life boats.' Soon we were out into the fast flowing river, heading for a dark misty horizon, that seemed full of incoming ships. Wrecks lined the heavily buoyed channel and little coasters, now manned by the RAF, flew their great silver balloons high above us all. Tossing day after day on the dark waters, watching Britain's western life-line parading past, theirs was a strange sort of existence.

Our boats' crews were piped away to cruising stations, as look-outs up on the forward twelve pounder gun. Armed with a fine pair of glasses, we watched the mist turning to fog. Just before it came on thick we saw a mine floating dead ahead. Quickly to our report, the ship swung away to starboard, circling while we fired our small arms, till it disappeared from sight.

Down below, at the teatable later, the monstrous blaring of the ship's siren seemed to make the mess vibrate with sound. In a way, it was rather lucky that we had not yet moved up to the sergeants' recreation on the boat deck, which after much discussion had been handed over to us as flotilla petty officers' mess. This much we had achieved, although being directly above the engine room and abaft the funnel, it had its disadvantages, as we now realised. Looking back in the light of my own stripes, I pity those officers. They must have found us rather a handful at times.

We went on watch again from eight till twelve, in a thick almost impenetrable black out, and we moved up into the eyes of the ship. It was really thick now and our speed was almost nil. We rolled into long beam seas, waiting almost expectantly for something to happen. The blast of another ship apparently passing right across our course, followed by an even louder siren from an even closer ship, keyed us up. Passing the homing convoy really was no joke. Sounds seemed to come in on us from all directions and when midnight and our relief came we felt done in. The mess was heavy with smoke, and very stuffy after the hours up in the bows.

It seemed as if I had just got to sleep when her sudden lurch, shot me out of my 'window seat'. There was a fearful crash and men were tumbling out of their hammocks in noisy uproar. A few seconds later the alarm bell rang and everyone seemed to be milling about in the dark, till the order 'Switch the bloody lights on' stopped the jostling.

The ship suddenly heeled over at an unpleasant angle – it was a nasty moment – and I ran out through the swing doors onto the now sloping deck, past groups of men, a few wrapped in blankets but the majority in their underclothes, and down to my boat, where men were lining up already in rows opposite. A heavy fog made the dark night more sinister. A searchlight was panning across what seemed an enormous ship – a ten thousand tonner, whose bow was now more than half way through us, just abaft the funnel. And on high, perched like a great sinister bird with wings outstretched, was a Hurricane Catafighter. It was literally an incredible sight, for none of us had seen a Catafighter before and nearly a year was to pass before the public saw even a photograph of one. The light from the bridge moved across her, then down. The fog swirled in eddies and all the while the sirens let off their baleful notes.

The engine man was working the electric motor lowering our boat down from above to this deck, and as she came slowly down, the seamen and I jumped on to haul her in tight against the ship's side. When we had made secure and the first lieutenant had seen that all was well and that the other port side boats were in position, he paced up and down past the waiting men, mustering opposite the boats four deep in perfect order. They looked a sorry lot, for their flat down aft had flooded at once; and they were grim and silent for before them lay the unconscious figures of their two engineer officers.

The commander, watching from the bridge yelled: 'Abandon ship, Number One, abandon ship!'

An awful moment. For a brief second the tragedy of losing our ship struck home, but was gone in the rush to get the men on board and lowered. Three other boats were slowly going down. Their weight made the ship suddenly heel over even more with a sickening lurch and ranks were broken as men fell against each other.

'Get the injured aboard first,' ordered the first lieutenant, and they were passed groaning across the gap and down into my boat. Whilst the remainder clambered aboard and went below, I darted up the steeply tilting deck back to the mess and grabbed an armful of blankets.

In there now, all was confusion. A few were packing madly, responsibilities to the ship forgotten, their thoughts bent on saving their personal belongings. The scene was amazing. Clothes were scattered everywhere, kit bags had been emptied, and into suitcases their most valuable items were being stuffed. It suddenly struck me, as I was seizing blankets, that I was doing a foolish thing – that my boat might be lowered without its coxswain – and that horrible thought sent me up with as much speed as my great bundles would allow.

The ship lurched once more as I staggered past the surprised first lieutenant, who called, 'Get your boat into the water as soon as it is full, and stand by with the others.'

I pushed the blankets through the small doorway in the canvas canopy and this raised a pleasant cheer of appreciation from the men. My boat was packed. Men were crowded everywhere, but some were in their underclothes and the night was cold. We slacked off the tackle, allowing the boat to play out from the ship. After some shouting we had managed to get an officer on deck to work the electric switch that would lower us into the water, and as we reached it we were lifted by a nasty swell. A frightened fellow yelled, 'Get me out of here. We're going to capsize!'

'Keep still and cut the cackle – give the crew a chance,' said a calmer voice, relieving me greatly for I did not want a panic. Then the familiar voice of the seaman and the engineman called, 'All gone aft. All gone forward,' and I put the helm over and we drew off. Our normal hooks had been removed for repairs after our last manoeuvres and we had been given shackles as a temporary measure so it was no easy job letting her go in a choppy sea: but they managed in great style. As soon as I felt the water under her I pressed the self starter and away she went. She had not been in the water for over four days and great was my relief at her response. Just as we drew away from the ship's side, the lights went out, the current failed and we only just made it.

The boat astern was luckily in the water, but could not get its engine started. 'Stand by me, Henty,' called their officer. We circled and got a tow across, then her engine roared into life and we cast off the tow and got clear as the searchlight went slowly out.

Steering past our ship we rounded her bows and went alongside the great ship which had rammed us, yelling for a ladder to be lowered.

The weather was worse here, and our over-loaded boat heavy and unhappy alongside. After what seemed like aeons of time, someone threw us a line, and a scaling ladder was unrolled on us. Men had just started up, when the great thing went full astern and we were swept off like leaves in an autumn gale, back towards the gaping side of our damaged ship; while the monster disappeared into the fog, her siren floating back to us. The din inside the boat was terrific – language for once worthy of the occasion.

I found the rest of the flotilla circling off the port side of the maimed ship, each following the one ahead. Joining in and passing from boat to boat I called out: 'Any orders?' The reply, 'No, sir, have you any for me?' was rather astounding for I was only still a petty officer. At last I managed to get into the circle of leaderless boats, at a loss and very disgusted. There was not even a sub-lieutenant amongst us to take command.

Then one boat broke the circle and went off into the fog, and all the others as if eager for a leader followed. Convinced that our flotilla leader had taken a grip on the situation, I conformed with this manoeuvre.

Old Arthur turned his gaze from them to me. 'Well! In all me days at sea I never thought I should be running off a ship and leaving me captain.' Neither had I. In the density of fog and night, new sounds grew in intensity. The awful noise of many deep foghorns grew nearer. We were obviously still in the path of a convoy, with big ships almost on top of us. The constant alarm of, 'ship ahead!' made things even more trying. The majority in my boat were stokers and their excited directions were always for whichever way they were facing – not from the boat's head – and therefore very conflicting and confusing. We could see no ships – just the churned up water round the stern of the boat ahead; and as it turned, I suddenly found that the others of our flotilla had vanished.

I was alone in charge of a boatload of survivors and beyond knowing what sea I was in, I had not the least idea of our position – not a pleasant situation.

Blanketed by the fog, we were still enclosed in a sound box reverberating with countless fog horns and sirens and the groans of the two injured men. When one of our boats loomed up and was about to pass, we yelled like fury and they stood by. In it there were three officers and a few ratings. They too had been looking for the mother ship.

I transferred fifteen of my passengers but surprisingly no officer volunteered to take charge of my boat. The second cook, who was with them, threw us over some of the loaves he had managed to snatch up before he left the mother ship, and someone else passed over eight packets of cigarettes. The engineer officer also came over bringing with him a sick bay attendant. The boat's officer, with a, 'Keep in touch,' to me drew away.

We were all more comfortable now with the extra space. The groans of the injured died down and most of the others wrapped themselves up in the blankets and tried to get a little sleep. We had been rammed at three a.m. and it was now four-thirty and a slight rain had set in. The fog was patchy and showed no signs of clearing. Several ships came so close that we found ourselves running across their still bubbling tracks.

I was very worried about the injured. We were steering due east and the sea, being on our port bow, gave us a pounding that added to their misery. And although the sick bay steward had done his best, no one had any idea of internal injuries and little could be done to ease their pain or make them really comfortable.

At eight o'clock, the fog was as dense as ever, but through it now filtered an uncomfortable glare. I wondered how much longer it would be before we struck land. It was lucky we had fuelled and prepared the boat so well for the raid, for we had a useful range.

Then we heard the foghorn. Its mighty booming breaking the silence that had been with us for so long. The engineer officer was convinced that it was a ship and would not believe me when I suggested, 'Land ahead, sir!' When at last some dark patches did appear ahead he said jokingly, 'You see, Bo'sun, I was right! A ship. Steer for her.'

I stood clear of the large rocks which did indeed look like the silhouette of a small vessel, but kept on in the direction of the fog horn. Suddenly – ahead and above – huge wireless masts grew in shape and we slowed down. It was baffling. The tops of the steel masts thrusting above the thick layer of fog was an extraordinary sight, so clear and stark they stood out: and as we went on, the rocky outline of the very rugged coast unfolded itself, and we were among little rocky islands and close to a tall white lighthouse. While the other boat decided to go north, we searched for a break in the wall of rock and were lucky to find a stone jetty where the lighthouse keeper stood to welcome us.

A great weight seemed to fall from me. I looked at the injured men sleeping the sleep of exhaustion, and hoped it was not too late to save them. We would now be able to send a signal for an ambulance.

The men scrambled ashore in great good humour. The lighthouse keeper and his good wife were wonderfully hospitable and soon the men were comfortably settled in several rooms around large fires, drinking great mugs of tea and eating slices of bread and jam; they enjoyed themselves.

An hour or so later escorted in by an RAF rescue launch through the harbour channel we arrived at last at a little town, where a small crowd watched us with some amusement. The men in long woollen underpants, in pyjamas, and some hiding their nudity in blankets, climbed up the stone steps of the jetty, where they were met by an army lorry and driven away to camp for a hot meal and battledresses.

I found the Senior Naval Officer in the hotel and reported my arrival. He was pleased and congratulated me. Aircraft were still looking for the other boats. We heard later that some had found themselves on the Irish coast.

X

My White Paper Moves On

As usual Lowestoft was windy and cold and the station was bleak in the black-out. Here and there a torch would flash on seamen as they mustered through the barrier under the watchful eye of the Duty Petty Officer, who marshalled them into groups for the lorry ride up to The Nest.

I had delivered my draft to their own base in the south and was now alone. I went on ahead by bus, very bucked at the thought of getting in before the others and my chance of choosing a decent billet. But when at last we arrived at the one-time theatre, the place was packed; where, on my last visit had been rows of seats, there was now a mass of sleeping forms.

There was no hope of a billet. I was given a station card and told to draw bedding. Below the stage a couple of Wrens were busy handing out blankets, hammocks and mattresses to a long queue of tired and very fed up seamen, who had converged on this depot from all parts of the British Isles.

Back in the middle of the hall where rifles were stacked, I joined a group of petty officers and chattered for a while. The loudspeaker cranked away and every now and then an order boomed out. Finally I found a free space in the orchestra pit, climbed in, and settled down for the night.

At seven came the order: 'All those who arrived p.m. yesterday are to proceed to the canteen for breakfast.' At nine, having returned our bedding, we mustered. There were a hundred or so of us, all petty officers and seamen – we were marched off to the 'oval' to have our cards stamped by the medical and dental departments.

Presenting my card, now stamped, on the stage again I was handed a billeting chit. Then I had to go to one of the sheds that was in use as a divisional office to report myself to the old three-badge petty officer and have my past Naval movements recorded, with my new address. My double-barrelled name which had caused a great deal of trouble in past correspondence, had stamped itself on several minds now, on my fourth return here. I had been greeted with, 'What! You here again? Struth! Have I got to write your ruddy name out.' And other remarks – witty but quite unprintable.

The divisional commander, after a chat and an enquiry into my movements over the past months, decided to get me before a board as soon as possible. Armed with a chit from the doctor – and taking the precaution to see that I was not to be drafted into the blue without his consent – I left for my digs for a much needed 'clean up' after my night on the floor, without the chance of a wash or brush up.

The usual crowd of small boys with push carts stowed my kit in a rickety contraption, and we set off for the billet – up Denmark Hill this time.

In this base all ratings were billeted out in houses. These houses were sometimes owned by patriotic citizens who had opened their doors to the Navy when the storm broke, and enjoyed doing their bit, but the majority were out for all they could get. This very unpleasant breed had taken their houses 'on spec' and with the scantiest of furniture, were always ready to put as many as they could into each room, regardless of the comfort of their paying guests – the Navy allowed twenty-four shillings a week for each man – so there was always a chance of finding oneself allocated to a double bed already occupied by two other sailors! Beds were sometimes jammed so tightly that one had to climb over the foot – no hardship in itself but a little upsetting if a couple of drunks happened to share the same room! And in this type of house no sheets were provided and the meagre blankets cried out for a visit to the laundry. After seeing the bedrooms I could always tell what food to expect. If there were sheets on the beds, one knew the owners were civilised and kindly and did not worry too much over profits.

On this occasion, a landlady took me to a room which contained nothing but a double bed, two single beds and a dressing table.

'I think you will be comfortable here,' she said pleasantly, 'I always do my best for the Navy. I've had ever so many and they always come again!'

Lucky lads, I thought grimly to myself. I plonked my stuff on one of the single beds – although undoubtedly the double was the better – and said quite firmly that I had no intention of sharing a bed with anyone.

We went down to the back parlour where four men were sitting around a large kitchen table covered with white oil cloth. The fifth – a large hefty Scots engineer, a perfect double for Wallace Beery in that magnificent film *Tugboat Annie* – took up the front of the fire. He had taken his shoes off, and with his toes sticking out of his unsavoury old socks, was toasting the soles of his feet.

Heavy green curtains and dark wall paper seemed to prevent any ray of the wan November light coming through the dirty windows. The electric light was on – without a shade – and a lead ran across the room from an additional socket to the wireless set, which blared forth loudly.

We nodded to each other with a, 'How do,' and 'What ho, mate,' and soon settled down to an awful meal which everyone ate in silence. All through the meal the 'Missus' or 'Ma' made excuses for the poor fare and talked of the difficulties of life these days.

I was glad to get away from her monologue, out in the cold weak sun again, and walked up to The Nest with the rest of the lads. From all sides the main street filled with men in blue – emptying out of their digs and surging in a steady stream up the hill.

The doctor's hut was just behind the theatre and a small line of new sheep– still in civvies – stood waiting to go in.

I found myself alongside a smart-looking fellow petty officer. We were both resigned to an indefinite wait and found the scene entertaining. The old chief outside was still droning away to his latest batch, the others inside – shirtless and cold – kept to themselves.

A bright, 'Afternoon, sir,' announced 'his' arrival. We both went in to our 'medical' wondering how stiff it would be this time – and because of the importance of the occasion – decidedly nervous. A light over the optical sign card was put on. 'Read the middle line,' said the sick bay Petty Officer. My companion, slightly rattled, started at the top. 'No! No!' interrupted the doctor, 'The middle one, man! Don't waste me time! Right oh! You next.' I duly obliged.

We were out in the sunlight again, somewhat dazzled by the speed of this medical machine.

'*What* a medical!' said my companion. 'I had been told so much about it that I even had a bath at lunch to freshen up.'

The commander took the slips of papers and we went to the next hut marked, 'Petty Officers Divisional Office' where a lieutenant was checking over names with an old petty officer. He told us of a navigation school he had heard was open to us. What about it? Would we like to polish up? It might be several weeks before the next selection board. We accepted with enthusiasm, and were told we could hop along and look round while he made arrangements.

Armed with a pass out, we went up the hill to a large house with a wooden sign, 'Welcome to Invalides!' It was now four forty-five and when a voice called, 'Petty Officers' navigation class fall in outside,' it dawned on us with something of amazement, that the class had been in our midst all the time playing billiards. We 'fell in' with them – in fours – and were marched by one of the squad down the hill again and back to The Nest. There the Divisional Petty Officer called us inside and told us to report in the morning at nine. Evidently we were not to be with this hard working class at all. Just as well, we thought!

Back at my digs I found my bed was just as I expected – dirty old blankets and filthy under sheet. I ended my long day with the most uncomfortable night I have ever had. Breakfast was just a slice of skinny bacon and a greasy potato.

George and I met beside the church and we went into the school together, where we found a crowd of leading seamen who were sitting for the Board of Trade Mate's Ticket – trawler section. Captain Balls, the master, handed us over to three other 'C.W. ites' who had been here for three weeks – and we had a cheery morning.

Captain Balls in action was a great sight. He sat at a desk with a host of men on all sides waiting for their turn to be called in to the examiners. Opposite him sat a seaman deeply intent on a model steamship and on a group of morse lights which the Captain played with great speed, fascinating to watch. Man after man sat down – Scottish fishermen from the Outer Isles, Yorkshiremen, Welshmen. The Navy had made it possible for these one time trawler men to study for their 'ticket' and all who wished could have a six weeks' course. Captain Balls was now giving last minute revision to the men who were about to go before the examiners. For a week they would be put through their paces, and he was anxious to see that they gave a good account of themselves, for this 'ticket' was going to mean a great deal to them when the piping days of peace came again, and they were very keen and very grateful for the opportunity.

Men who had spent most of their lives in drifters and trawlers as seamen were now sitting, and had sat for the last six weeks swotting; for, as one fellow confided to me, it would have cost him a hundred pounds before the war, to take time off from his fishing nets.

It was a most inspiring sight. Men with sextants, with complicated-looking nautical tables, morse lamps and semaphore flags, sat at chart tables with parallel rulers and dividers and worked away. It was a noisy room. Two fellows just behind us were checking each other over the international code using little wooden flags, which they dealt to each other. And every now and then a messenger would come in and say something to the captain, who, taking his ever smoking pipe would say: 'William J. Picket. Come on, me lucky lad! Show eeself, gosh! Seamanship for you!' The lucky lad with a sickly smile but inwardly shaking left us with a, 'Well, I've never asked much, I ain't, but I hopes I gets through this un!'

'Go on! Away with ee!' heartened Captain Balls loudly after the retreating figure, in a final effort to steer him on his way to the examination table. 'Don't forget what I been telling ee!'

We packed up at noon. George was going to spend the afternoon looking for another billet, for the disgracefully overcrowded tenement house he had been in for the last few nights was proving an adventure that he could no longer stand – five men in a tiny room with one double bed and a camp stretcher! Shaving in the sink amongst the dirty saucepans was one thing, but when the other four came rolling in from a binge and made sleep impossible, it was awful for him. He had won the DSM a few months before, and was due at the Palace in a few weeks' time. Another of life's little contrasts.

Back at the stage, hundreds of Naval 'sheep' filled the concert hall. On the stage, behind the wooden barricade, sat the shepherds – grand old salts of the Service with their rows of medal ribbons and three good conduct badges fixed securely beneath their petty officers' badges. They barked and shouted and swore at their ratings – conscript or volunteer were all the same to them. 'Get back there! 'ow many times 'ave I got to tell yer? Now get back!'

They sat and faced us as, crowded to the barriers, we jostled to hand in leave tickets and get our names down for billets.

When my turn came at the table, the petty officer looked up and roared, 'Blimey! You back again! Here's that double-barrelled bloke back again – can't we ever lose him?'

The poor fellow behind me, waiting his turn for attention, looked on patiently.

When all was found out that he wanted to know about the *49th Parallel* film, he suddenly caught sight of a name on his blotting pad. It was a new billet, just opened. 'A brand new place. POs only. You'll be the first,' he said, making haste to write out my billeting card. Places were getting rarer these days, he went on. Even old orders prohibiting two men sharing a bed had been washed out now. And extra pickets were on duty at night in the concert hall.

I soon had my things in a taxi, for the new billet was in the old part of the town. The driver knew the people. He had taken them there the week before. 'They're a bit of all right,' he said. 'You can always tell a good home by the curtains. Decent livin' folks 'ave clean curtains – and them's there only been in a few days – and them's got 'em!' We stopped. The door was opened by Mrs Moffat. And that was the start of the most comfortable stay in that town.

Her husband was a skipper, a Dunkirk man, now taking things easy after eighteen months at Dover. They were a wonderful pair – and could not do enough to make us happy. From the first day she never stopped worrying over good breakfasts and enormous lunches.

'Yes I know! I've three boys in the forces and I don't believe in profiteering. God has been good to me. My boys are safe, and I like to think that they are properly looked after too.'

Their hospitality was magnificent. There were five of us at the start. Three petty officers, a leading hand and a seaman. We called the tall hefty Scot 'Jock' and the old stoker petty officer 'Chiefie'. Both men were intensely interesting.

'Chiefie' had been in HMAS *Sydney*, one of the crew that took her out to Australia in 1911 to hand her over to the Australian government. He had never forgotten that voyage or the welcome in Sydney. Looking back on life, it was his one regret that he had not been transferred to the Australian navy.

The Great War found him in the Dardanelles. Sitting in the little room before a blazing fire in the evening. I listened to his story. After all these years he was back again in the Service – still as keen as ever; not in battleships this time, just a trawler. 'All I want now, mate!'

XI

The Board

After two long weary months of sitting about waiting my turn, the great day came at last. I was to meet the board which would decide whether I should be given a chance to go to HMS King Alfred and sit for a commission; or remain on the lower deck.

Several days before Captain Balls had handed me a slip of paper: 'One candidate to report to Divisional Office at two-thirty. Parade Dress.'

' 'Spec they mean you wearin' a clean collar – that's all,' he said.

On the great day – 13th December – it was snowing heavily. Four petty officers stood outside the little wooden shed, and I stood in line with them waiting for my officer to open his door. Then in the doorway to our great relief our officer appeared with the large C.W. envelopes, which had all our service particulars, tucked under his arm. 'Carry on up to the court-martial building, I'll see you there,' he ordered. It was now three o'clock.

We fiddled to kill time. Plans were made for each to hold the other's coat as he went in. In fact we all behaved like a lot of silly kids. Wrens passed and repassed: some began to recognise us but did not stop to talk. We were still 'lower deck' and their main concern seemed to be to get by at the double. 'Not very flattering,' said one fellow. 'Who do they think we are?'

A leading hand had appeared from nowhere: 'Wonters, Wonters, Where's Wonters?'

'Winters is the name!'

'Blimey, it's all the same to me, matey, but you're first in. Come along.'

We were silent, watching him go up the passage – very still, very erect – and round the corner out of sight. A heavy silence fell on all.

'God!' said one of the seamen further down. 'You would think we were going to be bloody well executed.'

'Nuts, don't try to kid us. Why, I can hear your bloody heart beating from here,' said a New Zealander.

'Come, come, gentlemen! Remember OLQ (Officer like

qualities)' said one yachtsman, now an engineer, and we all started laughing.

The first candidate came out perspiring although it was snowing outside. He was greeted with a subdued rush of questions. 'Who is in there?' 'What did they ask?' 'Did you pass?' 'Is he in a good mood?' 'Did Phillips ask anything?'

The fellow mopped his head. 'Same old rubbish,' he blandly replied. 'School, experience, private life. *You* know!' His manner was rather weary now, rather blasé too, 'Oh, he *did* ask what I would do if I saw a sub!'

The questioners stopped their catechism. We all thought, 'Well, what *would* we do?'

'Ram her,' said one.

'Absurd! The begger might be miles away.'

'Oh, hell! Do you think you passed?'

'Don't know. They don't tell you. Wonder if I should wait or carry on?'

'Oh, I should hang on if I were you.'

'No,' said a wise one, 'wouldn't do that. Not likely that. Not likely to hear tonight anyhow.'

The leading hand was with us again and a deadly silence fell. 'Costers next.'

'You mean Carstairs, P.J. Carstairs?' The leading hand was very patient.

'I bet I'm next,' I said. It was becoming boring. Of course *one* did not give a damn! Hell! My collar felt tight. The minutes rolled by. I should probably be at the end of the line – an awful thought. There were over twelve of us from seamen to petty officers. 'Wish I'd never started this nonsense. Awful waste of time!'

'Quite agree old boy, bloody silly isn't it?'

More silence ... I could feel my excitement mounting. Damn. This was silly. The heavy tread came back again. My heart was hammering. ' 'enty-Creer!'

'Right, I'm here.'

'Come on, mate. Your turn. Take your 'at off when you get in, and I'll shut the door for you.' Thoughtful fellow! The door opened. I was in.

Looking quickly round the room I saw four figures sitting at a long table. The commodore was in the middle, and my divisional officer was on his left.

'Put your hat over there,' ordered the great one. I did. 'Sit down.'

It was rather like sitting at the monkey house, only this time I was the monkey.

He fingered the papers. 'Hum! You are an Australian?'

'Yes, sir.'

'Nearly twenty-two?'

'Yes, twenty-two in March, sir.'

'What did you do after you left here in May?'

'I went down to T – sir.'

'Where is that?'

'Near F – outside Portsmouth, sir.'

'The actual place is W – ' interrupted a commander. I couldn't have remembered for the life of me.

'Ah, yes, I know the spot. What did you do there?' ... 'Oh! And after that?'

I could see that he was checking to see if my answers tallied with the statements on the sheet. And all the while they stared. One commander had his head on one side. I felt rattled. What did he think I was, a ruddy bird or something? My gas mask slipped off my knees. Damn!

'What is the difference between variation and deviation?' 'Can you pilot a course?' 'What do you know about tides?' I could scrape through those. 'Have you ever made a tidal correction.' No, I had not. 'No ... Raiding Craft. Don't suppose you worried much about that!' and they laughed.

'Know your rule of the road?'

'Yes, sir.'

'Well, there's nothing much to *that*. You can learn it by heart.'

'I have, sir.'

'Oh. Got a seamanship book?'

'Admiralty Navigation, sir.'

'Yes. Well ... ' He took off his glasses and sucked one of the arms. There was a pause. I breathed deeply. Suddenly he turned to the others. 'Any questions?'

'No, sir,' came from both.

'Oh!' I thought in dismay. 'They can't even trouble to ask me a question. I must be a certain flop.'

'Right! Carry on!'

I got up. 'Thank you, sir!' and grabbed my cap. They watched me leave. I bowed and gave rather a strained smile as I closed the door. Then, as through a haze, they all seemed to smile too. It was over. The door was shut. 'God,' I thought. 'Well that's over; of *course* I've failed! Oh hell! Who cares?' Then the others were around me with eager questions to which I could find no satisfactory answers.

We stood in the snow for a bit. Went around to the DV Office where old George, our divisional petty officer, gave us a cheery smile. 'Pass all right?'

'Shouldn't think so, George.'

'Well, hang on for a bit. He'll be back soon.'

We went outside again. 'Let's go into the POs' mess!'

'No. Couldn't do that. We are not staff POs.'

George confirmed this. 'Staff only. You will get shot if you go in there!'

We walked through the concert hall glad to be out of the snow. We looked at the noticeboards. There was nothing of interest.

Suddenly the alarm went. No one moved. Outside, staff fellows shouted: 'Clear the hall! At the double! Look alive there! Come on, lads. Shake it up, shake it up!'

The leading hand in charge of the library moved slowly to the door. 'Shall I clear the hall, chief?'

'Yes, clear the hall! Double up, man. The "crash" has gone.'

'Oh – em!' said one bitterly.

'Come on! Outside, the bloody lot of you.'

Just as I got to the door a large German bomber flashed over us with guns rattling. Our fellows opened fire from their several positions, but the Hun was lost to sight in the snowflakes and heading out to sea.

'Christ,' said a sailor, 'could have got him with my first three darts!'

'Yes,' said his chum, 'after you had had a couple.'

We made for the shelters. The all clear went at about five. Our officer was still not back so we gave up all hope of hearing how the board had reacted to us, and left the base very disconsolate.

XII

A Sneak Raider

I found a very shaken Mrs Moffat. She followed me into the front room and dramatically put two half-pennies and two farthings on the dining room table. 'There, Mr H-C,' she said triumphantly. 'As I stand here before you, with God as my witness, them's what saved our lives!'

I saw that there was no escape for me. I should have to listen to her account of the raid before she would bring the evening meal.

We had our tea at five-thirty and each fellow who came in had his story and each had come against red tape; each had been told that volunteers were not wanted, the official parties had the job well in hand.

There was one missing from our household – the Scot's engineer did not come in. He had told Mrs Moffat he would be back at four-thirty from a job on a trawler in the docks.

The meal was a quiet affair. The engineer's tea was poured out by mistake and no one would touch it. He had been a quiet old fellow. His lunch had been spoilt by an ill-tempered Wavy Navy lieutenant earlier in the morning, who had told him he was not fit to be a petty officer, and had caustically asked how he had been allowed to rise from an ordinary stoker! His deep Scottish voice had been blurred with misery and almost unintelligible when he told us. 'I nearly knocked the laddie down. All my life in the Navy too! Then these last eight years in charge of an engine room on trawlers! When they all said I was too old for sea? Why! Since I was twelve year old, I've been at sea. And that man there, a townie, with three months at sea and a wee bit of wavy gold braid, thinks he's a Nelson!'

We listened to the news at six. There had been a raid on an East Anglian town, slight damage to property and a few casualties. Yes we knew all about that! I went down town with one of the others to see if we could help. 'Hey, you Jack! Where do you think you're going?' a policeman called.

'Blimey, mate! To give them a hand!' A small band of sailors moved forward with the same intention.

'No you don't! None of you. Now get back! The official men are on the job and they don't need any help, see? And it's my job to see that you don't pass this rope! Get it?'

We 'got it'! If that was the official attitude, who were we to interfere? Somewhat nettled, we went off to the cinema across the bridge at the end of town.

Two hours later we came out into a dark, cloudy night without a star. But a bright glow rose from the centre of the town. Up the middle of the main street was a powerful lamp, shedding a yellowish light down on a heap of rubble that had been the row of shops Mrs Moffat had talked about. Clouds of thick dust hung in the air, as small gangs of men heaved on the ropes, pulling up girders to get at the trapped.

At this end of the street were more sailors and troops anxious to 'give a hand' but all were turned away. A small Navy party on the far side was on the job, having ignored authority. We cut up a side street to get to them and were stopped again. We were furious, for it was obvious that the town's red tape was going to be responsible for a lot of deaths.

'I'm reporting to an officer,' I lied.

'Carry on, sir,' said the policeman.

The NO was delighted to see us. 'Get all the men you can,' he ordered. He took us to a shoe shop. 'Crowd of people trapped in the cellar. See what you can do to help.'

We dashed back to the billet to change into working clothes. Mrs Moffat gave us some cocoa before we turned out. There were four of us.

It was an awful night. As the dead were brought out they were carried into the cinema, now a temporary morgue. Walls collapsed. Cries for stretcher or doctor went on through the hours. We tunnelled under the collapsed shoe shop without much luck, coming out of that choking air for an occasional breather. An errand boy appeared at midnight to tell us where the cellar was and disappeared again. The Mayor, wearing a red tin hat with CONTROL in large white letters, stood by for a while. Later on, he retired to the foyer and watched proceedings from a comfortable chair. This was not his first blitz.

Two days later a woman was to be pulled alive from under a heap of timbers six feet deep. A sailor was extricated from the toilet of a cafe, still with some life in him in spite of the fact that several floors had been above him for forty-eight hours. But that night the Chef was brought up in little pieces. The tailor's dummies gave unpleasant shocks to the uninitiated, and the shoe shop with its wooden trees and plaster feet, also caused some qualms and disappointments.

A few elderly ladies worked wonders in a small canteen nearby with hot soup, cocoa, sausages and mash, cooking away behind the counter, although the entire front had been blown in. While there, at two o'clock my curiosity was aroused by a small group of men who were sifting the earth with great care like beach-combers, while close to them a large group clustered round a safe, like crows round a dead sheep – a jeweller's shop had been above the spot and was giving some a pleasant night. A man hurried off into the night stuffing a heavy wad of notes into his pockets. 'It will be blood money,' said my leading hand who had watched the incident with disgust as he took great gulps of his cocoa. 'Never do them no good. Never!' He had just dug out two dead men and a mortally wounded young sailor. No doctor had answered his call and the boy died before the ambulance – wedged in by several lorries – could be reached.

Another of our lads, a stoker, had just seen too much and had been violently sick. There were so many hands and feet and other bits of human wreckage, bits of a pram mixed with other bits that no longer meant anything. Wiping his green face, he said slowly and bitterly: 'Never no more do I spare a Jerry! Never again will I pick up one at sea. Wipe them out wherever found! The dirty bastards!'

Next morning I went down to the base. An officer had taken the names of all helpers and new suits were to be issued. One fellow had a well worn suit under his great coat. He had ripped the cap and donned his oldest boots, for here was a chance for 'summat for mother!' I fell in behind him and watched a Wren taking his name.

'You *are* in a mess!' said the officer, surveying him keenly. 'What do you need?'

'A new suit, sir! Cap, boots, gloves!' He might have been ordering something from a store.

'Well, well.' The officer looked hard at him, 'We'll start at the top. How did you tear your cap?'

There was a silence. 'A beam fell on it, sir!'

'And you were underneath?'

'Yes, sir.'

'One coat, no suit!'

'But, sir,' said the startled fellow, 'my suit is ruined!'

'Yes, maybe, but not on rescue work. You will have to buy another. Show me your boots.' The fellow was very rattled by now, but he held up a well worn boot.

'Damn it man, you can't tell me you walked those holes in in one night! No boots! You just get one coat! Next.'

Outside the man gave vent to his outraged feelings and bad language filled the hall for awhile.

A few days later I was again on draft. Apparently I had passed the board, so going north once more would not be quite so bad this time. I hoped they would not lose track of my papers again!

I reported to the Drafting Master-at-Arms. 'Returning to your proper ship,' said he. 'Go and draw winter clothing and report back here at two-thirty tomorrow.'

The winter clothing was terrific. I had never seen such 'woollies'. There were two heavy singlets and two pairs of grey woollen ankle length combinations hand knitted in a thick wool, two pairs of gloves, a scarf and a balaclava. I went back to my billet and packed, wondering how a skin that had always fussed over even the finest wool, would take to these new garments.

On Saturday morning a taxi took my stuff down to the station, then I had lunch at the billet and made my farewells. 'You will always be welcome back here,' said kind Mrs Moffat.

XIII

Marking Time. A Shore Job

Two months of waiting about in a wrong base and at The Nest of all places.

The commodore had said: 'You are an SS rating, I can't have you sitting about down here. You'll have to return to your base in Scotland until you are sent for by the final board.'

I had used my time well. Thanks to Captain Balls and his zeal for imparting nautical knowledge, I had filled many gaps in my navigation and seamanship.

I arrived at Waverley station at five in the morning and went across to the Caledonian Hotel and had a bath. My next train was due at eleven-thirty and Edinburgh was hidden in a heavy snow storm. This journey north was always hell. By three-thirty we had finally arrived at a little station in the Western Highlands where three other ratings left the train with me. The RTO was taken by surprise and had to do some hard thinking. He might be able to get an army lorry to take us to the town twenty miles away, but he was not very hopeful.

By some strange accident a small van appeared at that moment through the howling blizzard, the driver an equally diminutive Wren wearing a large duffle coat. We all cheered and followed her into the RTO's office. Yes, even in this two-by-four station, that splendid service was functioning.

But she had not come for us. Who were we? She had no orders for us. We were wet and very cold and I had been on the move since eleven the previous morning. The other three were from Devonport and were properly 'browned off'! 'Might as well have sent us to Siberia – the bastards!' they grumbled savagely. They were complete with tropical kit and not at all happy.

The Wren wavered. She tried to phone through for orders but there was no response. The men she had come to collect were obviously adrift and certainly had not been on the train. It was getting dark and she admitted we could not stand about here all night. So loading up the tiny van, and with the other three crowded in on top of the kit we started off.

The country, heavily covered in snow, looked like a small edition of the Rockies. The wind howled against us and large snow flakes floated onto the windscreen. With no handbrake and a stick gear box, the little Wren had quite a job on her hands and she did it well.

We lurched and slithered down the valley, a frozen stream flanked us on one side some twenty feet below. No one will ever know just why we did not end up in it. Perhaps it was our Wren, a most splendid little driver. But the van was too small and kept nosing into piled up snow drifts. Three times we emptied it out and dug in the storm. But she got us to our base eventually and the loch looked magnificent, surrounded by snow-clad mountains.

I went down Admiral Saunders Road and stopped outside the

regulating hut. The old Marine sergeant – ex-colour sergeant – was our Master-at-arms, the only Marine up here. No one knew why, it really was most odd.

I reported to him and he surveyed me with a far away look: 'Huh, you back again!' It was two months since I had last seen him. 'Well! Well! The months do pass! Draw your bedding and report to the doctor in the morning. You might get some food if you hurry over to the mess.'

The petty officers' hut had a mixture of all trades and many dialects. The language was highly coloured and very much to the point. I turned in and was lulled to sleep by that great sound wave made up of motley human cargo, and the non-stop ruddy radio. Yes. I was back again!

Breakfast was in a saucer, a spoonful of beans and a slice of bacon. The bread was good, our supplies were out and the Poles were keeping us going from their liner in the loch. There were four long tables at the end of the petty officers' mess hut, covered with white oilcloth. There were not enough spoons to go round so we were all told to 'muck in'. 'Mucking-in' seemed to express the situation.

The old three button men – chiefs – sat at the top end and kept to themselves. They were mostly 'dug outs', now no longer anxious for the more active side of life. A few of them were 'going yachting' – instructing crews in the art of landing craft. Their days were spent out on the waters – not always very smooth – and their nights in the mess over beer and darts, or the occasional tombola! They had settled to a definite routine. It seemed to suit them.

I looked round the hut and thought about the will and power to win. A few had kept their swords bright and untarnished but the majority had long since lost their initial enthusiasm and become apathetic, and now only worried about the next leave. One could hardly blame them for this state of mind. The local contractors did odd construction jobs about the place when it stopped raining, on a 'weather permitting' basis, and were well paid for over-time, were believed to be on a thirty hour week, with a minimum of four pounds guarantee. Men could not help making comparisons. Life seemed very unequal and hard at times for those in the Service. The Glasgow bus strike had just ended and that too had thoroughly shaken the sincere volunteers – particularly those from overseas.

I stood in the sick bay at nine for the usual 'medical on arrival'. The sick bay attendant after fixing the cases, turned to me: 'There's nothing wrong with you, is there? Well there's no need to see the doctor. You can carry on.'

XIV

Camp Routine

The rain fell in torrents through the night, with tropical ferocity and never-ending roar. We had 'darkened ship' at eight-thirty and more men had arrived. As each new arrival came in he was sent to the bedding store and issued with two mattress covers, two pillow covers and a pillow, and he had to sign for the mattress which was already on the bed.

Now half the room was filled with two-tiered beds. A small washroom was at one end near the door, with bath and showers etc, each in its own little partition. The air was heavy with smoke and it got thicker until the lights went out at eleven-thirty. Then a few bold spirits took their black-outs down and opened their windows, to the great annoyance of a small section who, accustomed to the well sealed flat of a ship, did not take kindly to a little fresh air. By midnight general rowdiness had died down, and except for a few joke-makers, nothing but the everlasting rain and a symphony of snores disturbed our sleep.,

The camp woke at six-thirty when the seamen had to turn out. We others usually stayed in until seven-thirty, when a hectic rush for the few basins, carried us all in a flying muddle across the green and slightly boggy field, down to the petty officers' mess, above the door of which some enterprising fellow had carved the petty officer's badge on a plaque – crossed anchors surmounted by a crown.

The food was anything but a morning feast. Tea, a slice of bacon, an egg and sometimes a little marmalade to put on the bread and margarine. Late-comers were usually out of luck as far as marmalade was concerned, and cursed heavily. One saucerful was the allowance for twenty men.

By eight-thirty the camp, ship's company with the exception of the petty officers, fell in and were marched off to their allotted tasks.

This morning three of the boats were to re-fuel. My crew – the engineman and seaman – helped me to clean up the craft, and by nine-thirty our 'Looty' came aboard. We were a grand crew and got on very well together. The seaman, a fisherman owning his own boat, which was now of course in the Service, found himself posted to this particular section. He despised the craft he now had to handle. 'Them sore o'craft ain't fit for any as calls his self a seaman.'

This remark constantly reiterated, betrayed his nostalgia for his own trawler. The engineer petty officer owned a sizeable farm implements and motor tractor business, and the lieutenant had been a clerk in the accounts department of a big London Daily and loved every minute of it – this 'breather' from a routine office job.

We let go our moorings and with the other boats went speeding down the waters to the fuel ship. No one was quite sure what was going to supply us, but in a welter of flying spray and leaving a long churned up wake astern, we dashed in great style past the many ships until at last we saw one of our boats alongside a small canal tanker which had tied up to a trawler.

Boats already there were, to our horror, filling up from two gallon cans. These cans were dropped into her tank and after filling themselves, were then hauled up and passed over to the boat's crew, who tipped them into the large funnels and so into the tanks. An amazing performance.

The skipper of this little ship was furious. He had not been told what sort of craft he was to fuel and his usual system – although highly successful to men o'war – did not suit us. Time might be of no object to blue jackets but *he* had none to spare.

We were the last to arrive and when our turn came, the job took us well over an hour.

Passing one of the ships on the way, we went alongside while the 'Looty' boarded her to raid the canteen for duty free fags, rejoining us with a most satisfactory haul of chocolates, which he shared out.

These occasional turns of duty on the water made a welcome change from camp monotony. And were looked forward to by all spare petty officers awaiting draft or the arrival of their ships.

XV

HMSE … and Combined Operations: Back to the Water

With the suddenness of a tropical shower, a messenger found me on one of the 'fast' walks – one that had been taken purely with the object of conveying, whilst passing Number One's office, the idea that I was engaged on important work. It was the traditional method, and one passed on to me by a veteran over a glass of beer. The more experienced usually carried something in their hands, a notebook or a hammer, rather after the idea of a junior assistant director in a film studio – an impression being invariably better than solid fact. The 'quiet-but-efficient-fellow' had not a chance in this outfit. I was learning fast.

A small fellow swinging his whistle stopped me. 'PO, will you report to the Regulating Office right away?'

'Thanks, bosun's mate.'

The regulating office had been a lavatory and the petty officer's desk was pushed up against the two wash basins. There sat the Regulating Petty Officer, his left shoe against the urinals. His assistant, a junior petty officer, sat on an upturned box checking through leave warrants.

'Ah,' said the petty officer. 'A little surprise for you. You are off to the *E* – , joining the 8th Flotilla! Only temporary like. They ain' got no PO now, you see. 'Jimmy' says it won't affect your going down to Pompey.' He added kindly, 'Now return your bedding to the blanket store and pack your kit and report back here at three-thirty.'

My life of boredom was at an end and my only regret was that I was not off to a smaller ship.

With my draft of two ABs we jumped into the Naval truck and were taken to the village pier, joining the crowd of men who were fast filling the duty boat.

HMS *E* – a most unpopular base at that time, lay only a few hundred yards out and we were soon alongside.

'Back to the hell ship,' said one man.

'The bloody old *Altmark*, said another, and other far from

affectionate opprobriums flew around.

E – had been up here for months and always carried the overflow flotillas and of course the infantry training units.

I reported my fellows to the OOD and then went to the ship's office, to the acting Master-at-Arms, where we filled in the usual forms and were allocated messes.

She was a large trooper and the bosun's mate had to pilot us aft to the flotilla crew's quarters. Strange being back in a ship after months of shore bases. My old flotilla shipmates were all aboard, sitting down at one of the long wooden tables having tea. St Davids was there with another flotilla and it all seemed like old times.

There were four tables with various flotillas in a partitioned off area of one mess flat. Dozens of coats were jammed on the rows of hooks, duffles, oilskins and greatcoats; the place seemed packed. A number of small lockers were at the far end and someone kindly found me an empty one. The ports had been closed and the fug was terrific.

I had a cheery tea with my old shipmates and went along to cabin number four to report to my new officers. The corridor was full of Army and Navy officers going to their baths, some in coloured dressing gowns and others with just a towel round their waists.

Cabin Four was in the process of dressing when I arrived. The little darkish fellow was the flotilla leader, and his only officer a tall rather pale-faced young man. The lieutenant put on his tie and looked down at a pile of papers in front of him. I stood at attention with my cap under my left arm and waited. The sub-lieutenant adjusted his towel.

'Ah, very glad to have you, petty officer. This is Lieutenant S – '

The little fellow looked up. 'Well, thank God for that. We've got a PO at last! Now I am afraid you are going to have rather a hard time here. Have a cigarette? We've got the reputation of being the scruffiest lot on board.'

'Yes,' interrupted the sub. 'You are going to have to put your foot down.'

'Now, hold on, subby, I'm doing the talking. See?'

The tall fellow reached for his shirt, and the little man went on: 'Now, we have only been formed three weeks. Some of the lads are good, others are just a lot of barber's assistants. Only just joined up. Conscripts. In fact we have got to train them, see?'

'Yes, sir!'

'Some of them are bloody good!' said the sub.

The little man looked tired: 'Subby, I'm doing the talking. *None* of them are bloody good! Some of them are passably good perhaps, but none are bloody good yet!' He was a Merchant Officer, now an RNR, and I took to him at once. 'Well now, sometime tomorrow I'll give you a list of men. We're off on a party tonight. No need for you to come. See you sometime tomorrow.'

'Thank you, sir.'

'Oh, by the way. I think your boat had better be 211. The Stoker is a Welsh International. Good seaman, just joined. Wants training. See you in the morning.'

'Aye, aye, sir, good night.'

Indian stewards were running to and fro along the first class corridor. They were certainly looking after the officers.

I went below into the fug. This was Wednesday. Hugh was sitting at his mess table and I found the same old crowd. 'Got a hammock?' asked a friend. No, I hadn't bothered to draw one. 'Well now, look here, if you don't mind being bottled, we have a comfortable hideout down in the hospital overflow flat!'

I was in for anything! Definitely I would not lash up any hammock that night! Supper was not worth eating: We had some tea and bread and jam.

Soon after nine-thirty the hammocks started going up overhead; it was time to move. We took our several blankets and pyjamas and climbed on to the next deck, dodging past the OOD on his rounds, who gave his presence away by flashing his torch along the deck.

Our goal was the hospital flat and it was empty, with a heavy medical atmosphere distinctly pleasant after the fuggy air we had just left. Row on row of beds with comfortable spring mattresses, filled the place; it was almost too good to be true. The others had been doing this kind of thing for over a week. They said the fug down below was getting them down, or was it the ruddy hammocks?

Into the night orderly's cabin we moved like naughty school boys, undressed quietly, and quickly got between our blankets.

XVI

Interlude: Brass Hats for a Night

It was good to be in an hotel and heading for home. My train had got into Edinburgh early – four-thirty a.m. in fact – and my next would not leave till after eight. The wind howled over those wet cold-looking cobbles, and a few tired service men wandered about, for even the waiting room was suffering under the austerity rules and was dark.

The taxi splashed along up the ramp past the Art Gallery. The great towering mass of the castle, way up on the hill, was just a black silhouette against the grey dawn sky.

The night porter was sleepy: 'Ye canna take a bath till seven-thirty. No service, ye ken?'

'Aye, I ken.'

'The place is full up,' he informed me. 'If ye want to bunk down in the lounge, I'll gie ye a shake at seven-thirty.'

He led me across and I looked around. On two large sofas, sleeping under their greatcoats, were an admiral and a lieutenant-general. Feeling in good company, I stretched out opposite them, wondering what they would think when they woke later and found a young petty officer on the opposite sofa. The place *must* be packed. What amazing days!

Several hours later I woke to noisy shouting: 'Come, ye lazy bastards ... Up Wullie!'

I rubbed my eyes. Could he mean me? Then I saw the porter go across to the two figures who were still sleeping under their greatcoats. 'Get up this minute, man!' he said, shaking one.

It really was amazing – an admiral and a general too! Was I dreaming? The general turned over and snored loud and long. From the admiral came: 'Ha – Wha-s the time, Jock?'

I sat up and he sat up and we faced each other. He was old and unshaven and rather pathetic. 'Ga mornin' to ye!' he growled.

'Morning!' I said.

Standing up the coat slid to the floor. He put it on again hastily, covering the well worn and very dirty, long winter underpants and moth-eaten vest.

The head porter now arrived on the scene in his gaudy braid and brass buttoned jacket. 'Come along!' he said to the 'admiral'. 'There's hundreds of boots for you this morning!' Then turning to me, 'Ah, good morning, sir! I hear you would like a bath?' Turning to the other sofa he roared, 'Page! Page!' which galvanised the 'general' into action. That worthy now shot up, shedding his borrowed coat. 'What's the matter? – What's all the hollerin' about?' he asked peevishly.

He was a little dwarfed fellow and he got into his shoes muttering fiercely as he laced them up, and then with a magnificent sweep, wrapped the splendid coat around himself, trailing the lower ends along the thick carpet as he followed the 'admiral' into the cloak room where they hung up their borrowed plumes and then scrambled into their own coats, ready for the day's work.

Yes they had slept well – I hoped the owners of the coats had done so too.

The little fellow finished dressing in silence, then addressed me deferentially, 'Ye want a bath, sir? ... Aye ... Well, follow me, please.'

XVII

HMS King Alfred

Brighton station was filled with jostling crowds. They were a prosperous lot in their new spring frocks and light fur coats and their minds seemed far from the war as they chattered and joked. They watched us with not a little interest as we mustered under a large chalked up sign, 'Draft for King Alfred' at one corner of the station.

My train had got me here before the official time on my joining paper, and the tall weather-beaten 'chief' gave me a kindly smile as I walked across to report.

Several dozen others were already there and he made a space amongst the pile of cases for my kit. He was a quiet and very authoritative fellow.

'Your chum Clements been askin' fer you, 'e's gone off to 'ave a feed.'

'Thanks, chief, I think I'll go and join him.'

'Right oh, mate. Be back at one forty-five,' and he turned to sort a muddle of kitbags that was fast piling up and blocking the fairway.

At two o'clock we 'fell in' alongside three double decker buses and answered a roll call. A large draft of one hundred and thirty-five were soon trooped into the buses.

Several young 'subbies' from our northern base passed us, apparently on leave; passed us with less than a nod, although we had only left the place three weeks before. They were very conscious of their one wavy stripe.

We were carried up the steep hill behind the station and we were soon outside a large three storied school. The organisation was really good, so with the minimum of trouble we found ourselves free of kit and out on a large playing field facing the commander, a most impressive figure of stern authority – whose words on behaviour and deportment in and around this establishment – made the most tender-hearted quake! We were most definitely 'lower deck' and were there to learn the art of being 'Officers and Gentlemen' we were told.

From stage to stage, we floated along until finally, armed with our billeting cards and a large sheet of foolscap paper on which we were to write an essay on 'My most interesting and exciting experience since joining the Navy' we found ourselves out in the roadway again – a most efficiently managed afternoon with the best mass-production methods and fewer bottle-necks than we had ever experienced before.

The billet was a ten minute walk away. We had been alloted one large room with a double bed and a small table laid for 'supper'. It was five o'clock now and a garrulous Welsh woman showed us around the ground floor of this three-storied house off Old Shoreham Road.

It reminded me of my first billet at Lowestoft nearly a year earlier; in the sink was the same cracked enamel basin to wash in, the same outside whitewashed lavatory – and no bath!

We remembered how the commander had finished his speech with: 'The landladies know more about the routine and the boards than you will ever know – so get in their good books and you will probably get some tips!'

'If yer knows nothing and looks clean and tidy like ... See if I'm not right! ... You two've got nothing to worry about. Mark my words! I can always spot 'em!'

We wrote our essays and surveyed Brighton with a keen eye. Our months in the wilds of Scotland had left their mark and we knew we were going to enjoy ourselves. The list of banned pubs, dance halls and certain addresses out of bounds for us covered a full page of foolscap.

Each day some twenty or thirty fellows were called out to the boards and the remainder went on with marching, signals and squad drill. Our numbers grew less and there were days when a percentage was failed, so the general tension was terrific.

Those who failed slipped away quietly and without fuss. A messenger would call out some names and we knew that after half-an-hour, they would either be back again, or – hideous prospect – in the office of the Master-at-Arms collecting their drafting orders which would take them back to their depots and the lower deck for the duration. Many faces became a memory and we wished to God our turn would come soon so that we might be put out of our misery.

On Friday morning Clem and I found our names amongst a dozen for the afternoon board in the lower room. There were two boards, 9 and 9a – and word had gone round that the lower was the kinder of the two!

As the morning of signal practice went on we watched with interest and concern as the first ones on the list went off, and even noted that not all returned from the lower 9 board room! Had we been right after all?

It became increasingly difficult to concentrate on our little divisional officer, as he sent his messages on a morse lamp, out on the sunlit lawn, for through the window we could see the three backs of the great panjandrums as they talked to each candidate. Our eyes were constantly drawn to that window, away from the signal flashes.

Lunch at the digs was a strain. The landlady in her kindness had done her best to give us a good 'send off' as the eight baked potatoes on our plates showed, but the dish of ground rice and three tough

(*Right*) Henty in working
submarine gear
(*Below*) X-craft surfaced

(*Top*) The 51-foot long X-craft on the surface

(*Centre*) X-craft in training

(*Left*) X-craft diving

prunes was not up to the proposed expedition. I left a very disappointed landlady to eat them herself. I hope the punishment fitted the crime!

We three waited in the dental waiting room at two sharp – a silent thoughtful lot of three Bluejackets and three petty officers. The dentist made sure our teeth were all right before we saw the board – a quaint touch!

Clements was to be the first in. We followed him down three flights of stairs from the attic to that lower room and were mustered by a cheerful little three stripe able seaman with his last war ribbons and his greying hair, who looked us up and down critically. He had seen many thousands pass through before us.

The bell rang and in went Clements, with a nervous last minute tug at his jacket and a hurried look round at us all.

'Good luck, old boy,' and he was through the door.

The suspense was terrific. There was no talk at all and we could hear our hearts beat, as we watched with assumed interest, a squad outside doing gas mask drill. For fifteen long minutes this act went on and then the door opened. In those fifteen minutes they had decided a future officer and Clem came out looking slightly ruffled and rather hot. The bell rang before we could speak and he went in again to hear their decision while we others watched and waited without a word. Almost immediately he re-appeared all smiles.

'I'm through, ha, ha!' And he did a little jig. The one time colliery agent, after nineteen months a petty officer in raiding craft was well on the way to greater heights. 'See you later, I'm off to have a smoke!' he said and was off.

There was a slight pause which seemed to run to eternity! My turn next. I wondered if the first parachute jump could be any worse than this. The bell rang and I went into the passage.

'You're all right, don't worry. I can always pick 'em,' said the nice old able seaman, as he opened the door for me.

In the oval shaped room with their backs to the three windows at three large desks piled with papers sat a vice-admiral between an instruction commander and an RNVR captain. On a small Persian rug, spread out on the parquet floor directly in front of the group, sat a small upright chair to which the admiral waved me, I closed the door. I sat and faced the trio, doing a mental 'Quick pan' from desk to desk, hoping that my bearing and forced smile expressed a complete confidence I was far from feeling.

This was the climax of my first year in the Navy and my hopes were intense. One stripe meant so much more than just better conditions. It was to be a return to my more normal ways of life, of responsibilities regained after weary months a pawn in the hands of chief petty officers and some inefficient misfits of sub-lieutenants who – unused to responsibilities in civil life – found the task of commanding men, even bolstered up as they were by King's Regulations, beyond them. I would be an entity again and no longer a sheep to be jostled about in a mighty flock hither and thither. And more than all I would be a stride higher to 'Action Stations'.

I was asked about my schooldays, about my film career and what I knew about the sea. While the Admiral held the floor, the Commander read my essay and I was relieved to see I had drawn a smile.

'What is the 13 fathom mark on a lead line?' and 'What would you do if you saw a canbuoy dead ahead?' Were two of the Admiral's questions. Then two little brass model ships were manoeuvred on his desk, bringing the rule of the road into play. So far so good.

The commander passed my essay over to the admiral and I now felt far from happy. My writing had been awful. I had lost my pen on the way down to Brighton and had had to use the landlady's post office loot. I brought this up and raised a laugh.

The commander was interested in my Swiss schooldays; when he heard that no English had been spoken there, he did not bother to delve into my French, but stopped asking questions and said, pointing to the essay, which was now in the captain's hands, 'You really have quite a remarkable memory! If you can remember everything you are taught you should do very well!'

'Thank you, sir,' I said, hoping a smile hid my surprise.

The captain's turn came. He was very interested in my film days and talk went from my weeks in France with the BEF on the army film, in the days before the retreat, then across to Hudson's Bay and the *49th Parallel*. It was a most informal and pleasant talk, cut short at last by the admiral. 'Well, now, wait outside will you?' I left and closed the door quietly.

'What the devil have you been up to?' said someone.

'Blimey, mate,' said the old three-striper, 'You hold the record for time in that room!'

My allotted fifteen minutes had apparently stretched on to twenty-five. Now what was to be the result? I steeled myself for the worst. The bell rang and I was inside again and they were cheerfully smiling. 'I'm sending you up to Lancing on the 18th,' said the admiral.

My relief was terrific. 'Oh, thank you, sir!'

They beamed benignly. 'You will have to work now, and pass the exams all right!' sternly admonished the great one.

'I certainly will, sir,' I promised, inflated with gratitude.

'If you get amongst the first fifteen in your lot,' he continued, 'you are given a choice of ships. Otherwise you will automatically find yourself back in Combined Operations!'

With visions of an MTB of my own I said with great determination, 'I most certainly will, sir.'

'Carry on,' said the admiral.

Brighton was a merry place that night.

XVIII

First Day at Lancing

The second week at Mowden went by with great speed – partly because the board had been passed and we had come out on the right side of the door, and also because we now found ourselves amongst a hundred others, from all walks of life, looking forward with great interest to the next stage of this little drama.

We walked with a happy feeling of exuberance, and we watched with a lofty air of superiority succeeding batches of competitors go through the mill. During the day we practised on each other in a large playing field, had squad drill or attended classes and lectures on gas, signals, and elementary maths – an easy 'running in' period before the start of our course proper. At night there was the Theatre Royal or films.

On Friday morning a hundred names were put up on a board and orders were given to muster kit that afternoon. After lunch there was a lecture by the first lieutenant. We heard what we might expect and in turn what was expected of us. We could work hard but not *too* hard! We were darkly told that character and not marks, would get us out on top and we were exhorted not to worry too much. It was a most amusing talk and put us all in a really cheerful frame of mind.

Came the dawn and an early start. The two buses and lorries were loaded by eight-thirty and we were off down the road that stretched along the coast, with a 'Good luck lads' from the smiling chief in charge. He was of the old school and as this was the first time he had smiled since our arrival, our attitude to him changed too. 'Poor old blighter – fancy having to do this every week.' We all waved and gave him a hefty cheer.

Having been told by the officer that we were most honoured to be in the running for the coverted gold stripe and that we must not forget that we were still merely ratings and would be until the final posting several weeks hence, we felt that dignity could go by the board for the moment.

The large grey stone buildings of this old public school, standing stark and formal on a green hill top, looked most impressive and a hush fell on us all as we took in the pleasant surroundings. The white ensign flew lazily atop the small green square lawn in front of the tall chapel and our new divisional officer was standing on the 'Quarter Deck' as our bus climbed the winding slope.

Almost before the buses came to a standstill the voice of authority broke through our silent ranks, 'Come on now! Double up there!'

Our names were called and we found ourselves in four classes, all nautically named – mine was Nelson Division. There was a pause while the vans backed up to the broad steps leading to the lower quadrangle, then our eager hundred were told to grab cases and 'fall in'.

Our warden, a cheery and rotund chief petty officer, then marched us up to our respective dormitories, large airy rooms with double deck bunks. But we were not allowed to rest: we were off again to draw our bedding, marching up the long and winding cloisters in two ranks, to the bedding store where we signed for the blankets etc., under the eye of our tall, lean divisional officer, Lieutenant Wintle, and his assistant – an RNVR two-ringer. Then off again to our dormitory, falling in again through many turns and passages to the armoury store. Our hearts failed us when we drew full packs and equipment. By this time the Left, Right, Left, of our chief was getting us down, but our smiles returned when back once more at our bunks came the order, 'Right oh, lads, you can take it easy now. Get stripped for the doctor.'

The doctor and our divisional officer then came their rounds, while we – panting from all our exertions and rather flustered – stood naked in front of each bunk. Then a medical orderly inspected our feet and we dressed again, a few being picked out and told to report later to sick bay.

There was a thankful pause after this speedy moving in. Our warden gave us a few words while we dressed and made our bunks. There was more 'falling in' and we were in the drill shed – the old school theatre – listening to the speech of welcome read out by the commander. Then we were 'off-capped' while the articles of war were read to us; very impressive but rather trying, all this standing 'to attention' for what seemed ages.

Off we went again in a march round the establishment to the various sentry posts. We were to be the 'duty division' over the week-end. In four classes we were split into the defence scheme and by the time this was all settled it was twelve-thirty and lunch-time.

The large and very impressive dining hall with its panelled walls and arched roof, that once – not so very long ago – had echoed to the talk of school boys, looked down on the four white-clothed tables that ran the entire length to the top end, where they were met by the raised dais of the officers' table, stretching across from wall to wall.

After the austerities of the *E* – we savoured keenly the pleasure of being waited on by waitresses once more.

We were a motley lot, in bell-bottoms and petty officers' rig, ex-business bosses, men of means, clerks, salesmen and so on, down to the garage hand who had told the admiral he was a motor trade director – and got away with it.

To some, this first meal – as embryo officers and gentlemen – was an anxious occasion and in their efforts to behave in a manner expected of their future rank they put their best foot forward, with not altogether happy results.

We fell in once more after lunch and were marched to the science block for our divisional officer's talk. At first this officer seemed a veritable terror, but after half-an-hour the humour began to break through. In short crisp jerks, supported and supplemented by his assistant – a lawyer in civil life – this RN lieutenant talked of routine, dress, manners and morals. It was a good manly talk and we admired his handling of the business, but by now we were thoroughly tired and rather hot.

The powers that be had anticipated this, and the next move was to the swimming pool for the 'water test'.

A and B classes went first one after the other, some in swimming shorts and others in the little nature had given them, swam two lengths with varying skill. Our warden ticked off each name, as each fellow came out and once more we dressed and relaxed. But not for long. Off we went again, across the upper quad to the violet ray lamp. 'God, what a life!' said someone as we stripped and faced each other in a circle round the solitary lamp. Then we were mustered again and once more marched round the base to learn the layout of the class rooms.

After a short break for tea we moved into our lockers, and stowed our kit bags below in the baggage room.

From the hour leading up to nine-fifteen 'Fall in' for the first watch, the dormitory had been filled with little groups of men anxiously trying out 'Slope arms' and 'Present Arms' to the accompaniment of much barracking and good-humoured chaffing. It was amazing to note how few knew anything about firearms, in spite of their year in the Service!

'If Hitler could see our lot,' said one wit, 'he would be up the Thames tonight.'

We were marched off and given ammunition. 'Now if any of you lads is to lose this 'ere stuff, it will be off with those funny little caps what you wear, and up before the commander in the morning. Get it?'

'Do we load our rifles?' one queried.

'No, lad! You don't want no trouble, does yer? So don't try no mucking about. Leave it in yer packs and see yer brings it back. Get me?'

And we were marched off – cadet sentries on our first spell of duty.

I was posted to a trench in a sloping field. The sole occupant was a large tom cat, who carried on with his diversions during my watch. After a session of weird noises he would suddenly spring out and hurtle down the hedge, to the general annoyance of the bird and animal world.

Foxes called, the hedge moved and rustled, and a cloud obscured the new moon. I was fully expecting our divisional officer to be on the prowl, as of course he had promised, and I came to loathe that hedge during the next three hours. As it grew darker and the love calls of the Canadian soldiers in a nearby wood grew less boisterous,

I wondered just how much longer I would be able to stay awake. Before I could lapse, the officer arrived and with an enthusiasm, I was too tired to share, discussed the commanding field of fire. I tried to be interested, but was glad when he took himself off on his 'snoop cruise'. The lads at the main gate were kept busy halting cars and late-comers, but even they became quiet as the hours wore on.

At long last it was over. The tough voice of the chief petty officer called: 'Hey, you out there, come on in,' and a tall figure loomed through the dark to relieve me. His method of so doing had none of the tact we were told to expect, but he got his ammunition back! I turned in at one a.m.

So ended our first day – and what a day!

XIX

Welcome to the Brotherhood

We had left our studies with the gunnery chief in one of the small classrooms off the great hall, and individually made our way down across the two large quadrangles and the gravel quarterdeck to the captain's quarters overlooking the lovely valley and the sea.

Our warden with twinkling eyes, chuckled as he checked out names against a class list, his shining boots crunching the gravel to our heartbeats as we stood smartly in line awaiting our turn.

We had heard so much about this interview ... Rumour had it that this was one of the most telling moments in our five weeks course here. Everyone was out to give his best in true Navy style. Some had no ties to fiddle with; instead, the black silk and clean white lanyard came in for the usual nervous attention that always gives fellows away, no matter how calm they may otherwise appear.

The heavy oak door swung on its large hinges and pink-faced cadets came out with rather monotonous regularity and hurried back to the gunnery classroom.

As we waited by the old stone balustrade in the early spring sunshine, we watched the planes take off from the airfield below, beside the silver stretch of river. The warden paced up and down checking newcomers like a proud old broody hen; we were his charges and must not let him down.

At last my turn came and with that – literally – fearful interest in just what exactly I was to see on the other side of the door, I found myself in a large panelled room. Bright light flowed through the tall windows and the old parquet floor shone with dazzling brightness. As I moved into the centre of the expanse, a deep gruff voice said, 'Come in, Henty-Creer.' And I walked over and stood on a small Persian mat in front of a large desk. Interesting how very small a small mat can make one feel!

With his back to the window sat an extremely well-built man with pure white hair. At first as he sat in a dead black light it was hard to see his expression, but a long arm shot across the desk and we shook hands.

'Welcome to the Brotherhood, my boy,' he greeted me richly. Slumping back into his seat he looked at me appraisingly and relapsed into thought for a few moments gathering up his forces for the attack. Suddenly springing to a half rise, he said in deep solemn tones: 'You are about to become an officer ... About to place your feet on the lowest rung of a mighty ladder. Do you realise your responsibility towards your fellow men?'

'I do, sir,' I said with conviction.

'You realise that you are taking it upon yourself to lead men, perhaps to their death, men who will rely implicitly upon your every action, men who are trained to obey your orders no matter how fateful they may be, believing in the tradition of our mighty Navy?' His voice was shaking with intense passion.

'I do, sir.'

'Ah! And knowing this, you are prepared to lead these fine men against the bastard Hun and those bloody little Japs?' He glared with deep blue eyes that seemed to cut right through me, and then very softly added, 'Until victory is achieved?'

My 'Yes' caused no perceptible break in the steady flow of words.

'But only by hard training and industry and the banding together of our wonderful Empire will we be able to sweep them and their filthy followers from the face of the earth.' Raising his hand he pointed a hefty finger at me: '*You*, my boy, have it in your power to lead ... to lead and rebuild a better world. Knowing that the Royal

Navy is behind you, following its young officers to victory. Work hard. Never let up! Even after you have finished here, study and equip yourself, gather the knowledge that has been handed down to you, by your superiors from our long proud past and great traditions! Only by knowing that you do your job, will you ever get the full confidence of your men!'

He straightened up. '*You* have your feet on the bottom of our mighty ladder – *I*, am half way up. There is no top! Nelson tried hard enough God knows, but he never reached it.' His voice died down: 'The brotherhood of the sea expects a lot from you. Go back to your studies, my boy, and think of what I have said: for it is upon you to carry on our proud Naval traditions and take them to a new and greater glory – Goodbye!'

Turning his back he stared into the yellow rays of that morning sun out over the sea. I left, very moved by his splendid words and closed the door quietly.

When I entered the class room, the class stood up and chorused, 'Welcome to the Brotherhood, Brother!'

XX

The Final Hurdle

The examinations had gone on for four days and now we were reaching the final hurdle. The first few days had been treated with the respect they deserved, but later there was a distinct falling off in night work – the feeling of, 'what is to be' seemed to prevail – tempers became uncertain. Feeble jokes of the 'Back to Pompey' style were made, and most affected indifference.

These three months had gone quite fast really and now it was beginning to dawn on some that if the gods frowned, they might be back in Portsmouth barracks by Thursday afternoon – on the lowest rung once more, ambition blighted and with nothing to look forward to – back to where they had started among the ranks of little wooden faces. An awful thought!

On Wednesday morning we had heard the answers to several examination papers. In the afternoon that long row of houses, now taken over by many tailors, opposite the Naval establishment, had opened their doors for final check-ups.

The strain of study had left its mark, and various groups had got together and threatened to drink themselves under the table that night. 'Our last supper,' said one flippantly.

A party of a dozen of us had a cheery party at the Freemason's Arms in a little supper room. The Theatre Royal followed with Gilbert Frankau's latest show, then by buses back to Freemason's for a 'final'.

When for the last time the duty petty officer came on his rounds with a noisy, 'Nah then, you lads, get turned in,' and an officer followed up with, 'You're not over the hurdle yet. I'll give you two minutes to get these lights out,' we were jolted back to earth.

'No, by God, but why rub it in?' muttered one frightened reveller. We hoped the officer had not heard the fool; no one wanted any trouble!

On Thursday morning the dormitory came to life earlier than usual. The heads were crowded with pyjama clad figures having an early shave. After PT at six-forty we scrambled to return our bedding to the store – blankets – mattress cover and pillow slips; then we packed.

After breakfast a final tidying-up process followed. We had been ordered to muster in the large cadets' ante-room, that was to have been a municipal swimming pool before the Admiralty took over. There we would await the final board.

We did our last march past as cadet ratings and then on to the spacious place where the final passing out routine would take place. When we saw that our pay books had been stamped 'Temp. Sub-Lieutenant, RNVR' we hoped that this department was not taking too much for granted! Our officer's jibe the previous night about the last hurdle kept all but the most confident ones in an unpleasant state of fret.

We went through the necessary stages of the system from table to table, answering the questions of the Wrens and filling in the innumerable cards. The presentation of certificates was to take place at eleven-thirty and meanwhile we sat and read or pretended to read the daily papers.

At ten-thirty our old three badge warden came through the swing doors, and stood on the tiled stone walk above the smooth worn lawns that had felt the tramp of many thousands before us. Taking his sailor's cap off he held up his hand and a still hush fell on the lofty place that in peace-time would have been echoing to the splash and merry making of water revellers. We hundred turned intently as he coughed importantly.

'The following cadet ratings is to stand over here.' Five names followed – and mine was there. It would be an understatement to say I was shocked.

We five made our way over followed by the wondering and relieved glances of the rest. Their eyes spoke the same language in many different ways. Nobody envied us the distinction. One – Davies – we knew, must have passed brilliantly and no one had any doubt that he would be somewhere at the top, but what fate had in store for the other four no one could hazard.

We got together – sheep for slaughter – and the warden left with 'You're for the final board. Wait till I comes for you. And mind you don't stray.'

At times like this, cigarettes have a strange way of being lit and as suddenly snuffed out, and soon thrown nervously aside. In an isolated group we sat and waited for our warden's re-entrance. Old friends came over for a word to lighten the strain.

'Got nothing to worry about, old boy. Dead cert! You can't fail!' and with an over-friendly pat on the back – like visitors at a sick bed – they were off, inwardly thanking God that time was short and that it was obvious there would only be time for the appearance of the group of five – and no more!

The warden came at last and we followed him out and up the stone steps to a long corridor, where a chief petty officer stood waiting in the quietness. On a form against one of the walls we sat and looked across to the door where the chief stood sentinel. When it opened, a quiet voice said, 'Davies'. And it closed again.

Dave had been standing waiting beside our warden, who now opened the door with a most ceremonial air and bowed the first of our quintet in.

At times like these, minutes have a knack of becoming audible. I tried to read one of the latest Penguin booklets on Russia's internal reactions to the war, but mine were more shattering, and somehow the page would not photograph!

Davies came out at last, smiling, cheerful and gave the thumbs-up sign as he closed the door.

'I've passed – top of the division,' he said happily, and was off at speed down the stairs.

'Huh!' said the warden. 'He done all right, he has!'

And then the voice called out again: 'Andrews!'

The warden nodded to the second victim with ceremony. Andy was a broad Scot from the Lowlands whose ruddy comlexion was now crimson and white by turns. 'Good luck, lad,' said the warden as he closed the door on him. 'Blimey! Funny how some is easily scared.' He came over to me and spoke confidentially. 'I've seen some funny chaps sitting on that bench. Some as cool as you like – but the others, coo!' And he went back to the door with a knowing wink.

Then my turn came and I entered the panelled room with its long boardroom table, packed with many striped arms glinting in the bright summer light that shone strongly through the tall windows.

'Sit down,' said the admiral as he thumbed through some papers. I looked around the room with its double row of seated and standing figures. There seemed so many of them that faces became a blur and I was merely conscious of the light walls as a background to a dark blue circle of figures looking down at me! The admiral coughed. The silence was ghastly and I felt infinitesimally small, sitting on that straight-backed chair – the target of so many eyes. 'Huh! Well, Henty-Creer, think you could have done any better in your navigation?'

'Yes, sir – I could have.'

'Well, work at it, my boy – work at it!' There followed a pause as he looked at the others. And then: 'Congratulations, my boy! You have done very well indeed.'

I was quite startled and smiled in bewilderment.

'Congratulations, Henty-Creer. Very good work,' said the captain of the establishment. I got to my feet in sheer surprise and thanked him. Others said, 'Good show, good show!' I bowed to the captain with another, 'Thank you, sir,' and left, still shaken and very wondering. In fact I still am. I had passed out third on the divisional list of a hundred odd cadets and the shock staggered me.

The poor fellow who followed had the doubtful distinction of hitting the bottom rung of the ladder for the lowest marks of the division – an honour most of us had half expected and dreaded.

Back in the ante-room, 'stand easy' had been piped and coffee and biscuits were being handed round. After that we 'fell in' outside on the balcony in the order of our passing out marks and were brought to attention by our divisional officer as the admiral and party came out. The admiral stood there on the terrace overlooking the sea flanked by the captain and assisted by the commander with the certificates; and one by one we went up to the great man, saluted, shook hands, saluted again, received the small cards, then stepped back to the ranks.

After all this and a small speech, we marched in single file through the ward room and back to our dormitories.

For the last time dressed as ratings the order, 'Front rank, left turn, quick march!' was given by the divisional officer and the one hundred brand-new 'subs' marched off the terrace and through the ward room without a pause, with a confident swing down the stairs to the underground space.

The morning was over at last.

XXI

Greenwich Naval College

Excitement was terrific. The amusingly mixed accents and noisy, released laughter of the Royal Navy's latest additions to the quarterdeck, filled the underground dormitories where bunks were now piled high with packages and parcels from every tailor in town. Caps with their shiny new badges were tried on innumerable times to the accompaniment of hoots and jeers; the circle of stiffened cane was taken out and tops crumpled to take off the looks of 'new-ness'. Sailor caps were tossed in the air. We were free! It was amazing.

No one could really describe their spartan year in the lower deck as enjoyable. Later on some would look back with pride on having 'gone through it' but few who were accustomed to anything better would say, 'I enjoyed those days of swabbing decks and hammock slinging, and scrambled meals and the hideous lack of privacy and quiet.' I had been luckier than a great many others in becoming a petty officer which gave me some slight privileges and a collar and tie. But I often found food and conditions barely supportable. Perhaps others were luckier.

And indifferent as one might be to physical hardships and discomforts, no one of average mental development could do other than chafe at the mental limitations of the life. The assumption of the powers that be that lower deck intelligence and powers of reasoning were of the lowest order, was definitely degrading; and only a man with a 'dead soul' could be satisfied to be a two-legged number plate, a monkey on a string pulled up and down, by omnipotent authority.

The 'White Paper' routine had been a worrying business from start to finish; the starts and false starts, the long marking time periods before boards, the necessity of keeping a very watchful eye on one's papers: the strain of getting 'recommends' from each new set of officers in every new ship: the constant necessity of riding oneself on a curb, of forcing oneself to function as smoothly as an automaton, to run meekly with the herd of 'little wooden faces', had been hard to bear. My first papers had gone down with my first ship. My second lot – only started after three months under observation at a new base with fresh officers – were lost by the captain's office during a draft to another ship which took place at that period. Through these mishaps nearly a year was to pass before I put up the white cap band of a Naval cadet rating.

This period to some might have seemed a waste of time, but, to me at least, the great experiment had been worth while from the human point of view. I had met and mixed with men of every creed and class and country that together make 'This England'. It had been an education all its own and had broadened my outlook. It had done me, I hope, a lot of good, and it gave me an understanding and insight into human nature that I could not have got from many a tome on psychology.

Some were luckier than others. Those who were posted to Ganges and Collingwood and had their papers 'kept warm' while they did their three months at sea had the easier road, but they missed the practical experience of seamanship that came our way in small boats, trawlers, raiding craft, and the like. One 'competitor' on a cruiser, for instance spent his time carrying the tool bag of an artificer; others in the battleships hardly saw daylight, spending most of their time below deck; and although this period stood them well before the board, they looked apprehensively to their future as officers in the little ships that most of them would finish up in – and of which they knew nothing.

Our lot had been lucky – we had had a varied programme and we had got to grips with seamanship.

Some of us had not seen much of the enemy, but we had at least put in some useful sea time. And as very few indeed would ever get to anything bigger than destroyers, I for one felt no loss at missing the battleship routine. We had taken the rough with the smooth and were now ready for anything.

The final change over was made with a light hand, but many winced when the commander made a farewell speech, in which it was implied that – by Naval process and that alone – we had now become gentlemen, and, as such, officers and gentlemen, he wished us luck.

The 'brass hats' standing on the terrace watched us as we hurried with our suitcases to board the buses that would take us to Greenwich, where for a fortnight we would get our final polish.

The afternoon was hot and the men in those four buses fiddled with nervous hands at almost forgotten ties. In that class of a hundred only about a dozen of us had been petty officers. The new dignity sat heavily on some who sat in almost sombre silence politely smiling in meek gentility at normal jokes. They would get over it in time, but meanwhile this passing phase was rather odd to watch after the so very recent burlesque of life in bell-bottoms.

Every conceivable type of luggage filled the racks from the small green canvas Naval issue suitcases, and small brown things of composite leather, to expensive affairs from Piccadilly.

Some had costly greatcoats, others had been content to cut the belts from their rating raincoats; the Naval grant for the outfit needed a little management. Some had gone to the glory of silver-topped canes.

Greenwich, grey and formal behind the great iron railings, carried the war heavily on her outer facade. She was dusty and sandbagged, and fitted harmoniously into the misty river scene now heavy with industrial gloom and a sinking sun.

We debussed into the waiting arms of our young field training officer who wore a faded green band, and eyeing us with a cheerful grin – a happy change – promptly lined us up in our four classes. He, also, had a little word to say about the freedom of officers and what was expected of us during our sojourn in the establishment. We were no longer to be chased about 'like a lot of irresponsible kids' – had we been? – but to conduct ourselves like officers. Punctuality at lectures was to be our watchword for the next two weeks.

Men of the previous division then marched us across the great quadrangle, past the Queen Anne block now taken over by budding Wren officers, to see the lecture rooms, notice boards, regulations and the rest. And at last we were free to carry our bags up to our 'cabins'.

The building had been badly bombed and smelt of age. On my floor, plaster still hung in layers from the ceiling, much of which was in an extraordinary state of disrepair. There were two double-bunked bedsteads and two single ones, one large old deal wardrobe and two very ancient Victorian marble topped wash stands – for six officers. Heavy brown paper covered the low windows, open and level with the tree tops overlooking the park. Trams rattled and bumped along below and the evening crowds filled the pavements. It was strange watching the normal world of people passing on their way once more, whilst we up here, so lately snatched from their midst, were noisily 'moving in' along those dark passages.

The Painted Hall with its three long tables was a strange contrast to those other days. Armed with a napkin we had taken from a locker downstairs we sat where we wished. Wren officer cadets under training sat at a table in the centre. And overlooking us all, up some steps was the President's table.

Smartly uniformed little Wrens waited with speed and efficiency on us all under the eyes of their petty officers and chiefs. The painted ceiling glowed softly as the yellow light from the table lamps reached up. The food was excellent and varied, a change keenly appreciated by us all after our long period of culinary adventures in lower deck messes and unsavoury billets.

In the morning the commander said his little piece: 'We want you to absorb if possible the dignity of Naval officers here,' he remarked, 'so when you go into meals don't rush like a lot of hungry wolves; walk as if the stately charm of the place was a part of you. There is plenty of food – as far as I know. So you have nothing to worry about!'

He had watched our entrance – rather hurried I will admit – in to dinner the previous evening.

The surfaced X-craft at full speed

(*Left*) The harness worn by the officer of the watch on the deck of the X-craft. (*Right*) The narrow deck of the craft showing the hatchway into the interior

The interior of an X-craft, looking aft, where an officer is in the after control position. At this post, he could steer the boat and operate the hydroplanes, the engine and all the pumps. He is looking at a depth gauge while operating the hydroplane control. The large wheels in the left and right foreground released the mines from the side of the boat. The "joystick" on the officer's left was a four-way control for pumping ballast either from side to side or fore and aft trim tanks. The wooden handle on the right was an emergency hand-operated pump for bilges and internal tanks. On the deck beside the officer is the "gluepot" cooker – a double saucepan which could be used only when the craft was on the surface with the engine running to extract the steam. This was the only way the crew could have warm food.

An X-craft in dry dock, showing a practice mine attached to the port side of the boat. The black marks on the bow were priming for a paint touch-up. The hole in the stem of the craft carried a hollow steel towing bar, with a shackle at either end for the tow-line and release-gear. The telephone wire ran through the towing bar to a watertight plug. The fitting immediately below carried the shackle of a wire towing pendant, permanently rigged and clipped to the casing. The vertical tube is the air induction trunk, attached to which is a radio aerial. To the left of the induction trunk can be seen the night periscope, between two small guard rails. It had a wide range of vision and could be fully rotated, elevated or depressed. It acted as a lookout when the boat was on the surface in weather too rough for a man to stay on deck, and when submerged it provided effective underwater viewing. The scuttle (porthole) in the side of the dome to the right of the induction trunk provided sideways vision.

'Try while you are here,' he went on, 'to regain that feeling of quiet dignity, good manners, and above all, of gentlemen. Remember when you join your ships, you may find yourselves in foreign lands. And as such you will be watched by foreigners and judged accordingly. You are all ambassadors in your way, and your conduct as an officer in the Royal Navy is highly important. Never forget this and remember that the art of being a gentleman can be quite easily acquired, given a little study. Whilst you are here, look about you, let some of this ancient grandeur sink in. Take it all in. It won't do you any harm!'

Yes, some would have to forget saying, 'Wotcher, mate!' and all the rest. But they seemed to be doing it quite naturally now.

We were a large crowd and meals were arranged in two sittings, but although the commander had reminded us that the later sessions were the smartest – officers having their meals at a late hour – our appetites were prodigious, and the early sittings filled the great hall with extraordinary rapidity!

Those, with homes in London, disappeared after dinner. There were no station 'cards', no late passes, no book signing. It was wonderful.

London was at her best and everyone enjoyed themselves. It was all rather a joke really, but it was pleasant. And after a year of that other life, one felt it had come just in time. We wallowed in our regained freedom and the war took on a new and somehow more personal meaning. We hoped we would not let 'them' down when our turn came to command.

The two weeks which followed were wonderful. We did not learn much – but that was beside the point now. This place had another object and I saw it shaping.

The solitary little wavy stripe seemed to work wonders for some and how they revelled in it! – Their voices changed and they wore their new manner self-consciously with a little swagger, but with a great seriousness that was very warming. A mixed but a great lot.

XXII

Hymn of Hate

The last fortnight at Hove went by at incredible speed. After Greenwich it came as rather an anti-climax and somehow seemed to get in at the wrong end of the gigantic training sequence. For having been rather lulled into the quarter-deck atmosphere at Greenwich, the very intensive drill course which now took an important place in the scheme of things brought home very forcibly what our responsibilities might entail. That might have been the general idea of its position in the training schedule, for some of us certainly needed a reminder of the sterner realities of war.

Some fifty of us were marched off to the small green playing field on the sea front, into the waiting arms of the immortal Chief Petty Officer Vass.

Vass was a remarkable man whose fame as a field training expert, had spread far and wide — so far in fact, as to be almost global. Wherever an RNVR officer of King Alfred days happened to be, his name was sure to crop up. I had heard of him long ago as a rating. His name had come up at odd moments from various officers who knew I was marked down for King Alfred. All spoke of him with awe and left me in little doubt as to what to expect at his hands — and tongue.

During our weeks at Hove we had watched him. During that period he had not had more to do with us than bark an occasional correction during the temporary absence of our training officer. He was a small man with a bronzed weather-beaten face, from which shone with penetrating brightness and every ferocity — dark, all seeing eyes. He seemed to wear a perpetual smile that broke into unspeakable sarcasm at the oddest moments and with unpredictable suddenness. It was a smile that always fooled the newcomers and drew the unwary into his range of devastating invective. The popular idea of the sergeant-major had nothing on him; he was in a class of his own. On that green field he was entertaining — and knew it. His choice and use of the English language opened new doors to me. He was an artist at his job — and this he knew.

His long jacket, longer than most – curiously enough – gave him the air of a very small man, but the greenness of his gaiters and the brilliance of his boots were unmatched. Whale Island was stamped all over him and he had a right to be proud of that hallmark.

He had been waiting for us with obvious glee. Standing with his back to the sea, he slowly let his eyes travel down our ranks. Scorn was written all over him and at last he turned his back and looked out over the sparkling water, while we, in our long ranks, waited in various degrees of mental excitement for his attack.

After some seconds of meditation he rose up and down several times on his heels, then suddenly turned on us.

'Well now, gentlemen,' he began. 'We had better get to know one another. You know who I am – but I don't know *you*. I'm at a disadvantage there – but somehow that don't worry me. We have two short weeks ahead of us in which to learn what has taken me a *lifetime*. But there you are, the pick of the lower deck, the men with brains – the men who have *got* something! ... The Leaders!' He paused to give this time to sink in, then his voice took on a steely tone, 'Yes, The Leaders. And as you know, the Leader has to have qualities above the ordinary run of things. It is my job to give you these in two short weeks. Whether you like it or not, you are going to take it! And by the time you leave here some of you will hate me – *most* of you will hate me ... but that won't worry me! No! Not a bit of it! That is *my* personal tragedy.

'For years I have been hated – that is my lot. But when you go into action – up some foreign beach, or aboard some hostile ship – you will remember me! At least I *hope* you will – for your own sakes.'

He was a great little actor and knew the value of timing. 'Ah, yes ... The Leaders – What would we do without you? Now where shall we start on this stupendous task?' He paused again meditatively. 'Civilians ... ratings ... officers!'

For days we marched and counter-marched: We drilled and formed and doubled. The days were hot, and those hourly periods with him stand out of that period starkly.

To those who have gone through the usual Naval barrack training of all conscripts it was a strain. But to me who had only had one week of it and that over a year before it was more than a strain: it was a nightmare.

Each day some quaking soul was called to the front to carry out company drills.

On the final day, with fixed bayonets we marched up the ramp and along the road to that fearful sward where Vass stood waiting. He held a long stick which was padded at one end, and had a loop of rope at the other. Through the fence he watched our entrance.

'Left ... Right ... Left! Right, Left – put some bloody guts into it!' he called. 'You are still in the bloody Navy. And don't forget it!'

We broke off and formed-up in a circle around him. 'Now you all know what a bayonet is – you have held it for months! But what its *proper* use is, what its effect on the enemy is – none of you, as yet, knows. Am I right? Well, gentlemen – a bayonet is a *fighter's* weapon! In the hands of a Briton it has no equal ... I *know*, I've used it!'

His speech was long and got hotter and hotter. And so did we. 'Now I'm not telling you to *hate* the Hun – Oh no! Not a bit of it – *that* part of my job was cut out, some time ago!' He pointed to the large block of flats across the road overlooking the field and in confidential tones that lost none of their natural intensity: 'You see, over *there* live the Staff officers' wives. They didn't *like* it. But they don't fight wars, do they? *No!* So,' here his voice jumped several scales, 'I'm just telling you to *kill* the Bastards! There are various ways of doing this. Nice, quick, juicy ways, and the sooner you get the idea, the better! This after all is a *war* – not an *ordinary* war – not a bit! It's a war against those swines your fathers and all my generation thought they had beaten. Well, we didn't. See? Because we didn't *kill* enough of them. Don't think you can go running to the captain ... This isn't a hate talk. Oh no!' His voice, full of meaning, sank to a sinister depth. 'I'm just going to show you how to kill *hundreds* and *hundreds* of them!'

His excitement was intense, his little narrow eyes gleamed like balls of fire, he grabbed a rifle. 'Stick them in the guts, in the stomach, in the chest, the neck ... *anywhere* but *kill* the Bastards'. You can shovel around if you will – pull his bloody stomach out and make a job of it! Make sure the bastard never fights again!'

He was crouching on his toes as he moved, as if he was about to charge us. 'If you *don't*, it will be your blood he will carry on his bayonet. See? – Not his – Yours! *Your* bloody stomach trailing on the ground – not his!' His gestures were pinpoints of fire.

The picture he went on to paint made some of us feel sick. We advanced to his orders at an imaginary foe, to the accompaniment of his blood-thirsty exhortations: 'In the stomach – *in* ... Out ... Advance! – In – out – advance!' And other parts of the human anatomy were equally successfully mutilated. By the end of that hour I knew I should never use a bayonet – Never! The lowness and bestiality of war – was brought home with a rush. It was altogether too filthy. I thanked God I had joined the Navy.

The hour was over; that too was well.

PART TWO

The Attack on the Tirpitz

I

Submarine Sketches

by Henty Henty-Creer

The doctor had run over me, the ear specialist and the X-ray expert had all had their turn, I was ready for the tank where all submariners learn how to escape.

A happy, husky chief petty officer took me in charge and gave me a lecture on DSEA – Davis Submarine Escape Apparatus. Valve cocks and other gadgets were all taken down and explained in a most thorough way, occasionally interrupted by an annoying phone that insisted on breaking in and destroying the continuity of the memorising.

Suddenly, to my horror, the chief said, 'Right, sir! We have just time to try you out before lunch.'

With very mixed emotions I undressed and got into a pair of swimming trunks. The set was strapped across my chest and I lowered myself into the tank. When the outlet valve got below water I turned it on and took another step down.

With the rubber mouth piece between my lips, the nose clip on, water trickling into my goggles, and the set around my chest – not to mention the business of breathing oxygen through the mouth – I realised with some shock my utter dependence on the apparatus.

Down the iron steps I went, pausing opposite a notice marked 'Clear Your Ears'. Obediently I squeezed my nose and with the other hand gripped the air tube, blowing meanwhile, to put inside pressure on the ear drums, which by now were becoming very heavy. All this accomplished, I reached the bottom, where my instructor was waiting to make sure all was well.

It was a weird feeling, standing just off the bottom, learning to regulate the flow of oxygen in sufficient quantities to keep down and not shoot to the surface – the slightest misjudgement would send one shooting ignominiously up.

Then on the signal I switched on the air supply, and with my hands crossed behind my back, shot up to the surface, where the temptation to swim was quickly checked by the instructor, who ordered, 'Lie on your back and let the set take charge.'

I let in more air until some began to escape through the outlet valve, then switched off. Blowing hard on my mouthpiece I put more air into the buoyancy bag and found myself floating nicely on my back. Taking care to switch off the mouthpiece lever and clearing myself of all oxygen, I at last took the mouthpiece off, and breathed fresh air with a sigh of relief.

After lunch came the actual escape routine, when for the first time I was to realise what it felt to be imprisoned under water.

In all my life I had never known such fear. The strong, almost overwhelming desire to pull off the set and strike out, was only kept in check by the knowledge that I was bottled up in a flooded iron submarine chamber and utterly dependent on keeping my head and following implicitly the instructions I had received. I got in through a round safe-like door, then the water was flooded in and the door closed. The level rose higher and higher and at last reached my chest, then I had to switch on the outlet valve and give the 'Thumbs up' signal as the level of water passed my eyes.

Soft green light flooded through the port and the noise of flowing water drummed on my ears. Soon the pressure became offensive to my ear drums and water seemed to be dribbling between my lips and down the air pipe. I did not realise that I had forgotten to keep the bag supplied with air, and felt my last second had come.

I tried to steady myself, but water still came in and a dreadful surge of panic to add to all my other unpleasant sensations was rushing up inside me. I tried to remember all the instructions, but there had been so many. Then on a last hope, I accidentally did the right thing – though I did not know it even then: I gave more air to the bag. Now, instead of water getting in, air bubbled out, which was equally alarming to me in my ignorance of the apparatus.

It was a dreadful moment. I felt I was completely helpless in a flooded tank with all bulkheads closed, entirely dependent on myself – I did not learn until later, that the instructor could have emptied the chamber in a few seconds. I was biting the mouthpiece and had stopped breathing for a second or two which seemed like aeons of time. But at long last things straightened themselves out and a lever clanged at my feet – a reminder for me to pull it and open the hatch above my head.

I let in more air and, with my arms above me, felt for the escape hatch which was heavy and would not at first yield. Putting more pressure, I felt it give slowly. At last it opened and fell back with a clang and I shot through to the surface.

The sensation of escape was indescribable. For the first time in my life I had felt trapped. In the back of my mind the thought, 'You're finished, you really are drowning,' had surged forward in spite of all my efforts to be calm. In those few minutes I knew exactly what death below water was like; the past did not come racing forward to entertain me, there was only the stark present. I cursed myself alternately for going into this thing and for being so easily panicked. Never in so short a space of time have I said so many contradictory things to myself as I did at the bottom of that tank. There seemed to be two very forceful characters inside my brain, one driving me on to do the right thing and the other like some little black dog, snapping and tearing at the little morale I had left.

The feeling of panic had so completely gripped me, that I couldn't remember what I had done below. Spluttering breathlessly I pushed my goggles off and looked up into the faces of my instructors, now leaning calmly over the small iron rail. They were almost in darkness against the bright sunlight that shone through the great glass dome above.

What a lovely feeling to be back in a world of humans again! And then the thought, 'I wonder if they had seen how scared I had been?'

The instructor's, 'All right, sir?' jarred on my throbbing ear drums. I nodded. 'Carry on down again, sir.' And down I went again below the surface.

'Keep calm, you fool,' I kept telling myself, 'Keep calm!' As I reached the hatch, water again came in through my mouthpiece, but thoughts of fear crushed in on me again, and I flashed back to the surface. It was no good; my nerves were getting the better of me.

Up in God's good air I took off the mouthpiece and got to grips with myself. This would not do at all.

'What's up, sir?' asked the instructor.

In a choked sort of voice I said, 'How do you stop the water leaking down the ruddy pipe?' He told me and down I went once more. But immediately an indescribably dreadful fear took hold and everything seemed to be going round. His last words had been, 'Remember your drill sir! You did all right this morning. This is just the same.'

As I reached the hatch, 'Remember your drill! Remember your drill!' seemed to keep time with my beating eardrums.

I pulled myself through and heard the trap door clang shut above me. New directions were chalked up on a slate and held outside the tank, in front of the glass. But now there was another complication – my goggles had misted up and flooded. I thought back over his instructions. There were several handles and wheels to turn; the outlet valve had to be opened and the compressed air lever switched on. What next? What a fool I was.

In what order I carried out the drill, I do not know, but the pressure became terrific and my head felt as if it would explode, added to which, the noise of air being forced out and the continuous hissing made me feel that at any moment my eardrums would give out. What *was* happening? What should I do next? Suddenly I found that all was well. The water level sank to my chest, and I took my mouthpiece off when it fell below the entrance door. When I switched off and turned the flood shut, pressure on the equalising cock gradually lessened, the hissing stopped and the door opened; I was back in my own element again and relief was intense.

Psychologically, this had been an awful business for me – my first real encounter with fear. I'd always been at home in the water; in fact I could swim almost as soon as I could walk. I had been buffeted about by formidable Pacific surf before I was a yard high; I had been dared to swim in a dark deep mountain pool in Java, among unpleasant goggle-eyed carp of pugnacious mien, when not much bigger than they: and had shot on a banana leaf down the sliding rock of an almost perpendicular waterfall in a Malayan jungle, not much later. And of course there had been other thrills in various countries, which had all given me some heart beats, but those qualms had been exhilarating – I had known I could be saved if anything went wrong.

Down in the submarine tank with hatch closed, I was alone, shut in and entirely dependent on, not only doing the right thing in the right way at the right moment, but on a number of very urgent things that were indispensable to the smooth running of the apparatus – and to my very breathing. There were many exigent gadgets that demanded a cool head.

The awful sensation of claustrophobia that seemed to take charge of my senses – clouding my power of thought and making my heart beat heavily – as soon as the trap door shut me in, was overwhelming and had to be mastered. I knew at once that if I did not go through the whole ruddy business again, I never would. I had reached a crossroads with myself and knew with absolute certainty that if I did not take charge of my mental forces, and master my panic once and for all, I was lost and would have to get out of submarines.

'Do you mind if I do it once more, chief?' I asked. 'See if I can't do it without a 'muck-up' this time.'

'OK, sir,' he answered. 'But you don't *have* to, you know!'

But I knew better – so down I went again and all went well that time. I now knew my stuff. I felt a changed person when I went in to dinner that night.

II

A Brush with a Destroyer

We had left the wooden jetty and were heading out for our special area, some ten miles south-east of that flat sandy coastline with only the tall man-made hills of quarried slag to break the green horizon. In the rather crowded space between the shining blue 'tin fish' we sat on oil drums or sacks of cotton waste, in a smoke-laden atmosphere of warm oiliness, gently rolled by beam seas.

Before we left harbour the loud speaker had issued the order: 'Diving stations! Diving stations!' followed shortly afterwards by: 'Uncover all planes and auxiliary vents.'

'Testing klaxon! Testing klaxon!' reverberated through the space, the inevitable blast that in more serious moment, had sent men racing to their posts.

'Blimey!' said one of the crew. 'Jimmy's* a bit noisy today. Must have had a night of it.'

'Harbour stations! Harbour stations! Close all hatches! Close all hatches!'

---

* Naval term for a first lieutenant.

Apparently we were under way at last and outside the harbour entrance. Then as we passed, the loudspeaker blared forth: 'Red Watch Patrol routine! Training class supply all look-outs!'

A chief petty officer rallied his white-sweatered group of trainees, detailing them off to motor room, engine room, control room and the fore and aft planes, where they were to understudy the old hands, most of whom were at home for a spell of leave to take things easy after strenuous periods in Mediterranean and Norwegian waters.

A great draught of air came down through the conning tower hatch and was sucked off through the large control room to the two roaring diesel engines which were driving us along on the surface.

For some time we headed out to sea. Up forward, torpedo men were working on their great charges – polishing, painting, oiling.

As one wandered aft one passed the crew space with its motley collection of variously clad figures, then the petty officers' mess and the row of curtained bunks which lined one side of the narrow walk, and on past the wardroom next door, and the galley, so cunningly tucked between shiny valves and great white pipes in a corner all its own and from which came the smell of the mid-day meal and the quiet song of the young cook. On past the captain's cabin, the wireless office, and into the great complexity of the awe-inspiring control room with its innumerable valves, levers, wheels and twinkling indicator lights, white paintwork, shiny metals – spotless.

And from this silence – for submarine acoustics are quite extraordinary – one steps through the bulkhead into the engine room, down into the sudden roar of reverberating engines, where the crew of engineers, ERAs and stokers were busy ministering with oilcan and spanner. On again – for the noise is shattering after the peace forward – through another bulkhead to the motor room. The motors are out of sight under you and only the great switch board with its copper bars and glass ammeters are a sign of that other motive power which will come into play the moment we dive. There is little room here, one can hardly stand upright. A long leather-covered seat runs down the length of each board on either side. Here one stops, for further aft there only remains a cramped space of pumps, air compressor, tail clutches, a veritable welter of machinery, and in any case this is one of the comfiest spots in the boat.

Here above the motors between the tail and engine clutches men sat reading, waiting their turn which would come when the

telegraphs on that bulkhead suddenly clanged and the little pointer
swings round to 'stop', then on to 'out engine clutch'.

In the meantime a well used pack of cards is being dealt. At any
moment with any luck, a face may suddenly appear and say: 'One all
round.'

'Good old Jimmy,' says a keen smoker, for 'one all round' means
one cigarette; and a smoke at sea in a submarine is a luxury that
depends on the views of its commander – there are some who are
very rigid on this subject!

We could only spend a limited amount of time in each
department of the boat and after a few days we found that time was
on our side for there is after all, only so much to be learnt by
watching.

It wasn't until we went to another boat whose first lieutenant took
a keen interest in our time aboard that we spent whole mornings at
every position in the boat, from the simple one of merely opening
and shutting a vent to the more complicated post when a fellow had
a department on his hands. *That* was training in earnest and a
wonderful way of learning a particular boat.

But on this day things were over crowded and there were far too
many 'makee learns'. When we had settled below the surface we
were left in peace to go to various parts of the boat and worry the
different chiefs and petty officers for even more information – or to
dip into our supply of books which was fairly good, ranging from
Guedella's *Life of Wellington* to the usual novels and crime stories.

Occasionally an order such as, 'Red Watch, watch diving!' would
stop the polishing cloth of the crew, and as the klaxon blared, there
would be a scuffle as figures leapt about the space, manning valves.

'Open A inboard vent. Close tube compartment!' caused that lot
of bulkhead doors to be screwed down and those six gleaming white
torpedo tubes to be shut off from our view.

We were going down with a list now and watched the depth gauge
as the needle went slowly to twenty feet and down to forty. Evidently
the training classes were having difficulties!

But while these activities went on, a group of our fellows – whose
interest in submarines had, for the time being, lapsed – carried on
with the reformation of the world. Where would Russia be without
Stalin? Dictatorship and one man bands! Old man Hitler parading
across the world watched by uncaring gods. Murder purges. Each
gave forth headlines for a spirited argument. These discussions
would be interrupted by a sudden sharp angle of the boat –

inadvertently put on by an over-keen trainee at the after-planes. And overhead, condensation would form to drop into the arguments.

I wandered along to the crowded control room, where I found a certain amount of excitement; a destroyer had shown interest in our periscope and was on the way over to investigate. These little encounters could have their dangerous moments, and rapid identification was of great importance. Accidents had happened before now!

The captain's order: 'Down periscope!' sent the great brass tube into its deep red well. And when he called, 'Going up, Number One,' the first lieutenant reached for the phone and ordered: 'Diving stations! Diving stations! Shut main vents, open master blowers,' and so on, his orders flashed to various parts of the boat from the little switch board panels which he controlled.

We prepared to surface. The captain put on his weather-beaten Ursula jacket and crouched on the ladder with his hands on the lower hatch clips. Half way up the young signaller, a green football shirt showing above his oilskins, called out the depth as the depth gauge needle slowly moved foot by foot. The first lieutenant gave another order, and at twenty feet the lower hatch was opened and the captain raced up the conning tower and crouched below the upper one.

The signaller went on calling out the depths, and at last the upper hatch was opened and the rush of spray and cold air blew down on to the watching upturned faces of the first lieutenant, and those nearby.

After a few minutes, the wet, spray-covered signaller came below and we heard the upper hatch being shut. Soon the long legs of the captain came through the narrow lower hatch: 'Dive, Number One!' The first lieutenant took over again: 'Flood main line forward!'

I stood fascinated, watching the routine of a boat going beneath the waters. Soon we were thirty feet and he was steadying her and catching a trim. Orders were carried out and repeated, the port and starboard suction inboard vents were opened and shut, with regular monotony. Orders followed in quick succession to correct her trim.

Finally we were once more cruising thirty odd feet below the surface at about one knot, on one motor – and all was well.

The rating training class took the fore and after hydroplanes and the helm once more, and routine settled down again while all the officers under training, returned to the quiet forward torpedo compartment, for a lunch of beer and sandwiches.

III

Catching Trims

It was pelting down as we crossed the gang plank from the parent ship to our sub. A heavy squall of rain had come up, and now the town was just dimly visible through it all. Our number had decreased, some had gone to the dentist and our only lieutenant amongst our class of sub-lieutenants had apparently slept in, for there were now only two of us. How strange to find ourselves with this plumber's nightmare to play with on our own.

The usual training routine had rather slackened up and our party of some fifteen usually managed to arrange that there were always a few in the control room while the rest slacked off to the torpedo space forward or the warm and comfortable motor room aft, to read. Enthusiasm had cooled down slightly, for the training period allocated so many days to be spent at sea, and we felt we had run through the necessary knowledge required of us in the first week.

The first lieutenant fixed me with a cheerful eye. 'As there are only two of you today, you had better both be first lieutenants and catch trims.'

It was a wonderful idea and although extremely nervous as to my ability to do the job, I was delighted to get the chance before the course finished. We duly tossed up as to who would have the first watch and my luck was in.

This business of 'catching the trims' was rather like an airman's first solo, I felt, but with the difference of having to keep an even keel and proper balance with varying degrees of water fore, aft and amidships. For with hydroplanes for ailerons and fresh water patches for air pockets – the similarity was there indeed.

To keep the boat at her periscope depth, with fore and aft hydroplanes amidships with just sufficient speed to give steerage way, was our goal.

A few days earlier the first lieutenant had shown his ability by holding her for thirty-nine minutes on a stop trim. Both motors were stopped for this performance so there was little or no effect on the 'planes': we were perfectly balanced and just hanging motionless below the surface. It had been a good show.

I thought back over all I had learned and wondered what sort of showing I should make. We went down past the Isle of Bute and out to our submarine diving area. It was blowing in from the north-west and spray drenched the small conning tower bridge as we sped along at some twelve knots. A large aircraft carrier outward bound with her escorting destroyers seemed to flash past. I felt for a moment as if I had been a small car reversing under the shadow of a skyscraper! We wallowed in her wake like a great shiny whale as waves ran over our pressure hull and up on the casing.

Our captain, with a wicked gleam said: 'God, what a lovely target!' And silence fell on us for a while as we watched her into the distance and the rain. Our signaller watched her with scorn and the true pride of the submariner and crushingly remarked, 'She's got the legs all right, sir, but what a bloody great dirty box!'

We eased our speed about nine-thirty and waited for the weather to lift, for even in this submarine sanctuary, a definite 'diving visibility' was ordained before we were allowed to dive. Nearing ten o'clock the captain ordered 'diving stations' and the officer of the watch rang the bridge telegraph for 'Out both engine clutches' – which meant we were changing over to motors for the dive. Then: 'Half speed both.'

'Half speed both, sir. Both telegraphs showing half ahead, sir.'

The bridge was cleared and at last the klaxon blared. We stood in a rather crowded control room and watched as the main vents were opened and heard waters rushing into the saddle ballast tanks.

The first lieutenant watched to see the captain bang the upper hatch shut, and soon he too, was down below. For a few seconds we seemed to hover; then with a rush the depth needles began to move – ten, fifteen, twenty, thirty feet. 'Shut main vents,' I called.

The coxswain on the after plane spun his wheel to put a little rise on, and all was silence. Now something had to be done. The first lieutenant turned to me: 'She's all yours. Better do something fast!'

We were getting down by the stern. I clambered for my 'lines'. What the hell were the correct orders! What tanks would I use? With after planes at 'hard arise' and the bubble moving slowly forward I suddenly found my feet. 'Start the after pump. Pump on five auxiliary.' My order was repeated to the motor room. We waited for the answer and at last it came. The silent rating, with his ear to the shining brass voice pipe looked up. 'Pump running and sucking on five auxiliary, sir.'

'Very good.' I counted the seconds and watched for the bubble to start its move on the spirit level.

'Stop the after! Shut five auxiliary.'

'Stop the after pump. Shut five auxiliary, sir.' There was another pause and slowly the stern came up and the planesman began to level off with the bubble amidships.

'Slow both.'

'Slow both, sir. Both telegraphs showing slow ahead sir.'

'Very good.' I waited to see what effect our reduced speed would have on the planes. We were still bodily heavy and heavy aft. I started the after pump again, then called. 'Start the forward pump. Pump on Z.'

'Start the forward pump ... Pump on Z, sir.' This time by telephone to the forward crew space where the pump was operated.

'Pump running and sucking on Z, sir.'

'Very good.' I stood between the two periscopes and watched the depth gauge, the spirit level and the hydroplane indicators.

As we began to rise, the depth needle showed, thirty-three, thirty, twenty-nine. 'Stop the forward pump, shut Z.' For Z was our main midships tank and the most used. Of course there were others, X and Y, then the A and B and two tanks forward and again numbers 3, 4, 5, and 6 aft, to play with. But on this boat the forward one, A,Z under the control room and five auxiliary under the motor room aft, were the usual worker tanks. 'Both planes amidships,' was my next order. I watched what effect this had on our angle. The bubble began to drift almost imperceptibly forward – we were still heavy aft, but we were at periscope depth.

'Up periscope,' ordered the captain.

'Carry on planing,' I hurriedly ordered, hoping inwardly that they would hold her until I caught a perfect trim. 'Start the after pump, pump on five.' The bubble was moving forward again and I was terrified I should 'dip' him during his slow scanning of the horizon. 'Stop port!' My orders followed in quick succession, to be repeated by the rating. 'Stop port!' and the hand at the telegraphs sang down the order, 'Port telegraph showing stopped, sir.'

'Very good. Stop the after pump, shut five.'

Another pause. 'Pump stopped sir. Five shut, sir.'

As I watched the depth gauge I suddenly realised that I had done it! The planes were amidships, we were crawling at about one knot and keeping our depth.

The first lieutenant looked at me and smiled. It had not been so bad. The captain was looking through the periscope and I watched the bubble and needle anxiously. Would it stay still? I did not want to 'dip him' when he was looking through! The fresh water patches, were absent and we just sat happily. The petty officers and hands manning the various control points had watched me with interest to see how I would shape on my first trim. They went on talking quietly now. There was no doubt they watched us 'makey learns' with a certain amount of personal interest! For in this old boat, no one ever wanted to go below one hundred feet.

A week earlier they had been taken down by a new sub at a steep angle to 160 feet before anyone could 'pull her up'. Bulkhead doors had been shut for she was an old boat and her pressure hull, not so tough as it used to be, had given them a few anxious moments!'

I had not given them any thrills!

After a while a hollow voice came through the voice pipe and soon – 'Permission to pump out the after bilge, sir?'

'Yes, carry on.'

The first lieutenant looked at me to see what I would do next. It was going to upset the trim. He had been bending over the chart table flicking through some reports.

'Crack the after sea flood! Flood five auxiliary,' I ordered.

'After sea flood cracked, sir, five flooding.'

It was awkward not knowing the speed or rate of flood and one just had to guess. 'Experience will give you all that,' cheered Number One.

'Shut after sea flood, shut five.' And we were back again. It really seemed too easy.

The first lieutenant must have felt I was getting it all my own way. 'I'm going to mess up your trim for you,' he said. 'Stand by!' With a wicked laugh he 'cracked sea floods' and filling various tanks, handed her back to me – bow down and bodily heavy. I had no idea how much was in the various tanks after this, and I raised a laugh when I overflooded the midship tank. For, standing right over the inboard vent pipe, I caught a hefty jet of oily water in the seat of my pants!

'Ha! That'll teach you to flood tanks!' said the first lieutenant, and it certainly did! But I was able to tackle the situation. The water flowed down into the periscope walls, valves were shut off and the spectators regarded me with revived interest – but we were on our depth. The diminutive first lieutenant grimaced – 'I'm not going to let you get away with that! Pump out that tank and don't use it any more. Keep her trimmed with the fore and aft auxiliaries!'

After two hours of being put through 'all the works' I was really exhausted and thoroughly glad when we surfaced for lunch.

IV

A Spot of Bother

It is amazing how often accidents happen within sight of one's parent ship.

It had been a great run back from the diving area, the sun had made one of its rare efforts to please and we looked like going alongside a good hour earlier than usual.

The routine afternoon ferry across the estuary had passed, her deck crowded with the usual trippers in light hearted holiday mood; their interest in us never slackened. Our young captain, an RN lieutenant with flaming red hair and from the Channel Islands, doffed his cap as they cheered us on. The little examination vessel drew abeam as we passed between her and the shore in the entrance to our bay. The order came to 'Slow both' and then suddenly the worst happened – we were aground.

It was a humiliating moment, for we were not half a mile from the parent ship. Orders rapped out fast: 'Stop both,' and with great speed came the answer, 'Both telegraphs showing stopped, sir.'

'Full astern together.' And so it went on, but with little luck. We were held fast.

A motor launch passed, her small crew on deck watching as if we were some great floundering whale, and a small crowd began to gather on the promenade as our propellers churned up great white scurries of foam around us. The little examination vessel signalled, 'Can I be of any assistance?'

And then the long expected query came from our parent ship. 'Are you in trouble?' The captain looked at Number One, 'What shall we say to that?'

'Should leave it for a bit, sir.'

'Ah!' I thought – 'the Nelson touch!'

'No reply yet, signalman!'

'Aye, aye, sir.'

'Pump out everything aft, Number One.'

Number One went down the conning tower hatch and things began to happen. We were well aground and held by the stern and the helm had almost seized up. To add to our troubles, the rain came down.

'Cor – me!' said a voice from the after casing below the conning tower. 'Just our bleeding luck!'

The three deck hands who had been running out the after lines, took cover in the rope locker out of it all below the casing.

For five minutes the rain came down in torrents with tropical intensity, almost obscuring the watching parent ship half a mile away. The rain was cold and lashed our necks with horrible persistence.

After half-an-hour of concentrated effort, we were clear and signalled to our parent ship, with slight understatement. 'Have touched the ground but am now clear.'

'Fix your position accurately,' came the stern reply.

As we got near the little examination vessel the captain with a smile of relief said, 'Signal: Thanks for your offer; all's well.'

And with a cheery smile the skipper doffed his cap in a way that drew a laugh from us all.

V

Standing By

The days of examination were over at last – the long training months in class rooms and at sea were gone and I was glad.

I had an extraordinary sense of freedom as the train took the final turns up on that rain-soaked corner of the north-west English coast. It was late autumn and the last bright leaves were falling from the nearly naked trees. I wondered vaguely what my new life had in store – a new boat was altogether too wonderful and the longed for opportunity of standing by and watching her grow had come to me as an extraordinary piece of luck.

The great armament works covered the town in smoky mist and a steady drizzle fell as we left the station for our hotel. The bar of course was full. Officers in and out of uniform, were in holiday mood and their wives sat in groups in the lounge.

I found my CO behind a book over a late tea, in the midst of a knitting circle, wearing his customary frown and obviously he had not been able to settle down to the pages of Vicki Baum. The opportunity was too good to miss, and I made straight for him.

'Good show, you made it all right?'

'Yes, sir, just got in.'

'Let's have a drink.'

We left the buzz of Naval gossip for the twinkling glasses of Freda and the crackle of a large coal fire. The room was full of fellows I had not seen since early training days months before, and this 'standing by' period promised to be most enjoyable.

Dawn and a thick head found us walking the two miles of puddle soaked pavement through the town and across the bridge to the island.

The immensity of it all was staggering. Warships and submarines nearing completion filled the waterways and great billows of black smoke poured out of the tall chimneys, to drift lazily past the incredibly large cranes.

Block after block of red stone buildings, with their uniformed police on guard at all entrances, stretched out before one on every side. Lorries and locomotives with their squeaking wheels appeared from nowhere and, as soon, disappeared into this monstrous hive that was in itself, a complete city.

I had looked over various factories and plants before but had never come on anything like this. The night shift piled into dozens of buses, and hundreds of bicycles careered madly in the direction of the bridge.

It seemed unbelievable that all this could belong to one company – yet so it was. Nineteen thousand – a proud director told me – worked in these shifts, 'Sundays and all!'

I was taken through a maze of offices filled with hundreds of girls, whose mechanical typing at monster mathematical machines, was one of the most frightening things I had ever seen. The girls sat in rows reading figures from mammoth books placed on one side of each machine, from which great white sheets of endless paper poured out inexhaustibly. Their fingers moved with incredible rapidity and as I stood in a little glassed-off office – waiting for the first of many identification forms to be filled in – I watched fascinated, these units of a colossal accountancy system operating in the heart of this destruction factory. What were they all thinking about, sitting below those great yellow overhead lights, which put up such a bright show against the weak grey light that was almost too tired to come in through the lofty windows?

Small boys hurried back and forth armed with fresh volumes almost as big as themselves. Men too old to be called up after a lifetime in such a room or to be active enough for any other job, watched over them. There was no noise – just the occasional turning over of a page and the mass movement of hundreds of frantic white arms against a black background of machines.

I was extremely glad to get outside the building and away from these little slaves of such exacting soulessness. Perhaps this was foolish; after all, who was I to judge? Perhaps they enjoyed their work. But I couldn't help feeling that they were somehow a race apart.

Walking over cobbled roads that led to our boat, we passed shed after shed whose large open doors gave us an insight into another side of war. Great sheets of flame and white hot metal blazed in that inner darkness, where men became silhouettes as they tended their weird charges. The music of metal in all its stages, forged and struck with mighty living slabs of iron, echoed out to us as we passed on down the yards.

A couple of light cruisers lay fitting out – now scarred with great red patches of paint partly covering the deep brown of their new metal hulls. And ahead were submarines – glorious new submarines.

Men seemed to swarm over those long tubes; men welding, men with pipes, cables, instruments; large groups with their foremen; little gangs pushing and heaving. Lorries and trains rumbled continuously down to their sidings, and overhead cranes dumped fresh loads from the construction sheds.

My first few days went by in rather a daze. It was hard to make oneself believe that what appeared now just a collection of old iron, would in a month or so be a unit of the Royal Navy – spotless in its first coat of paint.

I moved about the different assembly shops and drawing offices, getting to know the men responsible for this hive of activity. After a few days when they realised I was personally interested in 'their' particular boat, their whole attitude changed and information and statistics came forth at the slightest provocation. They were wonderful. Even the foreman welder went to great lengths to satisfy himself that I understood their work on the boat! I was given samples and a demonstration and told proudly: 'That job there will go as deep as any – good first class stuff and no denying it! As good as ever I seen these last fifteen years.' And calling over one of his men with a, 'Hey, Bill!' he took me into his confidence: 'Bill and I been building submarines together now for as long as I can remember! I'm not saying as how we is the only good builders, but like as not, I reckons we can hold our own with any you like to put against us!'

Bill was a little man in brick red overalls. His happy smile and twinkling eyes below those hefty dark goggles, which he moved up into his perspiring forehead when he laid down his electric welder, showed a contented man. He was proud of his job and the position it held in the ship-building world. But above all – and certainly one of the first things to impress a stranger – was his deep pride in being a 'British ship builder.'

He assured me: 'Fred was certainly talking the truth! Why, all the lads on the job are that keen, why, I don't remember seeing it for many a job.'

Every ship was a 'job'. It was either 'this 'ere job' or 'that there job we done for the Turks' or 'before we started this 'ere' or 'that job we done for them South Americans, them comical fellows – you remember Fred!'

'The Brazil navy,' corrected Foreman Fred.

'Aye, that's right! So it was.'

'What do you think of America's ship-building?' I asked. At once I knew I had thrown down a challenge. They became deadly serious and looked at each other to see who was the most competent to 'defend the cause'.

'Well, now, I wouldn't be saying as how them fellows don't know how to build ships,' said Fred, pausing to savour this considered judgement. 'But mind you, they don't exactly *build* a ship – Why it's more like *blowing* it together!'

'Yes, that's what,' agreed Bill, and you could see that even Bill was amazed that any ship-builder could stoop to such a method.

Our ship-builders were staunch traditionalists and they felt they were doing as good a job of building now as their fathers had done in the last war.

'And we won then, didn't we? Yanks and all!'

'You bet!'

'Aye – And we'll do it again.'

'Why,' chimed in Bill, 'countries all over the world come to us, up here in "industrial Barrow". And them furriners is smart sometimes, you know! Them comics know what's a good job and what ain't!'

As the days went on and the boat gradually filled with more and more pipes and valves, and the maze of electric cables began to mean something, my confidence in myself fell hour by hour. Would I ever know the boat? Each day produced new gadgets and things seemed to get more obscure and I would go the drawing office to get an interpretation of it all.

At first glance some electrical drawings were just like early Egyptian hieroglyphs. But those experts would take me in hand and after a morning I would feel that at last light was dawning.

They were all the same, high up in their cloud of electrical knowledge which I sometimes found almost impossible to understand. Experts somehow have an unhappy knack of forgetting the elementary side of their job and flatter one with an intelligence equal to their own. Electrics – that all important subject in submarines – had never come my way in peace-time, and it was only during submarine courses that I realised the depth of my ignorance. I learnt a lot in the ship building yards of 'industrial Barrow'.

We watched the fellows at their laths and we thanked God that fate had not made us submarine fitters. These patient men moving intricate machinery into place inspired me with awe.

Our nights varied between quiet rests in the lounge or the dances at the town hall given by the various completed ships and boats, before they sailed away for trials and the war.

The hotel regulars eyed us with mixed feelings and no doubt chattered about our nightly escapades in the light of their own lives. They could not be expected to understand us; their side of the war, conducted from the fireside and the daily headlines, was poles apart from us.

The unfortunates who invariably got locked out of the hotel annex and were forced to 'come aboard' as they put it, up a drain pipe gave them some lighter moments! Some felt sure he would break his neck, but he always appeared next morning at breakfast.

The collection of girls which came in our wake often made an odd contrast to the rather more formal wives of the officers of the cruiser which was on a refit. But it was pleasant and the nearest thing to a holiday a lot of us had had for some time and we enjoyed ourselves. So did some of the directors of the colossal affair down on the island as we were soon to see – and in their own rich northern style.

Christmas eve and the days that led up to it saw an almost complete stoppage of work. The men were there all right but the men who mattered – the men at the top – were out of town and progress slowed down.

By noon on Christmas Eve in the offices lent to them by the company, so many officers of newly finished boats had given parties to the host of men employed on their boats, that the amazing sight of different foremen leading their men from office to office was quite a happy sign of the camaraderie that exists between the men who build and those who carry on where they leave off.

So many different groups surreptitiously pulled bottles of whisky out of their tool lockers and bags, to drink our 'health and success at sea' and so many made speeches ending with 'For he's a jolly good fellow,' that it became embarrassing; for we felt that it was *they* who should have been toasted – they had done well to give us something so splendid to fight with.

We hoped that when our turn came, we would not let them down. Yes, these workers certainly had a way of making one feel a hero long before his time! And when the final siren sounded, we were all very merry indeed.

But Northern hospitality reached new heights on Christmas Day, and following the night's revels as it did, was almost overpowering. Eight of us were invited by one of the newer directors of this colossal company to 'enjoy Christmas dinner with the family'. He was a fat little man on whom fell the responsibility of getting our boat out on time. His OBE won in the last war for breaking records in submarine construction, proved him a man of determined character where contract dates were concerned.

Our party was not altogether looking forward to this homely session. We hardly felt up to the strain, for the night had been very hectic indeed. In two's we walked in gloomy mood from the hotel and up the hill. There was no taxi in sight and we had cut things rather fine.

The road was deserted and a steady drizzle had a marked effect on our already low spirits. After several miles during which little was said, the gaps in our ranks grew wider apart and eight silent figures stretched over half a mile were slogging along. Suddenly a large car roared down the long straight road. Looking back I saw at intervals of a few hundred yards a naval figure standing determinedly in the middle of the road. By the time it had reached me, the car was packed with cheerful fellows.

'It's all right old boy, jump in, mine host's even sent this luxurious limousine to fetch us!'

'Might have warned us – saved me a lot of shoe leather!' grumbled a voice rather muffled under the weight of two others sitting on him.

We packed in; arms and legs were everywhere. By now we were in a happier vein as we sailed past the great wall with the small fort like entrances that marked the estate of the armament king, and on over a green hill to stop below a large bare modern affair, lacking the turreted entrances and other signs of circumstances of its neighbours but still a forceful place.

We fell out of the car and entered the green gate that led up many steps past terraced lawns to a limed oak door. There was a rustle of many feet over the parquet floor and the door opened. 'Don't forget to wipe your feet,' yelled a high-pitched voice in the background.

The door swung wide and with a delightful smile a girl in a red sweater and grey slacks said, 'Hallo lads – that's mother, come on in!' She was noisy and so were we. The other doors seemed to frame many faces. Calls of, 'Good old Navy, happy Christmas,' surrounded us as we took our coats off.

'The chain and thing is just through there if any of you lads want to wash and brush up,' said the bright young thing in slacks, as she helped to hang coats up.

The drawing room had many interesting things. It was a 'self-made' drawing room and not ashamed of the fact. The big window, we were told, was the largest of its kind for many miles around. 'Pop had it put in. Do you like our Pop? Isn't he wonderful?'

'Grand, simply grand!' bubbled over a mountain of fun sitting in a corner, who, we were afterwards told, was the manageress of a branch of big chain chemists in a large midland city.

All the young 'in-laws' were there too and – not to be outdone by this friend of the family – regailed us with Pop's virtues. There were other family friends too who joined in the eulogies.

A table held various bottles and our attention was called to one of Italian vermouth. 'Johnny over there just got the last dozen in the country – and isn't he grand – he gave them all to Pop!'

Fred and Bill – sons-in-law – competed with each other to keep glasses filled whilst other carried round large silver cigarette boxes filled with many makes of expensive smokes. On a piano stool sat a little man whose deeply lined face showed a lifetime of toil. He had been silent, but when the large lady overflowed out of her chair and whispered in his ear, we realised that he too was 'a story'.

'Now, Bubbles,' he said getting up and protesting, 'you know I don't play no more – I used to, mind, but not now!'

'Come on, lads. He's a great pianist is my little Irish Johnny. Give him a hand,' she turned to beam on the little man. 'You bashful thing you!'

But all the persuasion in the room would not move the family musician.

Suddenly the door opened and Mine Host appeared, gaily wearing a paper cap. A momentary hush fell on the room, 'Happy Christmas lads. Pleased to meet you all.' We all shook hands. 'I hope my little family are making you all at home. Sit down. Sit down.' And resting a fat little hand on the heavy gold chain that stretched across his midriff, he moved towards the fire. The family rallied around this lion on the hearth and various members placed a well filled glass, a cigar, a match and an ashtray, well within his reach.

'Play, Johnny – give the lads some music!' he commanded. 'That's our Johnny lads – and we are all very proud of him. He and I have kicked around these last forty years. Used to play once, only rheumatics have got into him and he ain't as good as he used to be!' We listened, whilst Johnny thumped along the keys with three fingers of one hand and an energetic forefinger of the other.

The airs of Ireland stopped when our hostess appeared, carrying a gargantuan turkey. Daughters-in-law helped her with the enormously large dish and for an awful moment we were not quite sure whether the bird was not going to make an even more dramatic entrance.

Pop came through the crowd and took command. 'Once round the room, mother! Let all the lads see before you cut him up!'

The turkey could stand inspection.

'Aye, he's a grand bird, is that! Had to drive over to Sir George this morning; our oven wouldn't run to him. Henry here suggested taking him down to the works, but Ma put her foot down. Said she wouldn't do no baking in one of my furnaces!' He winked happily.

We were all vastly relieved when the bird had withdrawn from the drawing room. He was far too slippery a wicket in such a crowded room.

'My, my,' said Bubbles. 'Did you ever see such a sight?'

No, we assured her. We never had! Johnny got up to leave. 'Were you responsible for that too,' asked Bubbles, scintillating towards him.

'Aye, thought he looked a bit lonely down south, so I tucked 'im under me arm and fetched 'im up 'ere!'

'You aren't half a wit, you aren't!'

'Aye, grand lad is John,' said Pop. 'Going to stay and have a slice?' he enquired.

'No, not me, bit too skinny for my liking.'

They tried hard to keep John, but he had his own home waiting for him, he said.

'I'm not forcing you,' said our host. 'But if you were to change your mind – ?'

'No, no. Ta-ta, folks!' and little John had gone. He was so much a part of the family that a sigh went round. Our host went back over the past.

'He and I went to school together. None of your fancy public schools either; just a little one here in industrial Barrow. We started off work together when I was eleven. That's a long way off now, you know. I'm not as young as I used to be.'

'Aye, but good for many years yet,' interrupted Bubbles.

'Yes, and with as much go as many a man younger than himself!' assured a daughter-in-law.

'Now don't you kids keep chipping so!' put in the great one

without a movement of a muscle. 'But take Johnny now – Irishman – never settle down to anything. Not steady enough to work. When he was eighteen gave up engineering and pushed an old clothes barrow round the town. Didn't do him any harm, mind you! That lad's got plenty of money now, although you might not know it by his appearance!

'Aye. He's made his little pile all right: Mind you I'm not saying he's as lucky as I was. But if any man was ever in trouble, why all through the years Johnny would see 'im through!' Flicking the ash from his long cigar he went on, 'We had to work in those days! Why I remember taking out the first sub we ever built. And that was forty years back. Not like me son here or Fred. I gave them a first class education, university and all, then I put them in my old engineering shop. *Now* look at them – son's only twenty-seven and he's in charge of five thousand men over at our aircraft branch. And Fred, he's done as well for himself – only thirty. I took him into the family when his dad died. Why he's got three thousand fellows and he's making big guns now. Big future for both of 'em!'

The two fellows were a little embarrassed, but quickly passed around the cigarettes.

'I'll show you the picture gallery.'

Several of us went into the large hall. It was panelled and on shelves running round its sides high above our heads, were dozens of silver cups. Our host waved his cigar in a wide sweep. 'Them's my canary birds' cups!'

There were big ones and tiny ones but the best were packed away under the stairs for the duration, we were told. 'Bombs you know! Why we had one in the field the other day.'

And under all these trophies were photographs, in each of which our host figured prominently. Foreign dignitaries, statesmen, and Royalties were there – and always escorted by a fat man in a bowler hat. 'Aye ... Good profitable days those!'

There were photographs of world-famous warships and liners. 'We made 'em all.'

On a small table by itself was a photograph of the King being shown round the works.

The women folk came bustling out of the kitchen laughing and joking, excited over their culinary achievements. The great moment was upon them. The long dining table was already filled with food. Large glasses of beer were filled and at last Pop came in having finally surveyed last minute touches in the kitchen.

The family sat at one end and we were at the other – large plates piled high were in front of us all. Pop said grace quietly and ended with, 'Now then, lads, slacken your belts and get on with it!'

At the other end the session went into full swing. They ate without a word whilst every now and then Ma hurried round with more stuffing, little sausages and even more turkey. There seemed no end. As fast as food dwindled on those large plates more and more was piled on. We who had been fairly talkative at first were silenced. I had never seen anything like it and said so. They were delighted. 'Have you slackened your belt?' asked our beaming host.

'Well,' said the lovely lady in slacks. 'now your top buttons!'

Pop had disengaged his heavy gold chain and unbuttoned his waistcoat. He perspired freely as he ate. With an occasional wave of a fat finger, he made sure the steady level of food was maintained. The glasses filled again and we were encouraged, 'Buck up, lads – have you forgotten how to eat?'

Even in peace-time it would have been a meal to marvel at. We were an exhausted group when we finally and very sleepily got up to hear the King's speech. And one or two found it an effort to regain their feet when 'God Save The King' was played.

The family – staunch patriots – stood behind Pop stiffly at attention with proud heads held high. We did not stand quite so smartly although we tried hard enough!

'Grand speech. Grand man is that,' said Pop.

'Aye grand and no two ways about it,' said his wife.

Some of the fellows moved into the kitchen to give the girls some help and Pop took me to see 'Them canary birds of mine.'

In an enormous aviary several hundred cages lined the wall – every bird a prize-winner. Here, surrounded by his hobby, Pop was a changed man. No longer the armament magnate, he became almost childlike, as, armed with a diminutive wooden rake, he moved bird after bird into a little gold cage for my inspection. He spoke to each one, he whistled softly, he soothed. If the little gold bars had not been in the way, his fat little fingers would have loved to stroke the golden plumage.

'Haven't done too badly this year. It's a grand hobby, you know. Why, last year I made £1500 out of these birdies of mine. Sent them all over the country. They always come back with the cups. Even yesterday I sold a couple for fifty pounds apiece.'

I asked about feeding problems. 'No trouble, not a bit of it. I can get as much as I need. Pay a bit more now perhaps. But it's good clean seed and they always get the best.'

He showed me the seed room where there were sacks of grain – he would be safe for the duration at least. He thought the birds kept him in good health too. 'Do the mind good. I come every morning before I go down to the job. Kind of soothes me and starts me off right like. Peaceful too, just me and them birds for half-an-hour. Then when I get in at night I come straight up here. Makes a nice change over after a hard day before going in to my family.'

The incredible contrasts of this man's life: On one side the simplicity of a bird-lover, a peaceful home-loving, family man; on the other the business tycoon absorbed in the job of turning out guns, tanks, planes, submarines – implements of death.

*

The governing board lunched us before we left and one of the six directors was Pop who in this setting had undergone a change. He was now a very formal host, who might have been formidable but for the furtive, genial wink he shot us when his associates were looking the other way.

We had a few very formal cocktails and then went into lunch. Liveried manservants silently served, whilst stern serious men talked of the weather. Iron-grey heads were coldly polite but distant!

This farewell lunch to a departing boat was to them a routine affair. It was a lunch without charm, without personality and completely empty of humanity. I felt afterwards that I had indeed eaten with men of death – men banking upon wars for their livelihood.

While they ate their lunch they could watch through the high windows, the tall cranes and towering hulls of future battleships, slowly growing day by day towards the one goal – ours and theirs. We who were to serve in their ships were incidentals.

Half way through cigars, the whistle went: They looked at their watches; they had a job to do …

So too, had we.

II

Training for the Day

by Henty Henty-Creer

Life suddenly speeded up one morning and we began to pack. The morning had its funny moments when one of the ship's officers was seen chasing cockroaches with a blow lamp closely followed by an attendant. But it was certainly a relief to be getting away from the Maltese stewards and their endless native backchat. They had nicknames for our small party for we were collectively known as 'the suicide boys'. This was whittled down to 'Seigneur Gingie', and 'Seigneur Hop-a-long' and other not so flattering titles. They were a noisy bunch and quite irrepressible. But just the same we were all rather glad to be leaving.

This had not been a happy ship and our being called 'the Glamour boys' had kept us apart as rather 'rare birds'. We seemed to keep to ourselves – it worked better that way – and anyhow we had no ties aboard and apart from the friends we made in *L-76* in which we lived for nearly two weeks, the rest of the parent ship's wardroom inmates were rather a clannish lot and made practically no effort to gather us into the circle. It was rather interesting to compare the different submarine bases, the atmosphere depended almost entirely on the sociability of our seniors. Some went out of their way to speak and be charming and others just ignored us completely.

The upper set aboard the floating base rather centered on the pay lieutenant RNVR whose family owned the island and consequently entertained the thick gold-striped fraternity. To us it seemed an interesting coincidence that his appointment was on his own family doorstep.

Our last week aboard had been filled in with mornings of diving and afternoons of lazy sleep – sleep we found inevitable after a morning in the diving boat. It was quite surprising how exhausted one became after playing about on the bottom under some 30lbs per square inch pressure on the body.

We left the ship after lunch and jumped a Naval lorry the two miles around Rothesay Bay to Port Bannatyne and the one time Kyles Hydro Hotel.

We soon found ourselves on the gravel drive outside the hotel overlooking Loch Striven and the lovely Scottish hills around the loch. The commander and first lieutenant were carrying chairs from a lorry and overall clad blue jackets were hard at work with beds and tables. There was obviously a large move on and we soon had to dump our kit and join in the fray.

It was Friday and the 'ship' was now officially in commission; at 4.30 'Clear Lower Deck' was piped down the long bare and now carpetless corridor of this luxury spa. We assembled in the ballroom – a ship's company of some fifteen ratings and half-a-dozen officers – and waited. The commander evidently was too busy to make an opening speech and we went on up to the first floor to arrange our ward and ante-room. A limited number of chairs and tables apparently had been officially allocated and of course the hotel looked empty.

The Scots pay lieutenant went from room to room with an official looking list and the rooms gradually became emptier. Long carpets were changed for bare little ones and the more expensive leather chairs were carried off to the senior bedrooms. Our ante-room outside the large dining room presented rather a problem – the lieutenant-commander was worried about the lack of screens, as the ratings had to pass to and fro to their 'mess decks' down a long passage leading to the kitchen – more known as 'the galley'. And they should not see what drinks we are having. So little screens were carefully placed out around green baize-topped tables.

The view was tremendous from our position, high up on the well laid out hillside of trees and shrubs. There were two hard red tennis courts and a nine hole golf course. Our feet echoed noisely down the stone corridors of this latest of Naval appropriations.

Monday came with squalls of rain and a further milestone in our rather novel lives. The gunner and his two rating divers came aboard and explained our plan of action and then climbed over the side of the large parent ship. We swung down the jumping ladder to a boat packed with all the paraphernalia of these underseamen. We pulled ourselves towards the shore and shallow water, anchoring over a four fathom patch of nice clear sandy bottom. With the iron ladder rigged over the stern, two of us took off our oilskins and were helped into the enveloping suits. They were canvas ones with light rubber wrists and took a certain amount of pulling and heaving to get on. Then followed the two monstrous brass boots which were lashed and finally strapped down.

My two experts dressing me had both explored the *Graf Spee* after she had been scuttled in the River Plate, and were full of interesting anecdotes of their job and kept the boat full of laughter.

Bit by bit the brass fittings were put in place and the nuts screwed home. Then at last the helmet. It was still raining hard and I was very glad to get the helmet on. I had been shown how to regulate the air escape valves on the right side of them. I clambered around to the shouts of 'mind my corns', from one fellow, to the ladder. The weight of the kit seemed terrific, and I bent over the top rung with a gasp whilst the two lead weights fore and aft were leashed on. With a total weight of 185lbs 'all up'.

I was in a very much happier frame of mind when finally the little face-piece was screwed on. For a few seconds pressure was rather high and then as I got below the surface the air escaped through the valve and a wonderful feeling of sinking through the water followed. With the exception of the slight hiss of incoming air there was almost complete silence. I touched the bottom softly and raised a small sand storm as I moved along. The helmet and top works no longer weighed down on me and regulating the air flow I controlled my buoyancy taking the weight off my very heavy feet. Crabs and small sand eels moved with speed as I moved along through the bright lit water. And the colourful anemone, and host of little fishes made a fascinating change to surface life.

It was all so new and full of interest that the fifteen minutes went by all too soon. Apart from the heavy work of walking and the water pressure on my body, it was good fun. Every few minutes one tug on the line asked me if all was well, and then finally four quiet tugs. This was my recall. Pushing in on my press button valve and walking over to get into position. I felt myself slowly rising. The boat loomed above me and I leaned back in time to clear it. A great kerfuffle of air bubbled all round as I found the ladder and started raising my self and those 185lbs up and up, to sag over the top rung whilst the lead was unlashed.

Then I saw Phillip, our only two-striper. He was standing by the pump without a cap, his oilskins open and his long seaboot stockings hanging round his ankles. He was soaked. He was a little fellow and they had forgotten to put the rubber 'Greys' on – additional rubber bands that fitted over the wrists to make a nice water tight fit on very small wrists.

He had just reached the bottom and the water had surged in as the air from the helmet bubbled out. Having the water trickling down his spine he felt something must be wrong and gave the four tugs on the rope for lift up. As there was little air in the suit and mostly water, he had been pulled up with his head carrying the weight, and with water halfway up the helmet, it must have been rather nerve-racking. The rest of the boat were still full of laughter over it all and the two divers ragged each other as they undressed me, 'You're for the rattle, mate – he may be a four striper one day.'

'Blimey, would I 'ate to be in your shoes!'

'T'ain't me – you said you 'ad put on them Greys!'

'Away and get stuffed! I never did.'

We pulled back for the ship and hot baths.

*

It was finally decided that the main lobby should become the quarterdeck and the conciergerie became the regulating officers. The captain's lavatory was soon marked off and by supper time and the arrival of a small party of Wrens; began to take on a more nautical air.

The large dining room looked cold and empty that first night as we sat down to a rather uninteresting supper – served by two, no doubt exhausted, little Wrens. Their small advance party had arrived four days before and with their usual efficiency had got to work so that the place certainly showed the feminine touch. There were flowers on the mess tables and the lack of after dinner coffee was soon replaced by large cups of tea.

They were brisk and businesslike and the commander was delighted that the entire place was to be almost entirely run by Wrens. The trucks, vans and motor boats would all be taken over – he was most enthusiastic about it all.

We turned in early that first night, wondering how 'the atom' was getting on. He, taking advantage of the move, had slipped off south to London and we hoped he would get away with it.

Our small party went diving the next day and some of us got down to 10 fathoms. My effort had been quite accidental – we had meant to anchor at about 7 fathoms and it was not until I got to the bottom of the shot rope and saw myself passing the heavy lead weight that I realised we were deeper. It had been an easy descent, I swallowed several times to relieve the pressure on my ears and waited to feel the bottom. It seemed darker than usual, with a queer stillness all about one. When I touched I did the usual quick turn round to make sure that there were no jellyfish about and walked away from under the boat.

It was only then that I realised that I must be quite a bit deeper, – for there some fifteen feet above me and showing darkly against the brightly lit surface was the anchor – hanging uselessly above. It was rather queer and reminded me of the Chinese pattern on household crockery, the dark yellow brown sea bed, with its rocks and black-looking seaweed, not a fish or crab moved and there all around at what seemed some ten feet off the bottom, was a soft white cloud effect as the weak light ceased to penetrate.

It felt strangely sinister and one had the feeling that here was another world below the bustling crowd of humanity, untouched and silent. I walked a few yards, the stirred up mud and sand rising to my cheek and hanging motionless, so that after some ten minutes wandering, I had laid a perfect smoke trail, that gradually in the distance merged into that upper soft white halo.

Always ahead of me was the invisible, impenetrable mass of dark water, for the visibility could not have been much above thirty feet. Occasionally the gunner above would give a hefty jerk on the keel rope and I would answer with the usual four.

The air wheezed into the helmet and bubbled erratically out through the outlet valve. I was happy and confident, and for once the outfit did not seem so heavy. But just the same, time dragged and when at last four hefty jerks came down that rope I was glad.

Then the fun started – in my wanderings the ground fog had made the overhead anchor invisible. Looking up I could just see the white rubber air line curve away out of sight to the surface and gradually followed its direction. Once under the boat I could only hope the shot rope was somewhere near. They had become impatient above and were obviously wondering at my delay.

I walked away from the boat and searched for the lead sinker that should be hanging somewhere above. It looked distant and the ruddy anchor hanging out of reach annoyed me – I felt like a climber that could not reach a rope.

Pressing down on the air valve I filled the suit and standing at what I thought was directly under the shot rope – waited to become buoyant. But buoyancy is a funny thing – before I knew where I was, I was on the surface on my back, having shot up like an express lift.

My air and best rope were foul of the shot rope and the gunner signalled me to go down and unwind it. As the air deflated I slid down once more and after what seemed like five hectic minutes of walking round the lead weight, finally cleared it and came up to the surface once more, and it was my turn to man the pump.

At twelve o'clock we stopped and pulled back to the *Cyclops*, tired, wet and glad to be through.

An odd assortment of submarines were lying on either side, American, Norwegian and British making fast astern. We stumbled up the jumpy ladder and just made the next boat ashore. Holiday crowds were disembarking from the ferry and watched us with idle curiosity, our oddly dressed little party in untidy submarine gear stood waiting for the truck to take us back to base. It rained, and storm clouds came morosely down through the Kyles and from the head of Striven and beat noisily against our windows.

Following our usual shipboard practice most of us turned in after lunch. It had been tiring – a morning on the air pumps was quite enough and anyhow we thought we deserved it, for after all it was a Saturday and memories of other more enjoyable peace time ones had long since vanished into a forgotten way of life. I wondered if we were getting lazy – both mentally and otherwise for this naval habit of sleeping whenever off duty during the day was very catching. It was encouraged during long submarine patrols as less air was used in the boat, but here in our luxury hotel it seemed rather shocking.

After a week of diving and little else the move up the loch was very welcome. There had apparently been room for four of us and on our last evening we drew lots.

Sunday had been a hectic day. The Irish doctor had taken us to the Hotel Victoria for a few drinks, and all no doubt would have gone well had we not run into two Glasgow pub owners enjoying a week-end jaunt. They were Irish as 'Paddy's Pigs' and full of life. It was really a disgraceful day; the first party finished at 1.30, another followed at three and as for 'John', our one time traveller in carpets, he did not get to bed until five on Monday morning.

We were all slightly depressed. The head of the loch had already somehow acquired an unpleasant reputation. The first three of our class had not hit it off too well with the first training class and we rather expected the worst on our arrival.

We determined to keep an unbiased mind, but nevertheless

maintain a solid front. We shook 'John' out of his sleep and as he had only turned in an hour before fully dressed, the problem of getting him down the steep hill to the jetty was quite a smooth operation.

We watched the efforts of two seamen in a small motor boat that broke down every few coughs, as they made their way out to the pinnace. Their language was ripe and full as only a matelot can make it at six in the morning when things go wrong, but at last she cast alongside and we were off up past the Kyles and into the loch. The waters looked cold and bleak and a heavy mist rose up off the steep sloping banks, the tops of whose hills were hidden in low cloud.

We sat up in the bows and morosely listened to the lap-lap of the bow waves as we splashed along at some five knots. The one or two whitewashed cottages in the bright green of their small surrounding fields, looked dead and very lonely as they stood on the loch side below these 1,000 foot hills of grey rock and dark purple heather. John, now in one of his 'back to nature' moods, took it all in with the pride of a live Scot, although his liver must have been in a hell of a state.

For over an hour and a half we surged ahead. Two months had gone by since our initial duckings in the DSEA tank at Fort Blockhouse and here at last was our big moment, around the last bend of the loch. We were all rather tense and just a bit keyed up, so many stories had filtered down. Some said you just couldn't see her – she was supposed to be so low in the water.

We waited and waited. The little drifter, her parent ship, so aptly named *Present Help*, was the only thing in sight. A thin plume of smoke from her galley wound up into the cold still air and it was just after 0800. As we circled her the first class were on deck and shouting about mail and laundry. One had the impression that here indeed, was utter desolation!

Lying alongside was a low flat object that looked like a long black drainpipe floating just above the water. That was all we saw before we were pulled ashore to the little concrete causeway. Then up and over the gentle green slope now covered with sheep, then through the modern iron gates to a straggling modern house in the imitation of the Dutch style.

The boards were bare and we trod noisily along the passage to a large room furnished with a bare kitchen table and a few leather chairs and garden canvas ones. They had all been brought up there in the little pinnace or aboard the *Present Help*.

The paymaster came in and surveyed my room; we had raided the wardroom and the large comfy leather chair did not seem to check with his list. He left, and peace settled once more. I dozed off, but in a few minutes he was back with our instructor lieutenant. 'Was I ill? Was everything all right?' Of course – and I explained that diving was not exactly quite the picnic they thought it was. Base staffs are a strange lot. Then fortunately a considerate little Wren came in with some tea and they left in rather a shocked silence. Then two men came in and removed the chair. Damn it all, was a fellow to have no sleep? I got up and put on my trousers – then the commander came in, 'What's all this I heard about your bed?'

'My bed, sir!' I was dazed – what the hell could be the matter with my bed? Followed by the pay lieutenant, he looked at the mattress. 'No sir,' he said, 'I think it's the other one.' They took the blankets off and prompted by the Scot the commander tried it.

'Yes, indeed – a damned good one.'

'Well, I think you ought to have it, sir!' He turned to me – 'Got the best bed in the hotel!'

'Really, sir?' And like two shoppers they examined the modern rubber mattress.

What an afternoon – the room felt rather like a public crossroads. I finished dressing and went out to help the doctor and others with a large kitchen table. Various others on the base staff were running up and down appropriating odd things like a lot of little kids, and were as quickly checked by the pay lieutenant. We only needed the Marx Brothers and things might have been more humorous! Men setting up house make the most pathetic sight I have ever seen!

The room was otherwise empty – the gallant owner had cleared the place completely, even to the wall mirrors which had been unscrewed in a moment of fury.

Our commander welcomed us and took us to our rooms, collapsible canvas camp beds, – used in private air raid shelters – this was the only visible sign that there were sleeping quarters.

Then down to breakfast. It was the first of many meals eaten in silence, broken only by the: 'Yes, sir', 'Of course, sir', 'Would you like some butter, sir', of the first training class.

We newcomers were ignored completely. To say that we felt quite ostracised was a mild understatement. We were furious, and had the feeling that we were butting in on private ground.

We walked down dejectedly to the lochside to get our gear. It was all, too, too private. We sat on the floor of one of the bedrooms and discussed the situation.

It was exactly as the first of our party had described – an atmosphere of coldness, almost resentment. It was fairly obvious that our first three had not played their cards right and we were reaping the wind of their work. I suppose these people up here thought we were going to turn out exactly like the others. Jealousy was intense between the two classes and had not been helped by our three starting in on the training before the first lot who had been waiting for months to be rounded up from various spots, found on their arrival our lot a week ahead in training. That week must have been intense, until three lads were sent down 'No room', had been the story.

Whilst sprawling on our bedroom floor our thoughts were startled by the sudden and very spectacular entrance of the commander. Two of us were stretched full out and completely relaxed when: 'Now then, what goes on?'

Philip, our senior, stood up: 'We were told to be at the swimming pool at 10.30, sir!'

'Well, the diving chief's down there now; you had better get along right away.'

'Aye, aye, sir.'

We met our old chief from Fort Blockhouse in the sun loggia, his lower paunch stretching his single-breasted rough service jacket to the limit. Two months had gone since those days and a different fellow greeted us after the commander had gone with: 'Call me when each one is ready.'

After asking the chief how things were he said: 'Well, I don't know, sir – I'm fairly chocker. This 'ere job 'as just about browned me off – do this – do that – 'an I does and it's all bloody well wrong – why, only this morning … Blimey, 'ow I wish I was back down south!'

The general atmosphere was unhappy, and the whole set-up seemed to be living up to its name, so early acquired.

One by one we were put into the swimming pool in the special suits. A suit designed by the commander. The CO watched us with an eagle eye as we floundered below. It looked exactly like an H.G. Wells dream of the ultra modern man with its tightly zipped rubber legs and metal body belt – its grotesque glass facepiece and of course the DSEA escape set strapped on the chest. It was uncomfortable, and oxygen continually escaped through the rubber seal around my face into the helmet, making me buoyant. The light rubber pad around my mouth seemed to bite in, and I came up exhausted after minutes of wild underwater swimming in vain attempts to keep below the surface.

So the forenoon of our first day went by quickly enough. Lunch was a painful meal. Our few efforts to join in were listened to politely, but there was no chance of anyone starting an intelligent conversation. We felt utterly miserable, and when at last the commander got up we hurriedly drank our coffee and went outside into the weak sunshine in the garden.

No effort had been made to gather us in – we were new boys. At 1.30 we walked down the muddy road through the new gates and down the sloping green field to the little concrete causeway. The motor skiff was waiting and we splashed out to the *Present Help*.

The young RNR Lieutenant Cameron was standing on her deck above the 'boat'. His air of quiet authority was refreshing and his eyes were full of humour as he smoked his enormous rough wood pipe. His cap looked altogether far too big for his small face with that pugnacious chin. We crowded round on the little deck and looked down on the rusty casing of the *Tiddler*, she was an impressive little thing and the very 'first of the few'. Only about 18″ of her bow showed above the water and with the inner feeling of hope and success we listened to explanations. The idea really was immense and one couldn't help feeling proud. Later, the words of that Yorkshire skipper of *The Isle of May* tender rather summed it all up. 'Man! If I was a few years younger – I'd play up merry – with them bastards, with a toy like that!' His faded last war ribbons and his pointed grey beard lent extra effect to the fierce glint in his eyes. Yes, he meant every word. It made one almost ashamed of being young and inexperienced. These old fellows who had proved themselves seemed to be eating their hearts out now that they were only allowed to do the pack horse jobs of the Navy.

My first impression was of the inside of a Wellington bomber – that maze of instruments, levers and electrical gadgets, the dim lighting and lack of standing room. The many cocks, valves, switches and pipe lines, pump motors, gyro, all so compact.

It was all there and as I sat between the 'Driver' forward and the 'Captain' at the periscope my head seemed to be in a whirl. I wondered if I should ever take it in. All the theory of the job at Blythe, our weeks out in the big subs, began to mean something. Lieutenant Cameron ran us through the boat – passing explanations at speed, whilst all the while the little motor hummed away. I came out mentally exhausted, and his 'Well, do you think you have got it all?' seemed altogether quite unnecessary! I laughed and got back aboard the little parent ship, with madly whirling brain. The others watching my expression of awe as I came through the hatch burst into laughter.

She was going to be all right – if one of us didn't manage to sink her in the meantime.

The carpet salesman, John, and I went for a walk after tea; our talk ranged back over the past few days. Our prospects were anything but good: we had cornered our instructional lieutenant in the hotel a few nights back. His submarine was in dry dock on refit and his very efficient presence amongst us was very inspiring if only for a few months. He took the full weight of our attack.

Rumours had got around – the lieutenant-commander who had signed us on at Fort Blockhouse had gone out East on another job, and all his promises seemed to be vanishing in thin air.

We nine had been promised the first operational boats – three of us would be made captains and the remaining six, the first lieutenants. We had worked hard for two solid months, now ... ideas changed with commands. There were now three classes and a small core of RN lieutenants to take these commands.

The temperamental outbursts of several fellows gradually worked us all up to a feeling of utter frustration. There was talk of 'Chucking up and getting on with the real job.' But when it came to bed rock no one was keen to throw his hand in! 'We are all going to be just a lot of bloody coxswains', was the general feeling. And this was not far off the mark. He had listened to us all and then given us the new set up, leaving us flattened and with only two alternatives. Either to face a long period of playing second fiddle with remote prospects of the first job, or throwing in. And as John and I walked down the loch we knew we had been double-crossed – it was no longer the RNVR show, and we now had to face up to 100% competition from the other classes. 'Wait and see,' was John's sound advice. It seemed a pretty good one.

Our dinner was a variation of lunch, only the commander's afternoon shooting was the official theme for conversation. We turned in early. This was going to be bloody!

Day after day we dived in the pool with hourly periods in the boat. We gradually worked up until on the fifth day when the first class were due to pass out.

I faced the moment with some fear and trepidation. It was one thing to go out with an expert and quite another to put one's life in the hands of someone who had only been on it for three weeks.

However our turn came after lunch. My 'captain' gave no orders at first, I sat in the seat and with a beating heart hoped for the best. He forgot about 'Opening up for diving' and other essentials. We seemed to be doing everything wrong. His constant alteration of course followed by 'as you were – port 20;' did little to calm me. And then at last, 'Dive' was the order.

So this was it. I opened up forward and down we went. For some ten minutes all went well at periscope depth – then all fogged up. Suddenly we hit a fresh water patch and she took a nose dive at a hell of a bow angle. With full rise on the after planes, I tried to bring her up. Nothing happened and with the speed of an express train we headed for the bottom out of control – 30 – 50 – 60 – flashed by on the depth gauge.

'Blow one's!' I turned the HP air blow to my forward tank. 'Blow two's,' The bow slowly came up. The gyro repeat was spinning round out of control. Then we headed for the surface, almost standing on our tail. It was so like coming out of a dive and going into a steep climb that all our new 'captain' had time to say was, 'Hang on, here we go!'

I heard afterwards that our return to the surface was spectacular in the extreme. I can believe anything now – it felt more than that.

'God, am I glad to be up,' said our young skipper. Unfortunately our return had evidently put the wind up the RN instructor, as at one stage just previous to our dive we had headed at some four knots straight for the rocky foreshore. I was not surprised to hear the angry banging on the hull followed by: 'What the bloody hell do you think you're playing at?'

Our first solo was at an end – I hoped mine in a week's time would be a little happier.

What a wonderful little thing she was! A lively little beast all right!

'Make sure you know what you are doing, and can see what you are doing and that the gyro repeat is in step with the master gyro!'

I took it all in.

We spent our evenings with duty periods and walks into the hills; the 'set' kept to themselves.

The first three days had been the most boring and egotistical I had ever spent – but this seemed to be at an end and a thaw was setting in somewhere now. It might have been because of the spells of duty we shared with other fellows – but nevertheless, we noticed now that we were gradually merging into two groups – that is, we RNVRs and our RN friends up here in this highland shooting box! The commander savoured every minute of the situation, for he was in fact responsible for the removal of the late tenant, whose lamentable cutting down and 'axing' of the Navy in those days between wars, was in no small measure responsible for the large numbers of RNVRs in the Navy today and the smallness of the pre-war fleet.

He was obviously enjoying himself in the multi-millionaire's house, although in turn the game-keeper levelled things a bit by stalking him, when one evening he looked like putting up some grouse! At the moment of meeting, the *Present Help* opened fire with her rifles on a short target shoot, and the poor fellow apparently bore down on the commander in great wrath imagining fearful slaughter amongst his birds. It must have been a funny meeting – our commander and the game-keeper.

The days went by – mornings of practice escapes and afternoons of practical boat work. It was most interesting and our sea time slowly mounted from the meagre four half-hour periods on the first week to four full hours in the second. Each day we went out to the escape pontoon with its replica of the job and were duly lowered away down through the centre to 15ft. The moments of darkness when sitting in the cramped little cell were soon over and opening the various valves and 'flooding up' until water pressures inside equalled sea pressure without. With a certain feeling of relief one unclipped the hatch and climbed into the greenness of the water.

It was amusing and competition was great, to see just who could come out with the minimum of bubbles – tell-tale bubbles which would give us away, perhaps fatally, later on.

The commander usually came out and of course 'took command' of the proceedings. The suits leaked and one invariably came up soaked, but the job progressed and our efficiency and confidence increased with time.

Day by day we followed a set routine of drills until the final Saturday morning – that was 'our day' and the climax of our first period of training.

With our instructors watching from the parent ship and escorting boat – which on these days followed the 'buff' more closely than ever. (The buff was a small buoy some 200 yards astern of our craft – in case the worst happened, to duly 'mark the spot'.)

We each had three-quarters of an hour as captains, with one of the officers of the next group as our first lieutenants and of course, one of our own ERAs.

Thinking of the previous week when I had gone out with a makee-learn, I felt sorry for the others, but they persevered with a steady calm that could not have been altogether inwardly backed with happiness.

It had been quite an eventful morning; one fellow had forgotten to fully surface and attempted to open the hatch when the craft was half submerged. Someone else had nearly run aground.

Now it was my turn. The escorting ship had broken down and we rowed for half a mile to take her in tow. Then we changed over with the previous crew and took out stations.

'Main motor ready, group down.'

'Main motor ready, and power.'

'Half ahead.'

'Half ahead.'

'Starboard twenty.'

'Starboard twenty.'

'Main motor going half ahead – twenty of starboard wheel on.' It was grand and we were off on a slow turn to get into diving position. All was quiet except for the hum of the gyro compass and the tic-tac of the repeater. I gave the order: 'Open up for diving,' Valves were opened up to the main ballast tanks, and good old 'George' took over the wheel on automatic steering.

I watched through the periscope and saw the great interest we were giving to our instructor. I hoped he didn't feel too worried – I certainly didn't. Then my moment came and I ordered, 'Dive!'

The vents were opened and we slowly sank to periscope depth. Her bows dropped and water lapped over the scuttles and we caught our trim, then all was quiet. We ran up our area and down again with always the little skiff in attendance. Then making our final turn before surfacing, we struck a fresh water patch and dropped rapidly. Stupidly leaving the helm on, I concentrated on getting her up again.

My first solo was over and life calmed down once more. We returned down the loch feeling less like students and happy with our new job. Later after several weeks of periscope navigation in two small yachts – we did our final weeks in this preliminary training period before a happy week in London on a gyro compass course.

The months had gone by and we returned ready for the advanced period that was to take us up to Christmas.

Then the accident happened. The fog thick and heavy with dampness, covered the waters of Kames Bay. We had returned from Wemyss Bay across the Clyde on a morning periscope navigation and dummy attacks on various shipping. The great liner *Queen Elizabeth* with her decks crowded with troops had looked down on us and waved cheerily. The little grey luxury launch passed down her sides – we might have been a harbour craft, for the periscope was well hidden and out of sight. Port Bannatyne pier with its several tugs was altogether empty.

As we made fast, the commander came hurriedly down and was taken to the diving ship *Tedworth* in a fearful flurry of speedy commands. I was dispatched up the hill at the double with a signal. 'Hands to panic stations' seemed the order of the day. I met the base's first lieutenant pacing the signal office whilst four fussed Wrens stood to their phones. He turned to me: 'Ex … Tripper' has just gone up!' He was flushed and my heart seemed to miss a step. This was the secret alarm signal calling pre-arranged rescue vessels to the head of the loch at full speed. We got a supply of petrol cans and hurried down the hill to the launch and out to the *Gedworts* as she let go her buoy. The commander came aboard and little was said as we sped northwards through the fog that rolled down Loch Striven. All sorts of thoughts flashed through our minds; the little crew – who were they and what depths of tragedy were we about to break in on?

After forty minutes we swept round the bend and bore down on the little *Present Help*. Out in the middle of that stretch of water bobbed the orange-coloured buoy. It looked so very ominous and meant so much to us all, marking the scene of the *Tiddler's* last dive. What luck to go out with those 200 yards of line and that little buoy. It had not been always so – often it had been forgotten, and always during dummy attacks it had been left aboard *Present Help*. I wondered just how long it might have taken to locate her in the depth of this gaunt mist-bound loch, with its tall shadowing mountains.

The commander leapt aboard the little ship before we made fast and hurried up the sloping deck to the fo'castle where the training commander waited for the conference with our two chiefs. We went below to the little wardroom to see the three survivors. It was a wonderful moment, full of smiles and handshakes. Snatches of, 'Good lad, well done,' and other complimentary phrases echoed

Four X-craft in dry dock

X-5 on the deck of Bonaventure

HMS Thrasher with X-5 on tow leaving Loch Cairnbawn

Operational and passage crews of *X-5* aboard the *Bonaventure*
(*Above*) Back row, l to r: Lt Terry-Lloyd (Pass CO), Sub-Lt Nelson (Op), Lt Henty-Creer (Op CO), ERA Mortiboys (Op); front row, L/Seaman Element (P), Stoker Garritty (P)
(*Left*) Back row, Terry-Lloyd, Nelson, Henty-Creer, Sub-Lt Malcolm (Op); front row, Garritty, Element, Mortiboys

round the little space. They were between blankets and smoking hard now, 'thawing out', after nearly one hour in the cold loch waters.

We began to get the story together and with it came those delightful snatches of English humour that always come to the top at dangerous moments.

She had apparently dived stern first 120 feet into the clay bed. Just after lunch watchers in the skiff had been horrified to see her surface almost vertically – standing on her tail for nearly three minutes before sliding slowly but surely out of sight beneath the waters. Then for nearly one hour nothing happened, only the orders of the young sub in command came up on the telephone line that was attached to the buoy. The instructor tried to contact them but no one seemed to hear his telephone rings. Then the training commander arrived on the scene and they waited anxiously. Below, the slow process of flooding up the forward compartment to equalise sea pressure without, was taking time, and all the while battery fumes got heavier.

They had tried everything to get her to the surface, but the pump could not keep pace with the steady rise of water and at last their air bottles were empty.

There was nothing now left but to bale out and, baling out was not an easy or pleasant job. The space was tiny and the awful wait for pressure to build up inside must have been fearful. The escape chamber was a small cramped affair, and usually meant a spot of planned thinking, but in the dark and knowing that the usual drill was now out of the question, sitting for nearly an hour waiting to equalise pressure which steadily rose to some 45lbs per square inch on one's ears could be quite a painful business. It must have been a glorious moment when the hatch at last fell open, but even then they seemed to keep their sense of humour.

I had lent a pair of sea boots to Guy, who after shaking hands with the other two, suddenly realised that he had kicked them off and promptly put them on again before shooting to the surface. Strange gestures and a credit to a calm mind. But then things seemed to liven up a little. The second fellow couldn't somehow make his DSEA set function properly, it could have been a nasty moment – chlorine gas was rising fast now and breathing without oxygen almost impossible. The sub-in-command kept his head superbly and fitted a second set on the man, but this too failed to co-operate with the feeling of the wearer. So with a mighty push he was shot through the hatch. How he held his breath on that journey to the surface, no one will ever know. But he appeared like a rocket from below and waving his hands madly in the air shouting for the skiff.

Here the laugh was on the commander, for he, thinking the fellow still had his escape set on, told him in no uncertain terms not to panic and calmly went about the job of getting the first man into the little motor boat.

But holding one's breath over the time it takes to come up from such depths left the survivor exhausted and they only got to him in time to prevent a complete tragedy before the third came happily to the surface.

We helped them into dry clothes and they were rowed ashore. In the meantime *Tedworth*, the diving ship, had followed up the loch and anchored over the buoy. Then the *Barfield* in a cloud of black smoke came up from around the point and with a superb show of seamanship dropped her stern anchor and turning to starboard came to a stop with her massive horns directly over the buoy. Wires were run out and she was held at right angles to the *Tedworth*.

The afternoon light faded and eight and a half hours after the sinking, the little *Tiddler* was raised to the surface.

Divers had worked hard and the two hoisting lines been made fast in record time, but at the first lift they had parted. Civilian riggers working under the orders of a Naval commander had done wonders, handling great wires as if they were string and all the while joking. One fellow, rugged and tough, talked to his section. 'Come on, ma wee Jessie – give, will ye – come to papa, ye bitch.'

The great wire was moved slowly through the horn above and slid like a great snake through the various blocks to the winch. Occasionally the brusque orders of the commander would break out through the glare of the lights that shone down on the light green water, as it came to life with great bubbles of escaping air and chlorine gas broke the surface.

Whether it was the usual order of the job and their own keenness to see what she looked like, or the inspiring way their officer spurred them on, they worked as few men have toiled, and she at last came to the surface in a great bubble of busy foaming air. Tows were thrown around her hull and a great pipe line ran down into her.

We bunked down in the little wardroom of *Tedworth* at midnight, I on the floor beside the small coal stove. The small group of officers who had been diving earlier during the day were still stranded aboard. We filled the leather side seats and overflowed into the passage.

Lieutenant Cameron, one of our instructors, was called at two and together we went into the *Tiddler*. She was a sorry sight, heavy oil covered everything, we slipped and slithered. He checked through in an effort to find out why she had gone down. At four we moved the pipe to the after compartment and gradually hour by hour the water level dropped, until at last at 6 a.m. we were able to haul the pipe lines to the various tanks and so drain the bilges. The mystery was baffling and remained so far unsolved.

The commanders held conferences and the small convoy of ships at last got under weigh and in the early afternoon the *Tiddler*'s career was temporarily ended. She was shipped to Kames Bay for the night.

There was a fearful lot of shouting, men scurried and yelled as small boats got her on the cradle. But when they took the strain, she wouldn't. She would not move more than half way up the slipway. We covered her up with large green tarpaulins and posted sentries around her. But she couldn't have liked her ignominy, as later next day the wires failed and with the horrified figure of the training commander standing on her casing – she sped with ungainly haste back into the water. His expression of shocked horror was for long the talk of the lower deck, that dashing figure hanging on grimly, whilst showing his thoughts of the next world to a hushed group of all ranks, who stood spellbound during those fearful seconds, whilst others jumped clear of that charging monster before she hit the water once more.

Next day we went on leave. Training was at a stand still – and but for the periscope navigation for the late arrivals, there was little to do.

The *Tiddler* had done well. Built as a test craft at a cost of some £100,000 she had lasted two months over the builders' guarantee of six months. She had worked hard at the hands of trainees and experiments – and now she faced a long refit. Poor little beast – she deserved it.

III

The Attack

by Frank Walker

Fortunately, prototype *X-4* had been delivered just before *Tiddler* sank, so training went on uninterrupted. *X-4* was put under the command of the experienced submariner Lieutenant Godfrey Place, DSC and it was not long before *X-4* demonstrated that these frisky little X craft were deadly, dangerous toys. One stormy night in December 1942, *X-4* was cruising on the surface on a training exercise. Place was relieved on watch on the deck casing by Sub-Lieutenant Morgan Thomas. While Place was scrambling down through the hatch, a huge wave washed Thomas overboard and the sea went cascading down the hatch into the boat. *X-4* canted perilously, its bows out of the water and completely out of control.

Place managed to send out a distress signal to *Present Help*, which again lived up to its name by racing to the spot and hauling *X-4*'s stern up so that the boat was again on an even keel and could be pumped dry. Sub-Lieutenant Thomas was drowned.

On New Year's Eve 1942, *X-5* arrived, followed within two weeks by *X-6*, *X-7*, *X-8*, *X-9* and *X-10*. With them came their new mother-ship, HMS *Bonaventure*, a former merchant ship with cranes strong enough to lift an X-craft bodily out of the water. Training for the actual attack could now start in earnest.

Focus of the attack was to be the largest and most powerful battleship in the world – the 45,000-ton *Tirpitz*. This formidable giant had eight 15-inch guns, with two two-gun turrets forward and two aft, twelve 6-inch guns, sixteen 4-inch guns, plus a huge battery of anti-aircraft guns. Her three turbine engines could power her through the seas at 32 knots. She was as long as two football fields, wider than two cricket pitches and drew ten yards of water. She had been launched on 1st April 1939 at Wilhelmshaven and the ceremony was performed by Frau von Hassel, grand-daughter of Admiral von Tirpitz, after whom the ship was named. Frau von Hassel's husband was then German ambassador in Rome. In 1944 Hitler had him executed for being involved in the assassination attempt of 20th July. The captain of *Tirpitz*, from its commissioning until February 1943 was Captain Karl Topp, who had been navigating officer of the German light cruiser *Emden*, sunk by the Australian cruiser *Sydney* off Cocos Island on 9th November 1914. It was in the wardroom of HMAS *Sydney* that Henty-Creer was christened six years later. Captain Topp's successor in command was tall, thin Captain Karl Meyer, who had lost an arm fighting in the revolutionary uprisings in Germany in 1919.

Tirpitz, the 32,000-ton battle-cruiser *Scharnhorst* and the pocket-battleship *Lützow* (sister-ship of the *Admiral Scheer* and *Graf Spee*) were lying in wait in the fjords of Northern Norway, ready to pounce on Allied convoys taking war material to Russia, or to make a dash into the Atlantic to prey on convoys from the United States and Britian. *Scharnhorst* and *Lützow* were both threats, but it was *Tirpitz* that concerned Britain most. Churchill wrote, in a minute to the Chief of Staffs committee on 26th January 1942:

> The destruction or even the crippling of *Tirpitz* is the greatest event at sea at the present time. No other target is comparable to it. If she were only crippled it would be difficult to take her back to Germany. The entire Naval situation throughout the world would be altered ... The whole strategy of the war turns at this period on this ship, which is holding four times the number of British ships paralysed, to say nothing of two new American battleships retained in the Atlantic. I regard the matter as of the highest urgency and importance.

*

Prime Minister Winston Churchill was the driving force behind the introduction of the midget submarine to the Royal Navy, which disdained the term 'midget submarine' and referred to it as an X-craft. He was spurred into action by the gallant and hazardous feat of Italian divers who had severely damaged two British battleships in Alexandria Harbour – HMS *Queen Elizabeth* and HMS Valiant. The Italians had ridden astride a two-man submarine that was so small that it would not even qualify as a midget – it was a miniature. They rode it like a motor-bicycle built for two and attached limpet mines to the battleships' hulls.

The idea appealed to Churchill. German battleships and heavy cruisers made only infrequent dashes to sea and were notoriously hard to sink when under weigh, with all water-tight doors closed and the crew on full alert. In harbour with conditions relaxed they were more vulnerable.

Churchill sent a memorandum to the Chiefs of Staff on 18th January 1942, demanding.

> Please report what is being done to emulate the exploits of the Italians in Alexandria harbour and similar methods of this kind. At the beginning of the war Colonel Jefferis had a number of bright ideas on this subject which received little encouragement. Is there any reason why we should be incapable of the same kind of scientific aggressive action that the Italians have shown? One would have thought that we would have been in the lead. Please state the exact position.

The exact position was that Colonel Jefferis had vainly suggested constructing a midget submarine which could penetrate enemy harbours, enabling frogmen to get out of the submarine and attach mines to enemy shipping. Following Churchill's intervention, a retired World War I submarine officer, Commander Cromwell Varley, DSC, drew up the designs for a prototype midget, which was built and given sea trials, both on the surface and submerged, three months later. It worked on the same principles as a conventional full-size submarine, with a tough inner hull, inside which were the machinery and the crew, and an outer hull of thinner metal. The space between the inner and outer hulls could be filled with water, which would make the craft sink, or with air, which would give it buoyancy. The depth of the submarine was controlled by the amount of water between the two hulls. To go to a greater depth, control valves let more water in and to bring the craft up, the water was pumped out.

On the surface the submarine ran on diesel motors, which could push the 35-tonne midget along at 6½ knots, and if the speed was kept to four knots they could cover 2,500 kilometres. The diesels, which were the same Gardner motors used in London buses, also charged banks of batteries, which supplied power to the electric motors used when the craft was submerged. When submerged, the midgets could get along at five knots for a short burst, such as an emergency. Their maximum range under water, without re-charging their batteries, was 130 kilometres at two knots. They could dive to 90 metres and stay submerged for 24 hours without running out of air. If they were close to the surface they could take in fresh air through the diesel induction pipe, which was normally the means of getting air to the diesels. Inside the craft's ventilation system was a container of a special absorbent which mopped up carbon dioxide. The crew also got clean air from cylinders of oxygen.

The main armament of large submarines is torpedoes, but these were not practicable for the 15.5-metre long midgets. Instead, they carried two large mines, each weighing two tonnes, attached to the side of the boat, and known as side cargoes. Each mine contained amatex, a sensitive explosive, with about the same force as a salvo of torpedoes. The theory was that the midget crews would manoeuvre themselves under enemy ships, set the time fuses on the mines by turning a gauge inside the boat, release the mines by turning a wheel, then make their escape. The mines would sit on the sea bed and tick away for anything up to 36 hours before exploding. Crews were taught to release the mines as close to the sea bed as possible so that they would not be carried sideways by the current.

The inside of a midget would have given the horrors to any plumber, electrician or engineer but a contortionist would have gone into raptures. It was a mass of pipes, gauges, dials, wheels, electrical conduits, pumps and levers. There were three water-tight compartments. The forward compartment housed the batteries. The centre compartment, known as the wet and dry compartment, had a hatch, opening at the top from which the diver could leave and enter the boat. He would enter the compartment with his Davis Submarine Escape Apparatus on, close the water-tight door behind him, flood the chamber, open the hatch and then float out, so that he could cut nets or wires to enable the midget to get through, then return to his compartment and pump the water out. In an emergency the entire crew could, in theory, use the same technique to escape from the boat.

The third compartment contained everything else – the controls for the gadgets that operated the boat, such as the steering gear, the hydroplanes which helped the boat dive or surface, the compasses, the periscope, the valves for trimming the boat and the pumps. The compartment also contained the control 'room', which is the equivalent of a ship's bridge. Above the control room, which was more of a control space than a control room, was the dome which housed the periscope. There were three small portholes in the dome – one on either side and the other on the top. The captain would use his periscope to run in towards the target, then dive deep and run by dead reckoning until he could see the hull of the ship through the portholes. Underneath the dome was the only place in the entire boat where a man could stand upright, provided he was 5 ft 6 (1.7m) or less. Henty-Creer was 5 ft 11½ (1.8m).

Repairs and maintenance to the engine would have delighted the contortionist. He would have had to wriggle onto a fuel tank only a foot (30cm) wide and when he got into position he had only a few inches clearance from the hull. Working the compressor was tricky and dangerous. With luck, a man could get his arm through the 6-inch (15cm) gap between a fly-wheel revving like crazy and the exhaust pipe. Without luck he would get badly burnt or lose some skin and bone.

Life on board the midgets was so demanding and so exacting that the Navy regarded 10 days as the most humans could stand. With special training they might be able to last 14 days, but the last few days would be little short of hell. Even the first few days were arduous. On the surface only one man could go on deck at a time, and even that was a mixed blessing. He had to be lashed to a stanchion or be washed overboard. He got fresh air but he also got a cold bath. One thing he did not ever get was warm. The only wash the crew had was the involuntary one when they were lashed to the stanchion on deck. The air inside the submarine was always foul, even when running on the surface, and always dank and humid. The bulkheads (walls) were always dripping with condensation, which played merry hell with the sensitive electrical gear. Food was not exactly cordon bleau. The only cooking device was a little electric pot and that could be used only when the boat was on the surface, otherwise the steam would add to the unbearable moisture in the boat.

*

In their anchorage in Kaafjord, at the innermost part of Altenfjord, the German ships were out of range of land-based bombers from Britain. They were protected by fighter squadrons at two nearby air fields, Bardufoss and Banak, and an attack by carrier-borne planes was therefore out of the question. To make doubly sure, the Germans had installed smoke-making equipment on the hills that towered over the fjord, so that the ships could be blotted out of sight if they were attacked from the air.

The only way to attack was by sea, but an attack on the surface would be suicidal. The attacking ships would first have to get through the minefields off the coast and in the sounds, then make the 100-kilometre dash up the fjords, running the gauntlet of artillery batteries on the cliffs and torpedo tubes controlled by

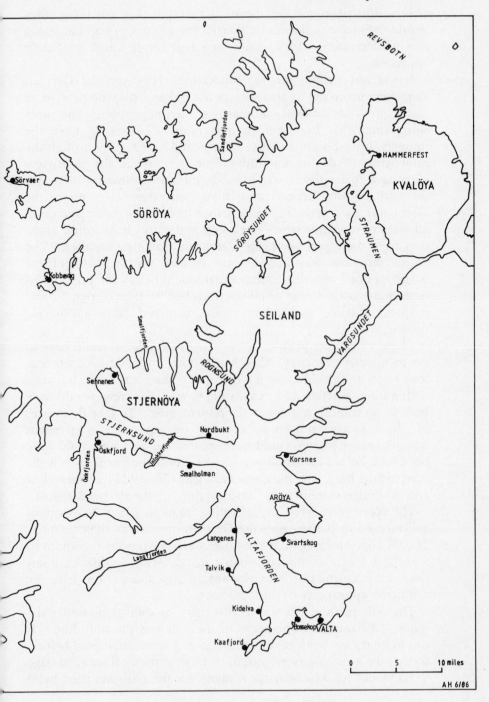

The Approaches to Altenfjord (now Altafjord)

observation posts on the shore. If they got through these, they would then have to face the withering fire of the German battleship and battlecruisers, which would have had ample warning of their approach.

It was obviously a job for submarines. However, the German ships were protected by anti-submarine and anti-torpedo nets, so an attack by conventional submarines was impossible. The only submarines that had the slightest hope of attacking were the midgets. It would not be easy. They would have to get through the minefields, evade the anti-submarine nets, evade the destroyers keeping a hydrophone watch inside the anti-submarine nets, get through the anti-torpedo nets, manoeuvre themselves under the German ships, release their mines, then unwind the entire process in an attempt to escape when every ship and patrol boat would know they were there and would be frantically searching for them. The entire shoreline was guarded by sentries on the lookout for periscopes or water disturbances that would betray the presence of underwater craft. Crews of all warships had been given regular and frequent practice using dummy frogmen and faked submarine noises.

There were other problems, too. First the midgets would have to get to northern Norway. They had a range of 2,500 kilometres at four knots and could make it – only just – there and back, but after such a long, exacting and exhausting voyage, the crews would have been in no condition to make the return voyage. To take them over in their mother-ship was out of the question – German reconnaissance planes would have spotted her and she would have been sunk before she could get anywhere near the fjord. Even if she survived the bombing, the element of surprise would have been lost and the midgets would never have got through the alerted defences.

The Navy considered using fishing boats in which Norwegians had escaped to Britain after the German invasion of their country. They found, however, that the boats were not powerful enough to tow the midgets at any reasonable speed. Also, the fishing boats were not from the northern Norwegian area and did not have the distinctive appearance of the local boats.

The only method left was to tow them by submarine under the water – a hazardous operation in itself. It was the only hope. It would be tricky. Nothing like this had ever been attempted before. So that the attacking crews would be fresh at the vital time, passage crews would have to man the midgets for the crossing, then hand over to the attack crews just outside the fjord. This meant training both submarine crews and passage crews in under-water towing techniques, as well as training the attack crews for the actual assault.

Timing was critical. The German ships were anchored five degrees north of the Arctic circle where there was no darkness in summer and no light in winter. Summer was ruled out for the attack, because although the midgets could have penetrated the fjords submerged by day, they would have had to surface at night to recharge their batteries. To try to use the induction trunk as a Schnorchel for re-charging would have been too risky – the sentries on the shoreline would certainly spot them if the patrol boats did not. Winter was ruled out, too. The midgets needed daylight to make their attack so that they could see their target by periscope and judge their release positions by sighting the target's hull through the tiny glass portholes in the dome. Also, if wire-cutting was necessary, the man making the cuts had to be able to see what he was doing at some depth below the surface.

To get the right proportion of daylight and darkness, timing was limited to the days in March and September when daylight and darkness are equal – the equinoxes. By March 1943 the crews would not have had sufficient training. The Navy therefore decided on September, somewhere between 20th and 25th September.

Henty-Creer had been given command of *X-5* and had supervised its construction, as had the other commanders. Lieutenant Ken Hudspeth RANVR got *X-10* and Lieutenant B.M. McFarlane RAN *X-8*. Lieutenant Place DSC, RN was given command of *X-7*, Lieutenant Cameron, RNR, got *X-6* and *X-9* went to Lieutenant T.L. Martin, RN. For both Henty-Creer and Hudspeth it was an outstanding achievement – they were the only two non-professional sailors awarded commands. Hudspeth had been a schoolteacher in Hobart before the war. Three of the other four commanding officers were permanent Navy men, and Lieutenant Cameron, as an ex-merchant service officer, was in the Navy's sea-going reserve.

Henty-Creer, always the Australian, called his boat *Platypus* – it was not only an Australian animal, but it swam under water and laid eggs, like the midgets. That remained its unofficial name, right to the end.

Crews for the passage of the six midgets to Norway were also chosen. Among them were two more Australians, a South African and a New Zealander.

Right through the spring and summer of 1943 the teams

practised, practised and practised for the day they called 'D-Day, which was later to be used for the Allied landing at Normandy. Navy experts laid out a course in Loch Cairnbawn with distances similar to those in the Norwegian fjords where the German ships were anchored. By this means the crews were able to make simulated attacks, using the old British battleship *Malaya* and other major warships as targets. The teams also practised towing with the conventional submarines that were to tow them to Norway and, it was hoped, back again. They practised cutting through the anti-submarine and anti-torpedo nets – a breath-taking exercise, during which the diving expert got out of the boat while it was under water, swam or crawled with cutters to the nets, made a hole large enough for the boat to pass through, helped the boat through and then scrambled back inside. One officer was lost during cutting exercises.

The young captains soon realised that as well as being deadly weapons, their boats provided unparalleled opportunities to have some fun at the expense of the senior officers. Naval custom decrees that when one warship passes another, the ship with the more junior captain must salute the senior captain. The junior ship sounds a whistle and the captain stands at the salute facing the senior ship. The senior ship then sounds a whistle in acknowledgement and the captain returns the junior officer's salute while all hands stand at attention. Then the senior officer sounds the 'carry on' whistle, the junior ship acknowledges by sounding its whistle and life goes on as before. The midget captains were most junior in any collection of naval ships and a passage down harbour to exercise at sea involved a gauntlet of salutes. This was more than the midget captains could resist. They would pass senior ships with their deck casings awash and the captain standing on the casing. He would then sound his whistle and salute the senior ships where all hands would stand amazed while their captains returned the salute of a man who was walking on water. It was, the X-craft captains found, well worth a couple of wet feet.

While the crews were training, the German ships and the defences protecting them had to be watched. There were two ways to do it – by getting reports from the Norwegian resistance fighters and by aerial reconnaissance. A Norwegian who had escaped to Britain was landed by submarine on the Norwegian coast near Trondheim and managed to get himself a job at Alta, where he could keep vigil on the German ships. Without knowing it, the Germans helped him get his reports back to Britain – he lived next door to a German officer and used the German's receiving aerial for his transmitter. The Norwegian, Torstein Raaby, later achieved fame as a member of the *Kon-Tiki* raft crew.

Photographic reconnaissance was quite a problem. It was outside the range of aircraft operating from Britain, so the Russians were asked for permission to station British crews at Vaenga, in northern Russia. The idea was to run a shuttle service by Mosquito aircraft from Russia to Britain for the preliminary reconnaissances, then to use Spitfires based on Vaenga for last-minute reports. In addition, Catalina flying boats would run a shuttle service to and from north Russia with the pictures. On 27th August the airmen and their photographic equipment left for Russia in the British destroyers *Musketeer* and *Mahratta*. The Spitfires arrived at Vaenga on 3rd September, only eight days before the X-craft were due to leave Scotland for the attack.

The final days of training were devoted to towing, slipping from the tow and recovering. The towing submarines were fitted with a special towing tube and a slipping device. The tow ropes were specially made with a telephone line running down the centre as a core. The ropes were of hemp, but a new nylon hawser became available just before the operation.

Several of the crews had their wives up in Bute, Scotland. Cameron's wife Eve was there, with their baby son. Place's bride, Althea, was there, too – Henty-Creer had been best man at their wedding only a short time before. Henty-Creer's mother, two sisters and the family giant St Bernard dog Sarah spent three months there.

They had been bombed out of their London home, which was on the direct route for German bombers attacking a major power station. During the raids they had crouched together – Sarah, too, – under a card table taken from the German cruiser *Emden* after it was sunk by the Australian cruiser *Sydney*. When all the windows of the house had been blown in and they were the only residents left in their street, Henty-Creer's mother decided it was time to go somewhere safer, so she rented a house in Sussex, only to find it was in the centre of the training area for the European invasion.

By this time Henty-Creer had started his training in X-craft. His mother and sisters sensed these might be the last days they would be able to spend with him, so they moved up to Bute and saw him in most of his off-duty moments. At first they stayed in a small flat overlooking the sea where they could watch the midget submarines coming and going on exercises. However, they found that the woman who ran the flats knew too much. She was always watching the boats through binoculars and was even able to describe how Henty-Creer always stretched himself every time he emerged onto the tiny craft's deck. That was no place for submarine people to foregather so the Henty-Creers moved to a farmhouse.

Then came the day when Henty-Creer had to say goodbye. He gave his mother a small wooden plaque with a platypus inscribed on it and the motto *'Dum spiro, spero, spiro'*. ('While I breathe I hope and while I hope I breathe') carved around it. This was a replica of a plaque he had fixed to his beloved *X-5*. They talked about where they would meet afterwards, as the family by then had no fixed address. They decided he could reach them through their bank.

*

On 10th September, the eve of the departure of the X-craft and their towing submarines, the admiral in charge of submarines, Rear-Admiral C.B. Barry, arrived at Loch Cairnbawn and spent some hours with the midgets' crews aboard the mother ship *Bonaventure*. Later he wrote:

They were like boys on the last day of term, their spirits ran so high. This confidence was not in any way the outcome of youthful dare-devilry, but was based on the firm conviction, formed during many months of arduous training, that their submarines were capable of doing all that their crews demanded of them, and the crews were quite capable of surmounting any difficulties or hazards which it was possible for human beings to conquer.

It was in this spirit that they went out into the night in their tiny craft to face a thousand miles of rough seas before they reached their objective, which itself, to their knowledge, was protected by every conceivable device that could ensure their destruction before they could complete their attacks. And the *Tirpitz* herself was tucked away close under the cliffs at the end of a narrow fjord 60 miles from the open sea.

At 4 p.m. on 11th September, the submarines *Truculent* with *X-6* in tow and *Syrtis* with *X-9* left Loch Cairnbawn. Two hours later *Thrasher* left, towing Henty-Creer's *X-5*, with Henty-Creer and the attack crew aboard *Thrasher* and the passage crew in *X-5*. They were followed by *Seanymph* towing *X-8*, *Stubborn* with *X-7* and *Sceptre* with *X-10*. Each towing submarine had to make its way independently to a position west of the Shetland Islands, and then sail on parallel courses twenty miles apart to a position off Altenfjord. On passage, the X-craft were submerged for the entire crossing, surfacing only for about fifteen minutes every six hours to get some fresh air.

Soon after they left, a Catalina flying boat arrived from Russia with pictures of the fjords taken by reconnaissance Spitfires. They showed that *Lützow* was in Langefjord, near the end of Altenfjord. The Admiralty relayed this to the submarines with the instructions that Henty-Creer's *X-5*, Cameron's *X-6* and Place's *X-7* were to attack *Tirpitz*. MacFarlane's *X-8* was to attack *Lützow* and Lieutenant T.L. Martin's *X-9* and Hudspeth's *X-10* were to tackle *Scharnhorst*.

The photographs also showed that across Kaafjord were two single anti-submarine nets, each about 400 feet long and probably secured to the sea-bed. The north-west end went right to the shore, but there was a gap at the south-eastern end where a boom gate was installed. Around *Tirpitz* was a double anti-torpedo net, stretching from the shore, down her starboard side at a distance of about 170 feet, then across her bow to a gate about 600 feet away from the bow. A patrol boat was keeping constant under-water watch by hydrophones near the gate in the anti-submarine net, checking all boats and ships entering the area. All this was relayed to the attack crews aboard the towing submarines.

Until 15th September, everything went well with the tow – the weather was good and the seas calm. But at 4 a.m. on 15th September the tow between *X-8* and *Seanympth* parted. *X-8* surfaced but it was not until 6 a.m. when *X-8* had been due to surface for fresh air that *Seanymph* realised what had happened. She turned back but could find no trace of *X-8*. Meanwhile the tow between *X-7* and *Stubborn* had parted. While they were passing another tow rope, who should arrive but *X-8*. *Stubborn* took *X-8* under her wing and radioed *Seanymph* to come and get her. By the time *Seanymph* arrived next morning, *X-8* had got herself lost again steering 146 degrees instead of 046 – the result of a hearing error in passing orders for the course when the watch changed.

By a stroke of luck, *Seanymph* managed to find *X-8* again at 5 p.m. on 16th September. The attack crew, under the command of Lieutenant MacFarlane, took over the midget to give the exhausted passage crew a rest. But things were going badly for *X-8*. First she developed a list to starboard. MacFarlane could hear the hiss of escaping air and realised that the buoyancy chambers of the starboard mine were leaking. There was nothing for it but to jettison the mine. He set it to 'safe' so that it would not explode, but fifteen minutes later it went off with a mighty bang about 1000 yards away from *X-8*. It did no damage to either *X-8* or *Seanymph*.

But *X-8* had not finished her wayward tricks. She developed a list to port and it was obvious that the port mine's buoyancy chambers were also leaking. This mine also had to be jettisoned. Since the 'safe' setting had proved decidedly unsafe, this mine was set to fire two hours after release. Instead, it went off one hour 45 minutes later and, at a distance of three and a half miles, flooded one of *X-8*'s compartments, broke pipes and damaged the boat's internal equipment so badly that she could no longer dive. Since *X-8* was now crippled and without mines, she could no longer play a useful part in the attack, so it was decided to embark the crew in *Seanymph* and sink her.

For MacFarlane it was a bitter disappointment. He was the son of a Royal Australian Navy commander and had been in the British battleship HMS *Queen Elizabeth* in Alexandria harbour when she was crippled by Italian frogmen who planted limpet mines on her hull. Later he lost his life in another X-craft, *X-22*, during exercises in Pentland Firth. With him when *X-22* was sunk was another of the *X-8* officers, Australian Lieutenant J. Marsden, who was also killed.

There was an even worse mishap during the crossing to Norway. While *X-8* was having trouble with her mines *X-9* broke adrift from her towing submarine, *Syrtis*, and was never seen again. The telephone link had failed and *Syrtis* did not know *X-9* had broken loose until several hours later. The tow had snapped close to *Syrtis*, leaving *X-9* with the full weight of the tow rope hanging from her bow. This could have put her into a dive that could not be stopped before the increased water pressure crushed her to death.

In the early morning of 20th September, the day the midgets were to set off on their own up the fjords, *Syrtis* sighted a submarine on the surface, only 3,000 yards distant. It was clearly German. Rarely is a submarine in the position to torpedo an enemy submarine, and this was a sitting shot. *Syrtis* had lost her midget, *X-9*, and was free from any encumbrance. It was just a matter of lining the U-boat up in its sights and firing the torpedoes.

The Admiralty's instructions, however, were just as clear as the U-boat's silhouette. In order not to compromise the operation in any way, no submarine was to attack anything smaller than a

The battleship *Tirpitz*

Tirpitz showing a close view of her protected anchorage

Tirpitz in Kaafjord. A photograph taken by the Norwegian resistance

Aerial photo of Alten and Kaa Fjords showing the damaged *Tirpitz* and other German warships after the daring attack

battleship. The submarine captain, Lieutenant Jupp DSC, RN therefore had to watch in frustration as the U-boat glided past his periscope sights at a range of only 1,500 yards.

At about the same time, the submarine *Stubborn*, towing *X-7*, while *X-7* had come up for air, sighted a floating mine right in its path. The mine slid harmlessly down the side of the submarine without bending any of the horns that would have made it explode. But the submarine's wake drew the mine onto the tow rope and it slid along until it stopped at *X-7*'s bow. Lieutenant Place, captain of *X-7*, scrambled along the deck casing of his boat and pushed the mine away with his feet. To get it clear he had to push against one of the horns, dancing a more nimble jig than any sailor's hornpipe in history.

By 6 p.m. on 20th September everything was ready for the final stage of the attack. The midgets that had survived the crossing – *X-5* (Henty-Creer), *X-6* (Cameron), *X-7* (Place) and *X-10* (Hudspeth) – slipped from their mother submarines and made their way independently towards the minefield – the first of many hazards between them and their target. Just as Hudspeth slipped *X-10*'s tow-line from *Sceptre*, an Admiralty signal ordered Hudspeth to shift his attack to *Tirpitz*, because last-minute reconnaissance showed *Scharnhorst* was no longer in Kaafjord – she had sailed on gunnery exercises. This was no problem for Hudspeth – he had been briefed for just such an eventuality. The mother submarine captains later reported that the crews of all four midgets were in high spirits and full of confidence as they set off into the night.

The passage crews were now on board the mother submarines. They had experienced nine days of extreme danger and almost unimaginable discomfort. The midgets were never meant for high seas. There was always the possibility that they would meet the same fate as *X-9* and plunge out of control to a depth where the pressure would crumple the hull like a piece of paper. There was always the possibility that bad weather would prevent them surfacing for fresh air – with a freeboard of only a matter of inches, any sort of a sea would cascade down the hatch the moment it was opened, flooding the tiny boat in a matter of seconds. If the weather kept them down long enough, they would raise the induction trunk to a vertical position and suck in air from six to eight feet above the sea level.

Inside the midgets, they had been cramped up, unable to stand, huddled over the controls while the midget was jerked by the tow rope, while it porpoised around and pitched and tossed. The air was putrid and it was always freezing cold. They had to eat at their posts, catch a few minutes' sleep whenever possible and amid all this they had to keep the equipment and instruments in order, so that they could hand the boat over to the attack crew in perfect condition.

After that, the inside of a full-sized operational wartime submarine seemed to them like a five-star hotel.

While the four X-craft crept into the fjords, the towing submarines patrolled the outside minefield. Their function was to torpedo any German warships flushed out of the fjords by the midgets, and to wait for the midgets to return. They would then take the attack crews on board and tow the midgets back to Scotland, with the passage crews in control of the midgets.

As it happened, only one midget returned. Even she did not make it back to Scotland.

*

Ken Hudspeth had come a long way to be in command of *X-10* as she slipped away from her towing submarine, *Sceptre*, on 20th September 1943. Soon after the war broke out, he had spotted an advertisement in a local Hobart newspaper asking for applications from 'gentlemen wishing to join the Royal Australian Naval Volunteer Reserve for training in anti-submarine duties'. Although he was sufficiently modest to have some reservations about whether he would qualify as a gentleman, he applied and was soon in training as an acting temporary probationary sub-lieutenant (provisional) at HMAS Rushcutter, the RAN anti-submarine training school at Rushcutter Bay, Sydney.

After a gruelling six-month course learning how to sink submarines, he passed his qualifying examinations, was allowed to drop the word probationary from his rank and, like many other Australians, was sent to Britain on loan to the Royal Navy.

His first ship was a corvette, HMS *Anemone*, on convoy duty in the Atlantic. However, Hudspeth found that although all the other corvettes seemed to be involved in dramatic actions, his was not. A notice in the Admiralty Fleet Orders caught his eye. Volunteers were wanted who were 'very fit, good swimmers and prepared for special and hazardous service'. Hudspeth was a good swimmer and hazards were just what he was looking for. He applied, and found himself training for service in submarines – midget submarines. The man who had learnt how to sink submarines now had to learn how to prevent them being sunk. The man who had learnt how to avoid attack by submarine now had to learn how to attack by submarine.

That was how Hudspeth came to be in Norway heading for a patch of water right underneath a German battleship, via a minefield, through heavily patrolled waters and under or through anti-submarine and anti-torpedo nets. For the name Hudspeth it was, in a sense, a return voyage – his ancestors had come to Britain from Norway as invaders and settled in the Durham-Northumberland area. Centuries later, some of their descendants had migrated to Australia.

Hudspeth had already given considerable thought to German battleships. When the *Bismarck* sank the British battleship *Hood* and made its ill-fated dash into the Atlantic, HMS *Anemone* was escorting a lightly-defended convoy that was right in *Bismarck*'s path. Thanks to a chance alteration of course by *Bismarck* the meeting did not ever take place. Later, in December 1941 and January 1942, HMS *Anemone* and her sister flower-class corvettes HMS *Abelia* and HMS *Veronica* were suddenly detached from an Atlantic convoy and sent at full speed to Hvalfjord in Iceland. There they were ordered to patrol between Iceland and the pack-ice extending to Greenland in case the German ships *Tirpitz*, *Scharnhorst*, and *Hipper* came out. If they did, the three corvettes were to send out sighting signals before being sunk so that British cruisers could move in and shadow the Germans until the British battleships could get to the scene. The patrol lasted two months, but the German warships did not front up. When Hudspeth set out in his *X-10* midget in September 1943 for Kaafjord, he was, in effect, keeping a postponed date.

His subsequent exploit is recorded in the following extract from the report by the Admiral (Submarines), Rear Admiral C.B. Barry, to the Admiralty, dated 8th November 1943. (All times are GMT).

'Narrative of *X-10*
'Paragraph:
'73. *X-10* (Lieutenant K.R. Hudspeth, RANVR) was slipped from HMS *Sceptre* from the slipping position – 70 degrees 40' N. 21 degrees 07' E. – at 2000Z on 20th September, and after a trim dive proceeded on the surface at full speed across the declared mined area in the direction of Stjernsund. The entrance to Stjernsund was identified at 2300Z from a distance of 20 miles, and at daylight (0205Z) on 21st September, *X-10* was in a position five miles from the west point of Stjernoy Island, when she dived.
'74. Difficulty was experienced in trimming, and the defect to the

periscope motor which was present on taking over from the passage crew had become worse. Further electrical defects also developed and the gyro compass failed. Lieutenant Hudspeth therefore decided to proceed into Smalfjord on the north coast of Stjernoy to remedy those defects. The choice of Smalfjord was made as it was considered there was less risk of detection there than in one of the small fjords in Stjernund in which it had been the original intention to bottom during daylight on 21st September.

'75. X-10 arrived in Smalfjord at 0700Z on 21st September, bottomed at the head of the fjord on a sandy bottom and spent the day making good defects. By 1750Z the defects had been sufficiently overcome to warrant proceeding – though they were by no means cured – and X-10 proceeded out of Smalfjord and at 2035Z entered and proceeded up Stjernsund, keeping close to the north shore. The only sign of activity was a small ship of fishing craft type which was sighted with navigation lights burning at 2135Z. She appeared to enter Storelokkerfjord.

'76. Altenfjord was reached by 2320Z on 21st September, and intending to press on so as to be close to the entrance of Kaafjord by daylight on 22nd September, course was shaped to the southward, keeping to the eastern side of the fjord.

'77. At 0110Z on 22nd September it was realised that the gyro compass was wandering. At 0135Z, the steaming lights of a vessel were sighted ahead, approaching X-10; and at 0140Z, X-10 dived to avoid being sighted. On diving it was found that the damping bottles of the gyro compass were not working, and on raising the magnetic compass the light refused to function. As this light can only be replaced by taking off the top cover from outside, the result of these two defects was to leave X-10 with no compass whatsoever. At 0150Z X-10 came to periscope depth; but on attempting to raise the periscope a brisk fire developed from the periscope hoisting motor, filling the craft with smoke, and Lieutenant Hudspeth was forced to come to the surface to ventilate and clear the craft of fumes. Dawn was then breaking and X-10 was almost within sight of the entrance to Kaafjord.

'78. Lieutenant Hudspeth then decided that, with the craft in its then condition, with no compass and no means of raising or lowering the periscope, he was in no state to carry out his attack. He therefore decided to bottom before daylight set in, in the only possible position within reach at the time. At O215Z on 22nd September he bottomed in 195 feet half a cable SE of Tommerholm

Island, 4½ miles from the entrance to Kaafjord, and took immediate steps to make good defects.

'79. At 0830Z – the exact time at which an explosion of charges might have been expected from the other craft attacking – two very heavy explosions were heard at a few seconds interval. Five minutes later – at 0835Z – nine further heavy explosions were heard at short and irregular intervals. These were followed between 0900 and 1000Z by a burst of about twelve lighter explosions, which were repeated, but this time louder and closer, at about 1100Z.

'80. The two heavy explosions at 0830Z would appear undoubtedly to have been one or more of the X-craft charges detonating, while the lighter explosions between 0900 and 1000 and at 1100 would seem probably to have been depth charges. It is difficult to understand the nine heavy explosions at 0835Z. They might have been some form of controlled mine, either in the nets or in the entrance, or depth charges: though it does not seem probable that craft carrying depth charges could have been got under way in so short a time. The possibility of there having been other X-craft charges should not be discounted, echoes and a possible miscounting of the number of explosions heard being responsible for the figures given.

'81. After spending the whole of daylight on 22nd September, the defects in *X-10* had still not been overcome; and Lieutenant Hudspeth reluctantly decided to abandon any idea of attacking and to withdraw. His decision was influenced by the explosions he had heard during the day, which convinced him that other craft had carried out their attack. At this time he still thought that all five of the other X-craft had been able to attack: he had no knowledge of the sinking of *X-8* or the loss of *X-9*.

'82. I consider Lieutenant Hudspeth's decision to abandon the attack was in every way correct. To have made the attempt without a compass, and with a periscope which could not be operated and must remain in the fully raised position, would have made any chance of success remote indeed. With the attack already compromised it would have been doomed to failure from the outset and would merely have been an unnecessary loss of valuable lives.

'83. *X-10* surfaced at 1800Z on 22nd September and made for deep water. At 1825Z on 22nd September both charges were jettisoned in 135 fathoms, set to 'safe'. *X-10* then proceeded on main engines out of Altenfjord. A darkened vessel was sighted at about 2100Z off the entrance to Langfjord but was lost to sight in a snow squall. The western end of Stjernsund was reached by 2350Z. As it was impossible to cross the declared mined area before daylight, X-10 proceeded into Smalfjord, where she arrived at 0215Z on 23rd September. As the fjord was completely deserted and snow squalls frequent, X-10 secured alongside the shore with her grapnel, considering the risk of detection negligible with shore and craft covered with snow. The opportunity was taken to get some rest and try to make good some of the defects.

'84. At 1100Z on 23rd September after the light in the projector compass had been replaced and with the periscope lashed in the 'up' position, X-10 proceeded out of Smalfjord and dived towards the southern end of the minefield. Surfacing at 1800Z, she crossed the declared area at full speed on the engines towards the recovery position, where it was hoped a submarine would be encountered.

'85. Recovery position FB was reached about 2300Z on 23rd September and a search was carried out. X-10 patrolled in the vicinity of the recovery position all day 24th September, spending some time on the surface in the hope of being sighted; and that night she carried out a further search. At 0430Z on 25th September, when no contact had been made, X-10 set course for Sandoyfjord, on the northern coast of Soroy Island. This was reached at 1200Z and by 1525Z X-10 was secured alongside the beach in Ytre Reppafjord, on the north-west of Sandoyfjord. This bay was completely deserted and here the crew got some much needed rest.

'86. X-10 remained in Ytre Reppafjord until the morning of 27th September, when Lieutenant Hudspeth decided to move to O Fjord, which it was expected a submarine would close that night. O Fjord was reached at 1550Z on 27th September and a search was carried out across the entrance after dark.

'87. At 0100 on 28th September contact was made with Stubborn and at 0150 X-10 was in tow. It was by this time too late for her crew to be taken on board Stubborn and the weather was none too good for the transfer, and it was not until 2200Z on the following day that the crew were taken off and the passage crew from X-7 took over X-10. By this time the crew of X-10 had been on board their craft for almost exactly ten days. They had been subjected to much hardship and disappointment, but were none the worse for their experience.

'88. Apart from the sighting of the three vessels mentioned, two of which (since they were burning navigation lights) may have been fishing vessels or small coasting craft, no patrol activity was encountered either on the inward passage up the fjords or, after the attack, on the way out; nor, apparently, was there any A/S activity or counter-measures in Altenfjord directly subsequent to the attack.

'89. *X-10* also reports that all shore navigation lights were burning normally and showing normal characteristics, and that the weather on 22nd September was ideal for X-craft attack, with the sky dull and overcast and a fresh breeze raising white horses to assist unseen approach.

'90. From these facts there appears to be no reason to doubt that other X-craft, free from defects, should have experienced no difficulty in making the passage to the entrance of Kaafjord.

'91. *X-10* also reports that before diving in the vicinity of Tommer-holm Island at 0215 on 22nd September, and again on surfacing that evening at 1800Z lights were observed in the entrance to Kaafjord which appeared to be of the nature of low powered flood lights, possibly for illuminating the net across the entrance to the fjord.

'92. The commanding officer expresses the highest opinion of all his crew throughout the whole time they were on board. They worked long and arduously in the face of ever-growing disappointment, and at no time did their zeal or enthusiasm fail. I consider the command-ing officer himself showed determination and high qualities of leadership in a gallant attempt to reach his objective. He was frustrated by defects for which he was in no way responsible and which he made every endeavour to overcome.

'He showed good judgment in coming to his decision to abandon the attack, thereby enabling the craft to be recovered and bringing back valuable information.'

The admiral's laconic report failed to mention that had *Stubborn* arrived just a little later at the point where she found *X-10*, the tiny submarine would have gone. Hudspeth had decided there was no further hope of rescue and was within five minutes of setting course for Russia, around the northern tip of Norway. He had already laid the course on his chart.

Stubborn took Hudspeth and his crew on board and the passage crew took over for the long trip home. Hudspeth warned Lieutenant Peter Phillip, the South African who commanded the passage crew, that a lot of things were not working, including the gyro compass, the periscope, the automatic helmsman and the pump in the wet and dry compartment, through which under-water escapes might have to be made. The magnetic compass worked only spasmodically, half the lighting circuit had gone, owing to a fire behind the electric switchboard on the passage across Norway, and the air compressor was leaking. Phillip later reported that he found the ship 'held together by bits of string and chewing-gum and the motive power must surely be by faith alone. Within half-an-hour of my taking over, the lavatory pump packed up, which meant using the bilges or trying to get constipated. The first mainline valve I tried broke in half in my hand and the number one main valve jammed open'.

After several days of difficulty with the tow, the weather forecast predicted a severe storm reaching gale force, right in *Stubborn*'s path. If the tow parted during the gale, there would be no chance of regaining contact. *Stubborn* was already using the last available towing wire.

Conditions in *X-10* had become so intolerable that Hudspeth and his first lieutenant decided to go back to the boat and take over from two of the passage crew who had become exhausted. Lieutenant Phillip stayed with the boat. But with the gale threatening and 400 miles still to go, there was nothing for it but to scuttle the ill-fated *X-10*. She had had her share of problems ever since the training days, when one night at her mooring she decided to sink to the bottom. The Navy raised her, pumped her out and sent her back to Vickers for repair and replacement of all electrical gear. She was the only surviving midget of the six that had left Scotland on 10th September. They buried her under 50 fathoms of water at 63 degrees 13 minutes north, four degrees two minutes east.

For his part in the operation, Hudspeth was awarded the DSC. He was later to earn the DSC twice more for his feats in midgets – once for taking a midget to the Normandy beaches weeks before the landings to get samples of the soil and once again for taking a midget close inshore two days before the landings and acting as a navigation beacon for the invading landing craft.

*

The admiral in charge of submarines, Rear-Admiral C.B. Barry, DSO, submitted three separate reports to the Admiralty on the attack on *Tirpitz*, all of which were declassified after the war and published in the *London Gazette* on 10th February 1948. The first was dated 8th November 1943, some six weeks after the attack, and was classified most secret. It was based largely on the report made by Hudspeth of *X-10*, who was about seven miles distant from *Tirpitz* at the time of the attack, and from RAF and Norwegian resistance reports.

The second report, also classified as most secret, was dated 2nd February 1944, nearly four months after the attack. It stated in its preamble that by this time it was possible to reconstruct the attack, and a footnote said it was compiled from information received 'from German prisoners subsequently taken and from other sources.' There was no explanation of these 'other sources'.

The third and final report was submitted to the Admiralty on 26th July 1945, nearly two months after Germany had surrendered. The preamble to this report said it was based on evidence given by Lieutenants Cameron and Place when they returned from prisoner-of-war camps and also from information from captured German documents, namely *Tirpitz*'s deck log and the German High Command War Diary. Since this report is the Royal Navy's last word on the *Tirpitz* attack, it is relevant that it should be published here in full. The text is as follows:

'*20th September, 1943* (All times are GMT)

'All these X-craft slipped from their towing submarines between 1845 and 2000, all being in good heart and trim. *X-6*'s starboard charge had flooded since 11th September, but experiments with stores and spare gear had put the ship into a working trim, provided that the inland waters of the fjords were sufficiently saline.

'The minefields reported off Soroy were negotiated on the surface successfully, although *X-6* sighted a patrol vessel at 2200.

'At 2315 *X-7* sighted another X-craft and exchanged shouts of good luck and good hunting. Although not definitely identified, the other X-craft was certainly *X-5*. *X-5* now, unfortunately, passes out of the picture until her sighting on 22nd September.

'*21st September.*

'*X-6* and *X-7* both dived between 0145 and 0215, each finding trimming difficult.

'During the passage through Stjernsund, *X-7* had to dodge several vessels and *X-6* started a defect on her periscope which was to prove a major handicap throughout, but a triumph of mind over matter to her crew.

'The advance through the fjords toward the agreed waiting and charging positions in Altenfjord went according to plan, neither X-craft experiencing any difficulty in the calm weather prevailing, and at 1245 *X-7*, taking advantage of a freshening breeze, was able to ventilate the boat through the induction tank.

'An occasional anti-submarine patrol vessel, and a solitary aircraft had to be dodged, but at 1630 *X-7* sighted a large vessel in the lee of Aaroy Island. This vessel is noted in *X-7*'s report as "believed to be *Scharnhorst*" and was thereafter disregarded. All thoughts were centred on *Tirpitz*, which, under plan No 4, was the target for *X-5, X-6* and *X-7*.

'*X-6* was the first into her waiting billet, arriving at 1845 one mile north of Brattholm where she spent a rather disturbed night, charging, making good defects (particularly to her periscope) and dodging traffic. This traffic became so trying that the Commanding Officer surfaced to continue his charge at 2145, endeavouring to make contact with other X-craft during the night.

'On inspecting the clock settings of his fuses at 2300, it was discovered that the port (unflooded charge) clock was defective. To guard against any hold up, both ten point plugs were released and the charges set to fire at one hour from release.

'*X-7* had also reached her waiting position and spent the night charging and making good defects. Among this "making good defects" was the fitting of the spare exhaust pipe, the discovery that it did not fit, and its eventual "make do and mend" with the aid of tape, canvas and chewing gum. *X-7* also suffered some inconveniences due to small boats and minor war vessels.

'22nd September
PHASE I: *X-7* left the lee of the Brattholm group of islands at 0045 to commence the penetration of the known and unknown defences of Kaafjord, followed an hour later by *X-6*, neither boat having made friendly contact during the night. Operationally such contact was not necessary and it had not been allowed for in the plan.

'At 0340, *X-7* straightened up for the entrance through the A/S boom defence gap at the entrance to Kaafjord and by 0400 was through, only to be put deep by an ML outward bound. As a result of this temporary blindness *X-7* got caught in the unoccupied square A/T nets, once used to house *Lützow* but now empty. *X-6* followed later, and having increasing trouble with her periscope, dodged a small ferry boat and A/S boom gap.

Meanwhile, life in Kaafjord in general and *Tirpitz* in particular pursued its normal course. Hands were called, normal A/A defence and anti-sabotage watch ashore and afloat were set, and boat-gate and the anti-torpedo nets were opened for boat and tug traffic, and the hydrophone listening office ceased to work, all at 0500.

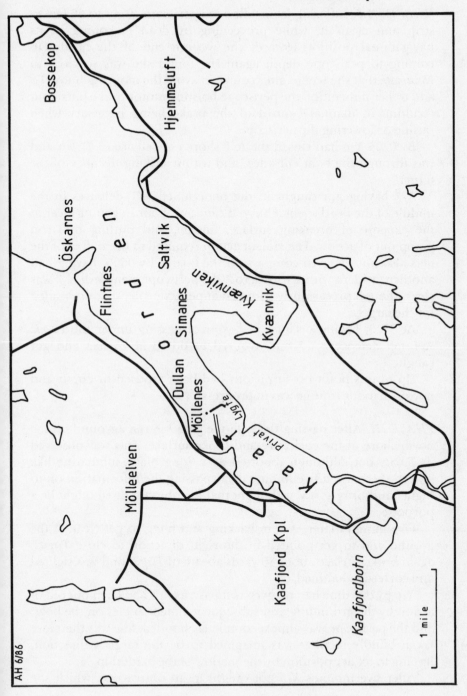

Kaafjord, showing position of Tirpitz

'*Phase II: X-6*, suffering from a flooded periscope, went to 60 feet to strip and clean it, while proceeding by dead reckoning of its navigational position towards the western end of the fjord. On coming to periscope depth again she found she was so close to *Nordmark* that she had to alter course to avoid the mooring buoy. To add to her difficulties, the periscope hoisting motor brake burnt out resulting in manual control of the brake being necessary when raising or lowering the periscope.

'By 0705 *X-6* had closed the A/T shore net defence of *Tirpitz* and was through the boat entrance, and within striking distance of the target.

'*X-7* having got caught in the unoccupied A/T defences in the middle of the fjord spent a busy, if cautious, hour in getting clear at the expense of breaking surface, unseen, and putting the trim pump out of action. The violent action required to break free of the nets also put the gyro compass off the board. By 0600, having had another incident with a wire across the periscope standard, *X-7* was clear, though precariously trimmed at periscope depth, and headed for the target.

'At 0710, having decided in favour of passing under the *Tirpitz* A/T net defences, *X-7* endeavoured to do so at 75 feet and got caught.

'Up to this point no suspicions had been aroused in *Tirpitz* and normal habour routine was in progress.

PHASE III: After passing through the gate *X-6* ran aground on the north shore of the enclosure and broke surface. This was observed in *Tirpitz* but, although reported as a 'long black submarine-like object' there was a five minute delay passing the information on to higher authority as it was thought that the object sighted might be a porpoise.

'Five minutes later, *X-6* in backing and filing to get clear of the ground and to get pointed in the right direction to close *Tirpitz*, again broke surface about 80 yards abeam of *Tirpitz* and was sighted and correctly identified.

'*X-6* by this time had no gyro compass, as this had been put out of action by the grounding and subsequent violent angles on the boat, and the periscope was almost completely flooded. She was therefore taken blindly in what was imagined to be the target's direction, hoping to fix her position by the shadow of the battleship.

'After five minutes *X-6* got caught in an obstruction which she took to be the A/T net on the far (starboard) side of *Tirpitz* but which was probably something hanging down either from *Tirpitz* or one of the craft alongside. Lieutenant Cameron straightened his craft up, manoeuvred clear of the obstruction, and surfaced close on the port bow of *Tirpitz* when a brisk fire from small arms and hand grenades was opened on the submarine. The submarine was too close to the ship for any of the heavy A/A (anti-aircraft) or main armament to bear.

'Realising that escape was hopeless, Cameron destroyed the most secret equipment, backed his craft down until the stern was scraping *Tirpitz*'s hull abreast 'B' turret, released his charges and scuttled the craft. *X-6* started to sink as a power boat from *Tirpitz* came alongside, picked off the crew of four and vainly attempted to take *X-6* in tow, but *X-6* followed her explosives to the bottom.

'On board *Tirpitz* and in Kaafjord the alarm had now been properly raised, and it is clear from the entries in the battleship's log that complete surprise had been achieved by our forces.

'Although the first sighting had been made at about 0707 (a note in the log states that times between 0705 and 0730 are inaccurate) it was not until 0720 that the order was given to close watertight doors, and the A/A guns' crews closed up. A power boat 'manned by one officer and equipped with hand grenades' left the ship about 0715, and was the one which took off the crew of *X-6*, having used her hand grenades, happily to no effect.

'Action stations was sounded, steam raised and the ship was prepared for sea, in order to get her outside the nets. This order was apparently not given until 0736, when watertight doors were reported closed. Divers were ordered to go down to examine the hull for limpet mines [limpet mines – explosives attached to the ship's side or bottom] but it appears that some form of charge dropped under the ship was also expected, as the extract from the log recording the preparations for sea reads "in order to leave the net enclosure if possible before the time-fused mines detonate". Destroyers in the fjord had also raised steam, and were requesting depth charges.

'While *Tirpitz* was making up her mind how to deal with the situation, *X-7*, so far unseen but stuck in the nets ahead of *Tirpitz*, was trying to extricate herself. The following is taken from Lieutenant Place's report:

'September 22nd: " ... 0710. Set both charges to one hour and released ten pin plugs. Went to 75 feet and stuck in the net. Although we had still heard nothing it was thought essential to get out as soon as possible and blowing to full buoyancy and going full astern were immediately tried. X-7 came out but turned beam on to the net and broke surface close on to the buoys, going astern to the northward.

' "We went down again immediately but had to go ahead towards the net to avoid catching our stern and the boat stuck again by the bow at 95 feet. Here more difficulty in getting out was experienced, but after about five minutes of wriggling and blowing, X-7 started to rise. The compass had, of course, gone wild on the previous surface and I was uncertain how close to the shore we were; so the motor was stopped and X-7 was allowed to come right up to the surface with very little way on. By some extraordinarily lucky chance we must have either passed under the nets or worked our way through the boat passage, for on breaking surface the *Tirpitz* with no intervening nets, was sighted right ahead not more than 30 yards away. 40 feet was ordered and X-7 at full speed, struck the *Tirpitz* at 20 feet on the port side approximately below 'B' turret and slid gently under the keel where the starboard charge was released in the full shadow of the ship. Here at 60 feet a quick stop trim was caught as at the collision X-7 had swung to port so we were now heading approximately down the keel of *Tirpitz*.

' "Going slowly astern the port charge was released about 150 to 200 feet further aft, as I estimated, about under 'X' turret. I am uncertain as to the exact time of release, but the first depth charges were heard just after the collision, which, from Lieutenant Cameron's report, would fix the time at 0722.

' "After releasing the port charge, 100 feet was ordered and an alteration of course guessed to try and make the position where we had come in. At 60 feet we were in the net again. Without a compass I had no exact idea of where we were; the difficulties we had experienced and the air trimming had used two air bottles and only 1200 lbs were left in the third. X-7's charges were due to explode in an hour – not to mention others which might go up any time after 0800.

' "A new technique in getting out of nets had by this time been developed. The procedure was to go full ahead blowing economically and then go full astern, the idea being to get as much way on the boat as the slack of the nets would allow and thus have a certain impetus as well as the thrust of the screws when actually disengaging from the net. In about the next three quarters of an hour X-7 was in and out of several nets, the air in the last bottle was soon exhausted and the compressor had to be run. When at about 40 feet, at 0740, X-7 came out while still going ahead and slid over the top of the net between the buoys on the surface. I did not look at the *Tirpitz* at this time as this method of overcoming net defences was new and absorbing, but I believe we were at the time on her starboard bow – we had certainly passed underneath her since the attack. We were too close, of course, for heavy fire but a large number of machine gun bullets were heard hitting the casing. Immediately after passing over the nets all main ballast tanks were vented and X-7 went to the bottom in 120 feet. The compressor was run again and we tried to come to the surface or periscope depth for a look so that the direction indicator could be started and as much distance as possible put between ourselves and the coming explosion. It was extremely annoying to run into another net at 60 feet. Shortly after this there was a tremendous explosion (0812). This evidently shook us out of the net and on surfacing it was tiresome to see the *Tirpitz* still afloat – this made me uncertain as to whether the explosion we had just heard was our own charges or depth charges, so X-7 was taken to the bottom ... ''

'This last excursion into the nets was apparently well on *Tirpitz*'s starboard bow and from outside. After getting clear X-7 sat on the bottom to survey the damage. Compasses and diving gauges were out of action but there appeared to be little structural damage. The boat was impossible to control, however, and broke surface on several occasions. On each occasion fire was opened on her from *Tirpitz* causing damage to the hull, and finally it was decided to abandon the boat. X-7 was brought to the surface rather than use DSEA (Davis Submarine Escape Apparatus), owing to the depth-charging that was being experienced. The boat surfaced close to a target allowing Lieutenant Place to step on to it, but before the remainder of the crew could escape, X-7 sank at 0835. Sub-Lieutenant Aitken was able to get out by the use of DSEA, at 1115, but no trace was discovered of the remaining two members of the crew. Both Lieutenant Place and Sub-Lieutenant Aitken were brought on board *Tirpitz* and well treated, as had been the crew of X-6.

'The first knowledge on board *Tirpitz* that more than one midget submarine was attacking came at 0740, when X-7 was seen just outside the A/T nets, having made her escape after dropping her charges. Hand grenades were thrown, fire opened from the 2 cm and 3.7 cm armament, and aircraft made ready to take off and carry out a search.

'As other craft were outside the nets in unknown numbers, it was decided not to take *Tirpitz* out of the enclosure, so the gate was shut, and the ship moved as far away from the position in which *X-6* had sunk by heaving in on the starboard cable and veering port. This brought the bows away from both *X-6*'s charges and the first of *X-7*'s, but left *X-7*'s second charge still under the engine room; those on board *Tirpitz* being unaware that a second attack had been carried out.

'*Tirpitz*'s log records at 0812 "two heavy consecutive detonations to port at 1/10 sec. interval. Ship vibrates strongly in vertical direction and sways slightly between the anchors." The first explosion abreast Section VII ("X" turret) about 6 to 8 yards away from the ship, the other 50-60 yards off the bow in the position where *X-6* sank.

'The weight of the charge was estimated at 900lbs, whereas, in fact, each of the four charges weighed 2 tons. It is not clear from this how many of the three charges laid off the port bow actually went off, although subsequent examination of the sea-bed failed to discover any of the charges, or even fragments.

'It seems likely, therefore, that all four charges detonated completely and that only the action to move the bows of the ship bodily to starboard on her cable saved her from far worse damage and even, perhaps, from destruction.

'Before dealing with the damage resulting from the attack it remains to be recorded that at 0843 a third X-craft was sighted some 500 yards outside the nets. *Tirpitz* opened fire and claims to have hit and sunk this X-craft. Depth-charges were also dropped in the position in which the craft disappeared. This was *X-5* (Lieutenant Henty-Creer, RNVR) which had last been seen off Soroy on 21st September by *X-7*.

'Nothing is known of her movements, nor was any member of her crew saved.

'*X-7* was salved, minus her bows, by 1st October, 1943, but there is nothing to substantiate a statement, made to Lieutenant Place by German interrogators, that the bodies of the two missing members of his crew had been recovered and buried with full military honours.

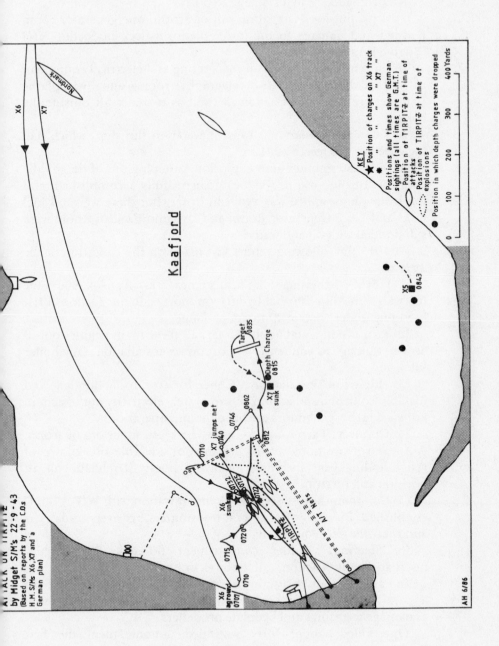

ATTACK ON TIRPITZ
by Midget S/M's 22·9·43
(Based on reports by the COs
H.M. S/Ms X6,X7 and a
German plan)

Kaafjord

X6

X7

Nordmark

Target
0835

Depth Charge
0815

X7
sunk

0802

0746

X7 jumps net

0740

0710

0812

X6
sunk

0705
0722

0720

0715

A/T Nets

TIRPITZ

X6
aground
0707

0710

X5
0843

KEY
★ Position of charges on X6 track
✳ "   "   "   X7

Positions and times show German
sightings (all times are G.M.T.)
⬭ Position of TIRPITZ at time of
attacks
⬭ Position of TIRPITZ at time of
explosions
● Position in which depth charges were dropped

0   100   200   300   400 Yards

AH 6/86

'Damage to 'Tirpitz'

'According to the first Damage Report:

'Port propulsion installation out of action, one generator room flooded and damage to the lower platform deck in Section VIII (Engine Room) and TS.

'In the whole ship nearly all the lighting and electrical equipment as well as the W/T [wireless telegraphy] rooms and hydrophone station were put out of action, as well as two aircraft outside the hangar.

'By 0833 there were 300 tons of water in the ship, which had increased to 500 tons by 0942.

'At 0900, 50 minutes after explosion, pumping out of the middle and port turbine rooms was being successfully accomplished, and the hydrophone office was again in order, but there were oil fuel leaks and No 2 Generator Room and Dynamo Control Room were still flooded with oil and water.

'At 1045 the following report was made on the condition of the *Tirpitz*:

' "(1) Schiffssicherung (Ship's safety measures): Approx. 800 cubic m. water in ship. Probable hits on port side in Section VIII. Flooding under control. Ship out of danger.

'(2) Propulsion installation: So far, all three main engines out of action. Damage to condenser in port power installation. One boiler hit.

'(3) Electrical installation: Generator room 2 flooded and dynamo control installation 2.50 cm. water, electricity out of action. Forward turbo-generators are brought into operation.

'(4) Gunnery: Turret A and C raised by blast, so far out of action. A/A control positions out of action. Considerable breakdown of range-finding gear including revolving hoods (Drehhauben), aft position and foretop.

'(5) Communications Section: Communication with W/T room C established. Breakdown of several transmitters, receivers, radar sets and echo-ranging equipment.

'(6) Steering: Rudder compartment flooded. Port rudder installation out of action, cannot be examined yet.

'In all sections breakdown (probably only temporary) of apparatus and electrical equipment through lack of current, as well as damage to casings and bedplate propellers.

'One killed, about forty wounded, among them the first lieutenant, slightly injured (concussion).'

'*Final effect of the attack:* According to an entry in the War Diary of the German Naval Staff for September 1943, it was decided that the repair of *Tirpitz* should be carried out in a northern port, and this decision was sanctioned by Hitler and the Commander-in-Chief, German Navy. It was, however, considered that the ship might never regain complete operational efficiency.

'Repair ships, equipment and a large staff of dockyard workmen were transferred to Altenfjord, and the services of a 100 ton crane were requested. The crane never arrived, however, being damaged by weather on passage, and only reaching the Namsos area.

'Much time, personnel and work were expended on improving the defences of Kaafjord, and *Lützow* was moved south to Germany. As this ship was overdue for refit in any case, it cannot be claimed that this weakening of the Northern Fleet was altogether due to the X-craft attack.

'On 22nd November, two months after the attack, again according to the War Diary, Marinegruppenkommando Nord reported to the German Naval War Staff that "as a result of the successful midget submarine attack on heavy units of the Battle Group, the battlecruiser *Tirpitz* had been put out of action for months", and the truth of this is borne out by the fact that not until April 1944, did the ship move out from her anchorage, only to be further damaged and finally destroyed, by air attack, from which she had been virtually immune in Kaafjord.'

(Signed) G.E. Creasy
Rear Admiral (Admiral Submarines)

PART THREE

The Search

by Pamela Mellor

Life is a narrow vale between the cold and barren peaks of two eternities. We strive in vain to look beyond the heights. We cry aloud and the only answer is the echo of a wailing cry. But in the night of death, hope sees a star, and listening love can hear the rustle of a wing. He who sleeps here, when dying whispered, 'I am better now.'

R.G. Ingersoll

I

The Search

When the war was over and the crews of *X-6* and *X-7* had received their awards, including the VCs for their two captains, it became clear that the crew of *X-5* had been written off as expendable. Henty merely received a mention in despatches. His mother took this matter up with Admiral Creasy in the strongest terms but all to no avail. Only the VC could be awarded posthumously and there was no one who could vouch for *X-5* having got in and laid her charges. Her crew was presumed dead and therefore qualified for nothing more than a Mention in Despatches.

In 1950 therefore, my mother decided to go up to Altafjord (formerly Altenfjord) and see for herself if she could get some evidence of *X-5* having completed her mission. Thus she and my elder sister Deirdre set off in a Hillman Minx to brave the terrible conditions then prevalent in northern Norway. They took with them bedding and mosquito nets, quite prepared to sleep out in the Arctic open. This in fact they did as often as not.

She found the small township of Alta trying to rebuild itself, as after *Tirpitz* had been put out of action by the X-craft, the Germans moved out the whole population of northern Norway and proceeded to lay the country to waste. Houses were destroyed, trees pulled up and roads devastated. A complete and utter 'scorched earth' policy was instituted, possibly in vengeance, but principally to delay any advance by the Russians across the top from Finland and Sweden.

Her visit was a source of amazement. Nevertheless she received the greatest welcome and co-operation from the authorities. Interpreters and launches were put at her disposal. Norwegian intelligence and the local police were most helpful.

As a result of her inquiries, she obtained a number of eye-witness accounts which were sworn before the local Lensmen. (Details and further comments are to be found later in this book.) To summarise these, however, shows the following series of events:

Firstly, when the charges went off under *Tirpitz* her whole hull, in particular her stern was lifted out of the water so that her screws were visible. Could the one charge laid by *X-7* under B turret have caused this? The other charge laid by *X-7* and the two laid by *X-6* were nowhere near the stern. Nor were they in fact under *Tirpitz* at all when they exploded. (See appendix.)

Secondly, the following morning a periscope was seen off Bossekop by a retired Norwegian sea captain. He had served in World War 1 and knew just what a periscope looked like. There were no German submarines in Altafjord at the time. German soldiers also saw this periscope and called out *'Unter see Britischer'*.

Thirdly, later in the day there was a further sighting half way down the main Altafjord. Later still, there was a sighting near Sternjoy Island. The times and distances involved in these three sightings are consistent with the possible escape of *X-5*. *X-10* (Hudspeth) had left the area twenty-four hours earlier and could not be confused with these sightings.

Fourthly, half way along Stjernsund (the exit route from Altafjord to the sea) there is a small isolated fjord called Inlokkerfjord. There is nothing in this fjord but a small fisherman's hut. The Norwegian authorities went so far as to take my mother and sister out to this fjord. It so happened that there was a fisherman there. He remembered finding a 'British Naval cap. But could no longer find it. 'Possibly,' he said, 'he might have burnt it.'

This fjord had been considered by the X-craft organisers to be a possible spot for use by escaping X-craft in which to lie up and re-charge their batteries.

Mother and my sister continued in their search north and east until they reached the Russian border on the north coast of Norway. This was as far as they could go and as the weather was deteriorating they returned to England.

On their return to England mother, for some unknown reason, did not pass on her findings to the Admiralty. Somehow she felt that Henty might still be alive and would re-appear to give his own account. One cannot but feel that this inaction was a great mistake.

At the same time the father of Henty's No 1, Sub-Lieutenant Malcolm, was equally dissatisfied with the Navy's attitude and he advertised in the Norwegian papers for any useful information. He got a very strange report from an eye-witness who saw four British sailors in the Alta POW camp shortly after the attack. Von Falkenhorst, the German overlord of Norway (who was executed after the war as a war criminal) had implemented Hitler's instructions that any Commandos, raiders and such like had to be executed immediately after interrogation. Such executions must in any case take place within twenty-four hours.

Germans are renowned for their careful documentation, but no trace of the 'British sailors' can be found in the official German records.

I had through the years thought the reports concerning the part X-5 played in the attack against *Tirpitz* in Kafjord Norway in 1943 very unsatisfactory.

In 1973 I saw an article in the *Daily Telegraph* by its Naval correspondent, Desmond Wettern, in which he wrote about the salvaging of a midget submarine which he said had taken part in the *Tirpitz* attack. I contacted him to discount this and subsequently he gave me the idea of getting together a search of Kafjord (formerly Kaafjord) with a team of divers. He put me in touch with Peter Cornish who at that time was a leading member of the British Sub Aqua Club and who was making a speciality of diving on and, when possible, salvaging wrecks.

It turned out that Peter had for some time been personally intrigued with the X-5 saga. He was shortly going to Norway with an RAF team involved in the salvage of a wartime Halifax bomber recently discovered at the bottom of Lake Hocklinger in central Norway.

He agreed to meet my husband, Gerard, and me later at Alta so that we could do a reconnaissance of Kafjord before getting a team together. We tried, without success to get some official interest from our own MP, the Australian High Commission and the British Ministry of Defence (Navy). Apart from these soundings, Peter wanted to keep this reconnaissance secret as he did not wish for other amateur divers to beat him to what promised to be virgin waters.

So in June 1973 Gerard obtained three weeks' leave from the Ministry of Defence, where he was working after a lifetime in the army, and we ferried our faithful Humber, a small pup tent and necessary stores for the trip.

We had heard about the high cost of accommodation in Norway, which we found to be true, from cucumber at two shillings an inch to whisky at twelve pounds a bottle! But we did find remarkably well-equipped camp sites, although they varied widely in their sanitary facilities.

Our first port of call was Lake Hocklinger where we arrived just as the Halifax bomber, with Peter astride the fuselage, broke the surface of the lake. We hoped that this would be a good omen for the future.

We then continued our long treck northwards, through Narvik of wartime fame and through the most stupendous scenery. Alas, many of the roads were unmetalled and had a profusion of potholes, possibly among the finest in Europe.

Eventually, however, we arrived safely at Alta and signed in at the camp site there. This was called Saga camp and was situated a few miles from the town. There were several long huts divided into a number of cabins. We rented one for ourselves and another for Peter who arrived the next day by air complete with his diving gear.

Much later we discovered that this camp site had been used by the Germans as a POW camp and was the same place where one eye-witness reported as having seen four British sailors the day after the attack.

As soon as Peter arrived and settled in we all drove out the twenty-odd miles to Kafjord where we were lucky enough to find a fisherman living just close to the site of the *Tirpitz* anchorage. His father had been in a small boat at the time and witnessed the attack. His efforts for self-preservation, however, prevented his being able to recall any really relevant facts. However, his son had a good motor-driven boat which he agreed to hire to us so that Peter could carry out some reconnoitering dives. These were done over the next three days with most encouraging results (apart from one day which was spent up in Hammerfest where Peter had to get air for his diving bottle – this we got from the fire station as there was no other place at the time where one could get compressed air.)

The fjords water was clear, the bottom level at some 140 feet and littered with war debris, untouched since the Germans had left some thirty years before. Amongst the litter were discarded crockery and beer bottles as well as a largish number of canisters which looked as if they might have been unexploded depth charges, but which, more probably were discarded smoke canisters. The Germans used to let off large quantities of smoke whenever there was an air raid warning. This was highly successful in hiding *Tirpitz* from any intruding aircraft.

Peter's enthusiasm was kindled and he became determined to organise a full-scale expedition as soon as possible to fully explore the whole bottom of the fjord. And suggested that if I learned to dive he would take me down.

By June the next year Peter had succeeded in getting together a party of about sixteen experienced divers, a woman anaesthetist who acted as camp doctor and a highly experienced marine geo-physicist together with sophisticated sonar detection equipment. He had also succeeded in getting a number of sponsors who provided camping and diving equipment as well as rations. Individuals however, gave up their own holidays and paid their own expenses to go on the expedition.

They all flew up to Alta. Gerard and I followed by car arriving a couple of days after they had settled in. This time we took a larger frame tent in place of the pup tent. We also travelled up via Sweden and Finland as easier road but utterly dreary scenery.

On arrival we set up our tent in an abandoned German gun site with a fine view straight down the fjord. This was a perfect spot until on our last night we had a terrific gale and were blown inside out at about two o'clock in the morning. We evacuated to Saga camp to dry out.

As soon as the expedition had settled in they hired the same fishing boat we had used the year before. A careful triangulation was made of the whole fjord which was then used to carry out a thorough sonar search of the bottom. This threw up a large number of 'anomalies' which were carefully plotted by the geo-physicist. Divers were then sent to identify them.

This revealed many interesting items, including the wreckage of several aircraft. But of X-5 there was no sign. Then on their very last day (we unfortunately had had to go a day or so earlier as our leave was up) one of the anomolies turned out to be the nose cone – approximately the forward third – of an X-craft. Was this from X-5 or X-7? There was no time left for anyone to make a detailed examination. It was lifted up, photographed and then lowered back again.

A further expedition was clearly necessary.

Two years were to pass before the repeat expedition could be organised. This went up in 1976. Based on earlier experiences there were many improvements. Many individuals of the 1974 expedition came up again including our geo-physicist. There were also a number of new faces including several from other countries and a team of Royal Engineer divers for whom it was an excellent exercise and who were specially fitted for the task of salvaging any heavy objects.

The first task was of course the lifting and salvage of the X-craft nose cone. This was filled with silt but in amongst the silt was a quantity of miscellaneous artefacts e.g., boots, diving gear, rations two pistols a telephone and above all the boat's sextant, still in its mahogany case. It was soon evident however, that this cone came from X-7 and not X-5.

Meanwhile the sonar examination of the fjord was again carried out even more meticulously than before. An enormous number of dives were made on all the anomolies discovered. In spite of tremendous efforts of the various divers there turned out to be no trace whatever of X-5. The dives went on far down the fjord, way beyond where the attack took place. Here the fjord became too deep, too dark, too cold for any further diving. Even then many of the divers went down to depths never before thought possible for Scuba type divers.

While all this work was going on, the Naval liaison officer with the Norwegian Army then stationed at Alta offered to take Gerard and me by boat to Inlokkerfjord, where we would dive. Altafjord is some twenty or thirty miles long. At its inmost end was the small Kafjord. *Tirpitz* was anchored at the landward end of the fjord whilst *Scharnhorst* was anchored near its exit to the main Altafjord.

Inlokkerfjord was some four hours from Kafjord by motor boat. This was the spot my mother had visited in 1952 and where a British naval officer's cap was found. A more desolate and remote spot I have yet to see; there was no access by road.

Did *X-5* make it back here? Does she now lie somewhere at its bottom? Were her crew found here and taken back to Alta and oblivion? Or did *X-5* make it out to sea again only to perish before contacting her mother submarine?

After his two expeditions Peter Cornish was able to say with complete conviction: 'Neither *X-5* nor her remains lie in Kafjord.'

*

After writing up our experiences the family was approached by Frank Walker a former press attaché at the Australian Embassy in Bonn, Germany, who could speak perfect German. He was interested in Henty's exploits and suggested he should get hold of a German armament expert and together with our findings join together in completing this book. He then went back to Australia and Gerard and I took on the long and sometimes frustrating task of going through reports at the Record Office. These findings were photocopied and the copies sent to Frank to amalgamate later in this book.

II

The Eye-Witnesses

Norwegian eye-witnesses made statements after the war confirming much of the Admiralty account of the action. Their timings differ somewhat from the Admiralty's, even allowing for the fact that the Admiralty report used GMT and the local Norwegian time was then two hours ahead of GMT. Following are certified translations of their affidavits:

Sven Hertzberg, Vesteraalen Steamship Company, Stokmarknes – Norway
'On Wednesday, 22nd September 1943, I was on board m/s *Stamsund* in Kaafjord which was riding at anchor about 400 yards from *Tirpitz*. Immediately after breakfast about 9 a.m. or 9.30 a.m. (7 a.m. or 7.30 a.m. GMT) I was on deck and noticed a parade on board the battleship. Suddenly all available batteries opened fire on the area of the sea which was within her own submarine net, and submarine alarm was given simultaneously from all sirens and in the air on all flag halyards. The fire ceased after a short while and was then directed towards a point just outside the net. I noticed several small submarines emerging at various places, we counted three or four, one of them passing so near us that we could estimate her length to be about 30 feet.

'Not many moments afterwards I saw a huge explosion just below the foremost tower of *Tirpitz* and saw how the colossus rose at least 1-2 yards, and at the same time the troops lined up on the foredeck, jumped high every time the deck heaved forward. I heard tremendous shrieking and yelling from the ship, and a large tugboat nearly rose almost on end. I could see a large part of the keel, and then she tilted over the first big wave, which gave me a bird's eye view of her enabling me to look directly into her funnel. I suppose the electric current had been destroyed by the explosion because after the Germans used only light guns, which could be turned by hand, and salvos were fired into the sea every time the submarine because visible.

'Halfway between *Tirpitz* and *Stamsund* a large target was lying at anchor, and between each salvo, from which we had taken shelter, we ran forward to get a view, and between two salvos I saw a great deal of bubbling in the immediate neighbourhood of the target, and then I perceived a soldier climbing on to the target. The firing at him was like a hailstorm, but he was not hit. When the firing stopped he lit a cigarette and walked up and down the target. At first a tugboat approached the target, but then backed. Then a motor launch arrived and took him prisoner.

'As one of the anti-aircraft personnel on board *Stamsund* had been mortally wounded, *Tirpitz* was signalled for a doctor, but we got the answer that they were too busy, and we were ordered to run alongside *Altmark* which was also riding at anchor, as she had a doctor on board. Later we had to leave the harbour as *Stamsund* was lying right in the middle of the firing line.

'Various motor boats, two or three destroyers and other vessels were busy laying depth bombs, but on leaving the harbour we could not see whether they had any effect. We were ordered to return in the afternoon, and the *Tirpitz* had sunk further. The officer on board a motor launch, which came along to take a chief lieutenant on board, told us that four more men emerged later in the afternoon and they had been taken prisoner.'

– Sven Hertzberg
At present captain of M/S *Andenes*
(rubber stamp) 19th February 1946

Leif Remme, Vesteraalen Steamship Company, Stokmarknes, Norway.
S/S *Rost*, Stockmarknes.
'On 22nd September 1943 I was a steward on board S/S *Stamsund*, and some of our cargo was consigned to Altafjord. When SS *Stamsund* had arrived at Alta on 21st September and discharged some of the cargo, Captain Hertzberg was ordered to go to a place in Altenfjord called Kaafjord where *Tirpitz* was stationed, in order to discharge some motor cars which were to be transported by a lighter from the ship and taken ashore at that place.

'Captain Hertzberg protested and would not go there because it was a German order and moreover a place used as Naval base for German forces. It was also difficult to approach the place mentioned, there being three or four marine nets which had to be passed through.

'In spite of our protest we had to go to Altenfjord on 20th

September at 2 o'clock p.m. A German naval ship led the way and the submarine nets were opened. We passed about 14 large and small warships before arriving at the place indicated, about 400 yards from *Tirpitz* on her starboard side.

'On 22nd September at 9.30 a.m. the submarine alarms sounded and some of the destroyers lying further out in the fjord, and which we had passed on the 20th at 2.17 p.m., at once approached *Tirpitz*. About ten minutes after the alarm had been given the submarines emerged on the surface about 100 yards from the stem of *Tirpitz* on the starboard side, near a netting fastened to a buoy. About three minutes afterwards the submarine fired at *Tirpitz* on her starboard stem, and directly after the firing a man from the submarine crew emerged and climbed into the netting near the submarine which submerged immediately afterwards. Whether the submarine had been hit during the firing from the destroyers, or whether *Tirpitz* had been able to fire at the submarine, I am unable to say. When the submarine had submerged, the destroyers began to attack and lay depth bombs around the area of the sea lying inside the last submarine net which we had passed. The man who had jumped into the netting from the submarine and kept hanging to it was taken by a German boat. He seemed to be unhurt when taken by the Germans.

'It was a miracle that S/S *Stamsund* was not sunk by the fire, and only one person on board was seriously injured. The warship *Tirpitz* was so heavily damaged that it was no longer in fighting condition. (Rumours said that a great many of the crew on board *Tirpitz* had been seriously injured.)

'Depth bombs were dropped during the next thirty minutes, then all was silent and a guard vessel came up and ordered S/S *Stamsund* to leave immediately. A guard vessel led the way and S/S *Stamsund* followed till we were out of the danger zone. S/S *Stamsund* proceeded to Bossekop in Alta.

'This is what I know of the happenings of 22nd September 1943. A courageous and splendid achievement on the part of the submarine crew. It would have been a pleasure for me if I had been in a position to give better and further particulars to the relatives of those brave heroes.'

Leif Remme,
S/S *Rost*
12th February, 1946.

Ingvar Dlaaen

'I was staying in Kaafjord, Alta, where *Tirpitz* was stationed when the attack took place, and thus I am able to tell you what I, along with several others witnessed that day. I was standing about 500 yards from the place, so I was not actually an eye-witness myself, but people nearby said that the stern of *Tirpitz* rose one and a half yards when the explosion occurred.

'Already a couple of days before this attack the Germans' attention had been drawn to something extraordinary further out in Altafjord, but they paid no heed. On 22nd September 1943 both submarine nets blocking the narrow inlet were opened to let in a coal-boat *Stamsund* bound for *Tirpitz*, and one of the submarines followed in her wake. Some believe there were two, personally I think there was only one. One theory tells that a torpedo had been fired at the stern, but in those narrow waters I consider this to be impossible.

'Another version, that the submarine had managed to place a bursting charge between the propellers, I consider to be more correct. What occurred thereafter is unknown, until two Englishmen emerged near the ship's side, and immediately afterwards two more on a wooden raft some distance away. They were taken on board *Tirpitz* and the explosion occurred the very next minutes with a thundering report all over Kaafjord.

'The Germans went absolutely crazy firing with revolvers and throwing hand grenades into the sea. No guns were fired.

'The Germans kept the Englishmen on board for a couple of days. They had some festivals on board, as they considered this to be a real achievement on part of the Englishmen. Perhaps they wanted to know how they succeeded in getting out of the submarine.

'When they drove away in motor cars – it was said to Narvik – they were sitting in couples in each car smoking long cigars and looking quite happy.

'Two of the *Tirpitz*'s propellers were damaged. The propeller shafts became cracked. Several hundreds of skilled workmen arrived here from Germany and were busy repairing all through the winter until 3rd April 1944. Then the bombing started, until ultimately *Tirpitz* left our harbour in the end of September, bound for Tromso, where she met her final fate.

'The submarine was raised and placed on the wharf in Kaafjord. What was left of her when the Germans had unscrewed all available gadgets, was a hull about 6 yards long and 1.8 yards in diameter.

Captain Sarilla, photographed in 1950, pointing to the spot referred to in his sworn statement reproduced on page 194.

(*Left*) Raising of bow of
sunken X-craft at Kaafjord

(*Below*) Nigel Kelland
interpreting the results of
electronic soundings

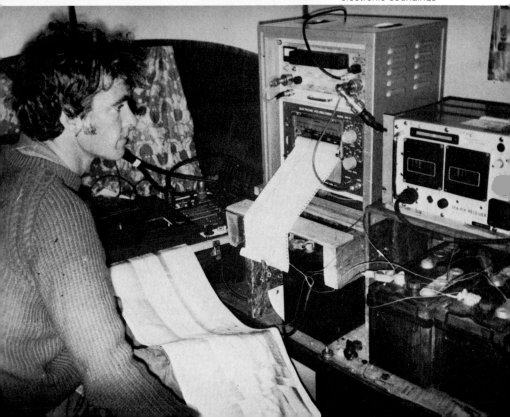

The submarine had no periscope like usual submarines, but looked like the upper part of a motor car with front glass.

'The Germans also believed that a releasable charge had been placed on the stem of the submarine. This accounts for the theory of an explosion instead of a torpedo at a few yards' distance. It was certain, however, that the Englishmen submerged on board the submarines came inside of the submarine net, one of them must have managed to pass under it, as it had been closed the minute the coal-boat passed through.'

Ingvar Dlaaen

Paul G. Leinan, Alta

'The undersigned was in Kaafjord the day this happened, 22nd September 1943. I was also there the day after in order to find out exactly what happened, as I carried on quite a lot of espionage against the Germans.

'The submarine which was below the battleship *Tirpitz* and placed the charge went out through the torpedo net, and two men left the submarine and on to a float in order to observe the explosion. These two men surrendered as prisoners to the Germans. The submarine was also taken by the Germans and beached near the *Tirpitz*.

'There were also two other men, from another submarine who escaped on shore and were taken prisoners by the Germans.

'These members of the crews were then taken to Elvenakken, and placed in a prisoner of war camp at a place called Saga.

'I followed the events and proceeded to Elvenakken, where I saw these four Englishmen marching through Elvenakken under German guard. My attention was also specially drawn to it by watching through an office window of a German building – Inspector Haussa, who beamingly related that 'Here we have Englishmen as prisoners.'

'These four men were later transported from Alta, further south probably to Germany.

'If you have heard nothing from them since, then it may be feared that they have been shot by the Germans. They were not shot here in Alta. The number of the submarine I am unable to give as it was impossible, owing to the strong German watch, to get near enough to observe it.'

(signed) Paul G. Leinan,
2nd February, 1946.

Lars Mathis Aleksandersen Sarilla, born 19. 2. 1880 in Alta, a former Arctic skipper, living in Bossekop in Alta, testified:

'On 23rd September 1943, at about 8 a.m. – the day after the British submarine attack on *Tirpitz* had taken place in Kaafjord – from the window in my home in Bossekop I became aware of something ranging up from the sea by Boissekopberget which I presumed was the periscope of a submarine in the underwater position. It moved rather fast in the direction of Krakenes (the other side of the fjord). The sea was quite calm (shiny surface) and I could clearly see a foam-stripe on the water after the periscope.

I stood and followed the periscope till it was in about the middle of the fjord and I could not see it any more because of the distance. I think three to four minutes (five at most) passed from the time I became aware of the periscope by Bossekopberget till I lost sight of it out in the fjord. By this time a few other persons who were present in our home also saw what I have explained but I am not able to remember who they were at the moment. If I can remember later I shall inform you about it.

When the periscope of the submarine passed the area near my house, some German soldiers, who were working a shore house near my home, became aware of the periscope. They pointed at it and shouted to each other: 'British submarine.' A couple of them ran to the telephone room in the store house probably to report to their superiors. However I could not see that anything was done by the Germans to destroy the submarine.

It had to be mentioned that once, during World War 1, while out fishing I saw a submarine passing in the underwater position with the periscope above the water, and because of this I could with certainty say that what I saw move from Bossekopberget towards Krakenes on the morning of 23rd September was the periscope of a submarine passing in the underwater position. I have nothing else to explain.

Read and agreed
(signed) Mathis Aleksandersen Sarilla
July 5, 1950.

PART FOUR

The Case for the VC

by Frank Walker

The Case for the VC

What happened to X-5 ?

In analysing the events of 22nd September certain technical factors must be borne in mind. These are:

(a) The two mines X-craft carried each contained two tons of amatex, a high explosive similar to amatol. Large masses of explosive are difficult to detonate evenly and in the case of the mines carried by the X-craft there was an additional problem – their shape was determined by the shape of the boat, not by detonation effectiveness. The usual criterion of optimum shape for maximum detonation did not apply. The experts resigned themselves to the fact that detonation efficiency probably lay within the range of 25 to 65 per cent. One hundred per cent was highly unlikely, in view of the shape of the mines. This was demonstrated when *X-8* had to jettison its mines on the way to Norway. One, set to 'safe', should not have exploded at all, but it did after 15 minutes at a range of 1,000 yards. It caused no damage. The other, set to fire in two hours, went off one hour 45 minutes later at a range of three miles and did such immense damage that *X-8* had to be scuttled. Hudspeth's mines, which he jettisoned from *X-10*, were perfectly behaved – they were set to 'safe' and did not explode.

(b) The two tons of amatex in each mine were secondary explosives and needed the impetus of a powerful shock wave to detonate them. This shock wave would normally come from a firing mechanism consisting of a detonator and primer, but it could also come from a direct hit by an artillery shell or from other shock waves such as a depth charge exploding very close to it. In surface ships the mechanism could be removed from the depth charges in emergency, such as the sinking of the ship, but in X-craft the firing mechanism was housed permanently in the mine – the captain needed only to set the timing device and release the mine. The fact that the firing mechanism could not be removed from the mine made it even more vulnerable to an unscheduled explosion and was a compelling argument for jettisoning the mine in emergency.

(c) X-craft were brutes to trim in any waters. In fjords, where unexpected patches of fresh water brought about sudden changes in temperature, salinity and hence water density, trimming was even more difficult. Where *Tirpitz* was moored, a river of fresh water flowed through the fjord less than half a mile from *Tirpitz*, thus adding to the trimming problems of the tiny boats. It is significant that when *X-5* broke surface at 0843, she was at the precise spot where the fresh water mixed with the salt water in the fjord.

(d) As the Admiralty reports show, X-craft were susceptible to technical failures, particularly in their periscope and compass equipment. This is understandable, since the boats were a new conception and there had not been sufficient time to find and iron out all the faults. It should be pointed out, however, that Henty-Creer's boat was practically fault-free. Of the four X-craft handed over to the attack crews outside Altenfjord, *X-5* was the only one without technical defects. That may have been pure luck. It may, too, have had something to do with Henty-Creer's obsession with technical perfection which he had learnt as a cameraman with Korda – the cameras had to be in perfect working order, as it cost money to keep film stars hanging around waiting for repairs to be made; and

(e) the anti-torpedo nets proved more formidable than intelligence reports had forecast. Instead of being single or double nets hanging down only enough to cover the battleship's hull and therefore leaving a gap underneath, they were triple nets hanging right down to the sea bed.

The chronology of events on the fateful morning of 22nd September was as follows (all times are GMT), based on the Admiralty reports and *Tirpitz*'s deck log:-

0400: *X-7* (Place) passed through boom defence gate of anti-submarine (outer) net, but became entangled in underwater obstruction.

0505: *X-6* (Cameron) passed through same gate.

0705: *X-6* got through boat entrance of anti-torpedo (inner) nets.

0710: *X-6* broke surface 80 yards abeam of *Tirpitz*. *X-7*, having freed herself from underwater obstruction, tried to burrow under anti-torpedo nets and became entangled again.

0720: *X-6* released its mines off port bow of *Tirpitz*.

0722: first depth charges and hand grenades dropped from German patrol boats.

0725-32: *X-6* surfaced. Cameron and crew surrendered.

0740: *X-7*, after getting through anti-torpedo nets, released its mines under or near *Tirpitz*, slid over top of anti-torpedo nets on surface in attempt to escape, was hit by machine-gun fire, dived, then ran into anti-torpedo nets from outside.

0812: British mines exploded. Shock waves freed *X-7* from net. Boat difficult to control and kept breaking surface. Each time hit by shellfire from *Tirpitz*.

0835: *X-7* surfaced outside anti-torpedo nets. Place got out onto pontoon, *X-7* sank.

0843: *X-5* surfaced outside anti-torpedo nets, about 500 yards from *Tirpitz*, was fired on and almost certainly hit by shells from *Tirpitz*.

1115: One member of *X-7*'s crew escaped from sunken boat using Davis escape equipment and was taken prisoner.

But what had Henty-Creer been doing while *X-6* and *X-7* were making their attacks? Did he make an attack? Nothing is known for certain, but sufficient research and exploration has now been done to probe every possible theory and to draw conclusions that are unchallengeable.

Several theories have been put forward:

Scenario No 1 assumes that for some reason or other, Henty-Creer decided, after clearing the anti-submarine nets, that he would not make an attack. After Cameron's *X-6* surfaced at 0710, all hell broke loose. From the ensuing explosions, which even Hudspeth in *X-10* heard seven miles from the scene, Henty-Creer would have known that the operation had been compromised. Perhaps this led him to decide that to attack in these circumstances would be futile and even suicidal. Perhaps his periscope or compass had failed. Perhaps he lost his nerve. But this hypothesis, along with the others just stated, has to be rejected, because if Henty-Creer had decided not to attack he would have beaten a retreat from the area long before 0843 or at least been preparing to retreat. In either case he would have jettisoned the mines to give him extra speed and manoeuverability during the retreat. But the sensitive mines did not explode when the Germans systematically depth-charged the fjord after the alarm was raised. And the underwater expeditions did not find any mines when they scoured the sea-bed in 1974 and again in 1976 – they could not possibly have missed metal objects as large as the mines. A two-ton mine cannot vanish unless it blows up, and no such explosion has ever been recorded in the area, apart from the ones that blew up alongside *Tirpitz* at 0812. The 2,400 pairs of eyes and ears aboard *Tirpitz* could not have failed to notice if it did, nor could the local Norwegians.

Scenario No 2 is that Henty-Creer was delayed after clearing the anti-submarine nets and before reaching the anti-torpedo nets. This delay may have been due to technical trouble with X-5, despite Henty-Creer's meticulous care with his boat. Or it may have been due to being caught in some underwater obstruction, as Place's X-7 was. As a result of this delay, says the scenario, Henty-Creer decided to wait until after 0900 so that he could attack during the second scheduled attacking period. From 0710 onwards he would have known that the attack had been compromised. From 0812 he would have known that *Tirpitz* had been attacked but had not sunk. He therefore decided that it was his duty to carry on with an attack, to succeed where the others had apparently failed, and regardless of the extreme hazards this would entail, he was manoeuvring to start the attack when he accidentally surfaced at 0843. But if this scenario is correct, his mines would have been attached to the boat when he surfaced at 0843. They must have behaved themselves during the 0812 explosions which sent shock waves strong enough to dislodge X-7 from the nets. They must have behaved themselves under the hail of fire from *Tirpitz* at 0843. They must have behaved themselves during the depth charging by German destroyers after 0843. But would they have behaved themselves? Their track record was far from impressive. They seemed to have a will of their own, as X-8 had demonstrated so dramatically. The possibility that X-5 still had its mines at 0843 seems very remote indeed.

Scenario No 3 contends that some time before 0812, perhaps even before 0710, he got through the anti-torpedo nets, released his mines under *Tirpitz*, then attempted to get away through or under the nets to the south of *Tirpitz*, just as X-7 did. He then experienced the same trouble with the nets as X-7, but managed to free his boat at about the same time as X-7 got free – if the shock waves could have freed X-7 they could also have freed X-5. In attempting to escape after clearing the nets, Henty-Creer ran into fresh water that streamed into the fjord about 500 yards from *Tirpitz*, lost his trim and was then fired on by *Tirpitz*. This scenario is almost identical with the experience of X-7. Why could it not also have been the actual experience of X-5, which surfaced only eight minutes after X-7 a few hundred yards from where X-7 surfaced? The combined evidence of underwater searches by the Germans in 1943 and 1944 and British underwater searches in 1974 and 1976 establishes that Henty-Creer did not jettison his mines in Kaafjord. He would not have attempted to escape from Kaafjord with his mines still attached. It is significant that Hudspeth jettisoned his mines before making his escape, but he had not been detected by the Germans and was by no means in the same desperate predicament at Henty-Creer. What, therefore, had Henty-Creer done with his mines? The only rational explanation is that he laid them under *Tirpitz* and that they exploded with the other mines at 0812.

Tirpitz's log states that the underwater explosions (that is, the mines) occurred at 0812, the first abreast of X turret, which the Germans call C turret, about six to eight yards from the ship's port side, and the second, about one tenth of a second later about 50 to 60 yards off the port bow in the position where *X-6* sank. The explosions off the port bow would have been caused by the two mines released by *X-6* and one of the mines released by *X-7*. The mines were closer to the bow at the time the midgets released them, but *Tirpitz* was winched away to starboard before the explosions took place. The explosion abreast of X turret would have been *X-7*'s other mine. These explosions were all on the port side of the ship, but were there any explosions on the starboard side?

Captain Hertzberg said he saw 'a huge explosion just below the foremost tower of *Tirpitz*'. Hertzberg's ship, the *Stamsund*, was on *Tirpitz*'s starboard side, about 400 yards away. It would not have been possible for Captain Hertzberg to have seen an explosion on *Tirpitz*'s port side unless a column of water had shot up at least above *Tirpitz*'s deck level. But *Tirpitz*'s log specifically states that there were no columns of water. This would indicate that what Captain Hertzberg saw was the disturbed water of an explosion on the starboard side.

Scenario No 4 accepts the theory that Henty-Creer laid his charges under *Tirpitz* and got back through the anti-torpedo nets. However, this scenario maintains that instead of starting his escape run down the fjord immediately, he deliberately waited around to see what happened. This is supported by two statements in the passage reports of two of the midgets. The passage report of *X-5*, after outlining the excellent condition of the boat when it was handed over to the attack crew, says:

Plan of attack: Lieutenant Henty-Creer's plan of attack was to spend the night of D+1 and D+2 in Brattholm Islands and to attack at first light on D+2. He intended to try and dive under the torpedo nets from the southward. After attacking, Lieutenant Henty-Creer intended to wait half way down Kaafjord in order to avoid being too close to *Scharnhorst* and *Tirpitz*.

(As it happened, *Scharnhorst* was away from her anchorage exercising. This would have affected Henty-Creer's decision on where to wait.) The report of passage of *X-8* which had jettisoned its charges during the passage states:

> It is of very great interest that the port charge should cause so much damage at a range of three and a half miles. This may well account for the failure of some of the first division to return, inasmuch as Lieutenant Henty-Creer in *X-5* intended to remain in Kaafjord after completing his attack. If he did this, his craft might well have been grievously damaged by the explosions of his own charges.

Thus, two separate independent reports stated that Henty-Creer intended to wait in Kaafjord after he completed his attack.

Why did he intend to wait? Why not get away while the going was good? There could be several reasons. First, that he wanted to be able to give Naval intelligence a first-hand report of the fate of *Tirpitz*, which would be more comprehensive than aerial reconnaissance reports. When he found that the 0812 explosions had not sunk her, he decided to wait in case there were further explosions from mines which had been set to fire later and had not been counter-mined. This would explain his presence when he accidentally surfaced at 0843.

Secondly, that he expected the explosions to sink *Tirpitz*, and in the ensuing chaos it would be easier to slip away unnoticed. The third reason is difficult for laymen and non-naval people to understand. It involves the almost unbelievably high morale of the Navy, particularly the submarine branch. It involves keen awareness of the Navy's tradition of audacity and boldness – the very spirit of Nelson. Henty-Creer, with his family background, would have been highly sensitive to this. He was superbly trained for the task and brimming with confidence. To him, staying back to watch the explosions would have been merely another phase of this intrepid exploit. It had probably never occurred to him that it might backfire and cause his death.

The damage to the Tirpitz

To relate the explosions to the damage done to *Tirpitz*, I sought the opinion of a recognised expert. I had been press attaché at the Australian Embassy, Bonn, before I retired from the diplomatic service in 1980, and speak German fluently. Through the Australian Embassy, I asked the German Ministry of Defence to nominate an explosives expert who could advise me on the *Tirpitz* operation. The Germans suggested Dr Guenther Sachsse, who had specialised in explosives after being awarded a doctorate in physics at Leipzig University in 1935. Dr Sachsse had gone straight from the university into the defence department and had concentrated on explosive techniques especially as applied to armour.

Together, Dr Sachsse and I studied *Tirpitz*'s log and her damage reports, as well as the Admiralty reports, following which Dr Sachsse authorised the following statement in his name:

'I have studied with great interest the log-book of the *Tirpitz* and the experts' assessment of the damage done to the ship by the British submarine attack on 22nd September 1943. I have also carefully examined the British Admiralty reports of the attack and the charts and diagrams attached to them.

'In forming my opinion on the cause of the damage to *Tirpitz*, I have taken into account the following factors:

'(a) the turrets were blown upwards but fell directly back on the ball bearings, indicating that the explosion came from directly under the ship. If the explosion had come only from the side of the ship, the turrets would have been thrust sideways and jammed outside the ball races;

'(b) the main turbines were blown upwards, tearing the bolts from their seating. The bolts were not sheered off, as they would have been if the impact of the explosion had come only from the side.

'The reports make it clear that when the mines exploded, three were about 50 to 60 yards abreast of the port bow of *Tirpitz*. A fourth was about five or six yards abeam of X turret, on the port quarter. In other words, none of the four mines known to have exploded was directly under *Tirpitz*.

'Each mine lay on the sea-bed, 40 yards from the surface. *Tirpitz* had a draught of 10 yards. The three mines abreast of *Tirpitz*'s bow would thus have been about 66 yards from the nearest part of the battleship's hull and the fourth mine about 33 yards.

'Damage to *Tirpitz*'s forward part was negligible, suggesting that at a range of about 66 yards the three mines were not effective to any major degree. Most of the damage was done to the after part of the ship, but one mine at a distance of 33 yards could not have done more damage than three mines at a distance of 66 yards.

'I have given considerable thought to the possibilities and consider it most unlikely that this one could have have caused such damage to the after part of the battleship. It is much more likely that another mine and perhaps another two mines exploded directly under the ship.'

In making his assessment, Dr Sachsse assumed that each mine exploded with 100 per cent detonation efficiency, thus providing the least favourable basis for the argument that Henty-Creer laid his charges under *Tirpitz*. Obviously if the mines exploded within the expected range of 25 to 65 per cent efficiency, there was an even stronger argument that more than four mines were laid.

What happened to Henty-Creer?

What was the ultimate fate of Henty-Creer, his boat and his crew – Sub-Lieutenant T.J. Nelson, RNVR, Sub-Lieutenant D.J. Malcolm, RNVR, and Engine Room Artificer R. Mortiboys, RN. As far as the Admiralty were concerned, they vanished at 0843 some 600 yards from *Tirpitz*, when the battleship opened fire on them. The Royal Navy made no effort to establish *X-5*'s fate, even after the war. Admittedly many ships and many sailors vanished without trace during the war. It would have been impossible to track down each of them.

But *X-5*'s case was different. The attack on *Tirpitz*, codenamed Operation Source, was hailed as worthy of the traditions of Drake and Nelson, one of the most audacious and gallant operations of the war. The deeds of the other two boats, *X-6* and *X-7*, and their crews were blazoned forth as feats of heroism of the highest order, as indeed they were. Cameron and Place were each awarded the Victoria Cross, as indeed they should have been. But Henty-Creer, the third of the intrepid trio, received no decoration at all – he was only mentioned in despatches. In other words, three captains took their boats in: two survived and were given the highest possible award for bravery: the third was killed and got no award. The one who made the greatest sacrifice – his life – received the least recognition. His name suffered an implied slur, because there was the sinister implication that for some reason or other he had failed in his mission.

There was a clear case for the Navy to try to find out after the war precisely what had happened to the third boat, if only to do justice to Henty-Creer. It would have involved no more than a search of the seabed of Kaafjord by Navy divers, some questioning of local Norwegian experts and consultation with an explosives expert. The Navy did none of these things, even though Royal Navy ships were in those waters after the war. They closed the file on Henty-Creer. It was left to his distraught family, his friends and admirers to find out.

Immediately after the war, Henty-Creer's mother advertised in Norwegian newspapers for witnesses to the *Tirpitz* attack, and obtained sworn affidavits from respected and responsible citizens. Then in 1950, she and her daughter Deirdre, taking turns at the wheel of their little car, bumped and skidded their way along the shocking war-torn roads of northern Norway to the scene of the *Tirpitz* attack and camped among the Lapps. They were following up the faint hope that Henty might have lost his memory and been living among the Lapps. In all they travelled 5,000 miles. They interviewed local Norwegians who had been in the area at the time and got more sworn statements.

In 1974, Henty's younger sister, Pamela, who had married Lieutenant-Colonel Gerard Mellor, went with him to Kaafjord with a team of divers from the British Sub-Aqua Club to search the sea bed. Pamela herself learnt to dive and joined in the grim, icy search. The expedition had with them the most modern and sophisticated technical equipment for tracing metal objects under the sea bed. Included in the team of sixteen were some of the most experienced divers in the world, mostly English, but some Australian and some American. They plotted the position of every object on the floor of Kaafjord, then dived to examine each piece. A second and even better equipped expedition made an even more thorough search in 1976.

Although the explorations and research do not establish with absolute certainty what happened to Henty-Creer after 0843 on 22nd September 1943, they do throw light on the theories that have been advanced over the years. The theories are:

(1) *'X-5' was sunk at 0843, about 600 yards from 'Tirpitz', by heavy gun-fire from 'Tirpitz' and depth charges from patrol boats and destroyers.*

This theory can be completely disregarded. The two British diving expeditions made a minute search of Kaafjord and found absolutely no trace of *X-5* or any part of her. They did find the bow section of a midget, but it proved to be Place's *X-7*. They also found many pieces of equipment – pistols, goggles, breathing apparatus, a Nescafé label, remains of tinned food, a telephone, a sextant (Place's), binoculars and a tidal almanac – but none of these were from *X-5*. All were in the bow section of *X-7*.

The expedition's leader, veteran diver Peter Cornish, told the London *Daily Mail* on 24th August 1974: 'We now know that, contrary to what was thought, *X-5* escaped from the fjord after the attack. We can say categorically that she is not inside Kaafjord.' After the 1976 expedition, he reported in a letter to Mrs Mellor:

> We never found *X-5*. I think I can now quite definitely say that she does not exist in Kaafjord at the 58-yard depth limit. Where she is, is now pure conjecture. She could be anywhere and it ceases to be a diving task. We tried very hard to find her but she is not there. [The 58-yard line stretches right across the entrance to Kaafjord from Altafjord.]

At 8.15 p.m. on 12th October 1943 *Tirpitz* had sent a signal to German High Command stating:

> Because of the current, heavy silting and the depth of water, the search of the third boat *(X-5)* had been abandoned without result. Destruction of the boat seems certain because of the numerous shell hits reported by impeccable witnesses, the depth-charging of the spot where the submarine dived, the boat's limited ability to withstand an attack, the long-lasting oil slick and the cessation of knocking from within the boat after 24 hours.

This does not constitute proof that *X-5* had been destroyed. It would have been almost impossible for German divers not to have found the wreckage of a boat about the size of a tram when they knew the precise spot where it should have been.

(2) *'X-5' got away, but foundered later about a mile away, where the Germans later found some wreckage.*

This is highly unlikely. The British underwater teams found the wrecks of many ships in the fjord, and the wreckage the Germans found could have been any of these. None of the wreckage found by the Germans was identified as coming from an X-craft other than

X-7 and no bodies or papers relating to *X-5* were ever found.

(3) *Henty made good his escape to a point much further down the fjords in a seaward direction.*

There is strong support for this theory, namely the evidence given to Mrs Henty-Creer by locals who lived in the area at the time of the attack. These statements were in the form of affidavits, with certified translations (See pages 189 to 194).

(4) *Henty-Creer, with his boat so badly damaged that it could not make the rendezvous area, scuttled it in deep water where the Germans could not salvage it, got ashore and made his way overland to Sweden or Russia.*

It is quite certain that Henty-Creer did not get to Sweden. The Swedes were friendly neutrals and would have handed him over to Britain or interned him until after the war. It is equally certain he could never have got to Russia. It would have involved a tramp of about 200 miles over some of the most inhospitable country in the world and he and his crew would have been in no position to make such a journey – they had very little food, no snow-boots and no equipment for crossing fjords and rivers or climbing mountains. Even if by some miracle they had got to Russia, there was no reason why the Russians would not have handed them back to Britain. In any case, in briefings before the operation, crews were advised to contact the Norwegian underground. None did.

(5) *Henty-Creer scuttled his boat, got ashore suffering from loss of memory and was adopted by the Lapps.*

This bizarre theory can be completely discounted. News of a drama of such rarity would have spread like wildfire among the tiny Lapp community, and when Mrs Henty-Creer and her daughter Deirdre went to Lappland, they could find no trace of such a story. It would by then have become a legend, known to all Lapps.

(6) *Henty-Creer scuttled his boat, got ashore, was captured by the Germans (perhaps handed over by pro-German Norwegians) and shot.*

This is a possibility. The German commandant controlling Norway, General von Falkenhorst, had issued orders that after interrogation, commandos were to be shot within 24 hours. Henty-Creer and his crew would certainly have qualified as commandos in German eyes. After the war General von Falkenhorst was executed as a war criminal, but nowhere in the German records is there any mention of the capture or shooting of Henty-Creer or any member of his crew. Although it is possible the Germans deliberately failed to record such an incident, that would not be consistent with their practice elsewhere in Europe. They kept meticulous records of events that they must have known would reflect badly on them, such as the minute details of gas-chamber atrocities. Also the Norwegian underground would have heard about it and reported it to Britain. No such reports were ever made.

(7) *Henty-Creer's boat sank to the bottom in deep water outside Kaafjord, taking all four of them to their deaths.*

This seems the most likely scenario. The boat had taken a fearful pounding after it broke surface at 0843. Apart from the shell hits claimed by *Tirpitz*, German patrol boats and the German destroyer *Z29* spent hours dropping depth charges all over Kaafjord. *Z29* also dropped fourteen patterns of five charges. Through their listening devices the Germans could hear knocking inside the submarine – obviously Henty-Creer and his crew trying to repair damage. It seems likely that *X-5* managed to creep away from the area, leaving the Germans to depth-charge empty water. However, the damage proved so serious that *X-5* foundered in water so deep that divers have since been unable to find her.

This is the only explanation that answers all the questions about *X-5*'s disappearance without trace.

Whatever the fate of *X-5*, one indisputable fact is that she took to their deaths four valiant young men who had willingly sacrificed their lives for their country. The question remains – was their sacrifice in vain? As far as the Royal Navy were concerned, it was. It wrote them off. The case for Henty-Creer having laid his mines under *Tirpitz* and escaping from the scene is overwhelming and it required only a little research, consultation with experts and some under-water exploration to establish it. Why, therefore, did the Royal Navy not do this? The files on the award of decorations for the *Tirpitz* operation show that the Navy was guilty of either rank indifference or callous negligence.

The Award That Was Never Made

The report to Admiralty from Admiral (Submarines), Rear Admiral C.B. Barry, of 8th November 1943, makes the following statements:

'Para 71: As *X-5*, *X-6* and *X-7* have not returned from the operation, it is impossible to trace their movements in their approach and subsequent attacks ...

'Para 71: That these three very gallant commanding officers succeeded in carrying out their intentions and pressing home their

Pam Mellor trains for sub-aqua diving under Reg Vallintine

Pam and Gerard Mellor at Kaafjord

At their request, Captain Roper, Chief Staff Officer, Submarines, came to see the Honours and Awards Committee and later sent them the attached x from the preliminary report on Operation "Source" in which X5, X6, and X7 carried out an attack on the TIRPITZ in Kaafjord.

2.   In the light of the report, citations and Rear Admiral (Submarine)'s very strong recommendation, the Committee consider that the award of the Victoria Cross to the Commanding Officers of all three of these craft would be fully justified.

3.   The following awards are therefore submitted:-

Victoria Cross.

Lieutenant Basil Charles Godfrey Place, D.S.C., R.N.
Lieutenant Donald Cameron, R.N.R.
Temporary Lieutenant Henty Henty-Creer, R.N.V.R. x

VICE-ADMIRAL
CHAIRMAN, HONOURS AND AWARDS COMMITTEE.
21st October, 1943.

I have discussed these proposals with Admiral the D.D.N.I and the C.O.S. to F.O.S. and am sure that the gallantry displayed by these three officers the award of the Victoria Cross.

I noted,
I suggest you might be to send for DNI concerning this.

fully concur with 2nd Sea Lord propose to approve 4/11

Concur

5/XI

x See da(s) for 3M055/6 of NID0050

Facsimile of the last page of the recommendation for the VC

attacks to the full, I have no doubt. But what difficulties and hazards they were called on to negotiate in the execution of the attack are not known. Nor is it known how some of them (if the German wireless broadcast is to be believed) came to be taken prisoner. It is certain that outstanding devotion to duty and courage of the highest order were displayed. The full story of this gallant attack must remain untold for the time being.

'Para 125: Finally I cannot fully express my admiration for the three commanding officers, Lieutenants H. Henty-Creer, RNVR, D. Cameron, RNR, and B.C.G. Place, DSC, RN, and the crews of *X-5*, *X-6* and *X-7*, who pressed home their attack and who failed to return. In the full knowledge of the hazards they were to encounter, these gallant crews penetrated into a heavily defended fleet anchorage. There, with cool courage and determination, and in spite of all the modern devices that ingenuity could devise for their detection and destruction, they pressed home their attack to the full and some must have penetrated inside the anti-torpedo net defences surrounding the *Tirpitz*. It is clear that courage and enterprise of the highest order in the close presence of the enemy were shown by these very gallant gentlemen, whose daring attack will surely go down in history as one of the most courageous acts of all time.'

This report of 8th November 1943, was published after the war in the *London Gazette* of 11th February 1948.

However, in the published version, some paragraphs of the original version were omitted. This is explained in the published version by a footnote, which says: 'The portion of this despatch, in which consideration is given to the extent of the success achieved on the information then available, has been omitted, in view of the Admiral (Submarines) later despatch of 2nd February 1944.' The omitted paragraphs contained the conclusions Admiral Barry had reached by 8th November 1943, 'based on photo-reconnaissance reports after the attack and on *X-10*'s report.' The conclusions were in the unpublished paragraph 134, which stated:

'(a) *X-5*, *X-6* and *X-7*, after being slipped from their towing submarines, at which time they were free from all defects, had no difficulty, in the absence of enemy patrols and the weather conditions at the time, in reaching the entrance to Kaafjord by the early hours of the morning of 22nd September;

'(b) that these three craft pressed home their attack and charges were released in close proximity to *Tirpitz* before 0800Z on 22nd September;

'(c) that the two heavy explosions heard by X-10 at 0830Z on 22nd September were the detonation of X-craft charges. (It is not possible to estimate the number of charges which detonated at this time. Countermining should have detonated all charges released in the vicinity.);

'(d) that the nine further heavy explosions heard by X-10 at about 0830Z may have been caused by enemy counter-measures. It must not be discounted that they may have been the detonation of further X-craft charges;

'(e) that Tirpitz has undoubtedly been damaged as a result of the attack. The extent of the damage cannot reliably be assessed from the evidence so far available, but from

'(i) The photo-reconnaissance showing the large amount of oil in Kaafjord round and extending from Tirpitz which was still present in large quantities 24 days after the attack, and

'(ii) the B2 report of 29th September, believed to be from a reliable source, that the ship was low in the water, had suffered much damage and that many had been killed by the explosion, it may well be that the damage is considerable;

'(f) that the denial by the enemy, before any claim had been made on our part, that any damage had been done as a result of the attack, followed, if any credence can be given to the Zurich report of 28th October, by a belated admission of damage, clearly indicates that the damage is more than the enemy first thought.'

The B2 report referred to in para 134 (e) (11) would have been an intelligence report from a Norwegian source. Its B2 rating gives it only limited credence. The Zurich radio news report mentioned in para 134 (f) stated that the German authorities had admitted damage to Tirpitz by midget submarines.

At this stage, Rear-Admiral Barry had already recommended to the Admiralty, on 14th October that all three submarine commanders – Place, Cameron and Henty-Creer – should be awarded the Victoria Cross.

Rear-Admiral Barry's memorandum to the Admiralty states:

I desire to submit for very early special recognition, the three missing commanding officers of X-craft.

There is no doubt in my mind that these three craft pressed home their attack to the full. In doing so they not only accepted all the dangers which human ingenuity could devise for the protection in harbour of vitally important fleet units.

The courage and utter contempt for danger and the qualities of inspiring leadership under these conditions of hardship and extreme hazard displayed by these officers are emphasised in the fact that none of them returned from their successful enterprise.

I consider that they all three merit the award of the highest decoration and I trust that the award of a Victoria Cross in each case will not be considered inappropriate.

The individual recommendation for Henty-Creer, states:

Lieutenant Henty-Creer, RNVR, was the commanding officer of His Majesty's Submarine *X-5* when she delivered an attack on the German battleship *Tirpitz* in Kaafjord on 22nd September 1943.

The attack necessitated penetrating the enemy's minefields, net defences, warning posts and gun positions. These were of an unknown extent, but must have been on a scale proportionate to the protection of the enemy's main units in one of his well established bases.

Cold-blooded coolness, determination and gallantry of the first order were essentials if this exceptionally hazardous attack was to be successful. It was also an outstandingly fine feat of leadership, required the highest degree of skill in handling the submarine and was performed by an officer who was for the first time in command of one of His Majesty's submarines.

I consider no award too high to recognise the outstanding bravery of this very gallant young leader in a successful pioneering and extremely hazardous operation.

The Admiralty's honours and awards committee agreed with the recommendations for all three officers on 21st October 1943. The Sea Lords also approved them and the First Lord of the Admiralty, Mr A.V. Alexander, approved them on 5th November 1943.

However, on 2nd February 1944. Rear Admiral Barry sent a memorandum to the First Lord, stating that further information on the *Tirpitz* attack had become available and that a fresh report on it had been prepared.

The memorandum added that it was now known that Place and Cameron were prisoners of war and recommended that the award of the Victoria Cross should still be made to them.

But in the case of Henty-Creer, a recommendation would be submitted 'at such time as a decision as to his ultimate fate has been taken,' said the memorandum.

The fresh report, dated 2nd February 1944, and classified as 'most secret' (see appendix A), outlines the exploits of Cameron and Place in much the same terms as the report published on 26th July 1945, after Cameron and Place returned from prisoner of war camp. It seems obvious that Cameron and Place had been able to smuggle reports back to the Admiralty. This would not have been terribly difficult. There were periodic exchanges of prisoners – most chronically ill cases – and they could have carried reports back with them. There were also periodic inspections of prisoner of war camps by officials of neutral countries and by International Red Cross representatives. It would have been possible to persuade one of these representatives to smuggle reports back. Also, the prisoners themselves could send back coded messages in letters. Cameron's wife once remarked that her husband's letters were sometimes rather strangely worded. Doubtless they contained messages which the Admiralty would have decoded before allowing the letter to be sent on to her. The first message to come through was relayed immediately by the Admiral (Submarines) to the First Lord of the Admiralty, Mr A.V. Alexander in a memorandum dated 6th January and marked 'most secret'. It said:

I know you would like to know straight away that we have just got the names of the six fellows in SOURCE who are prisoners of war. They consist of all the crew of *X-6* (Lieutenant D. Cameron, RNR) and two of *X-7* (Lieutenant B.C.G. Place, DSC, RN). Their names are:

Lieut D. Cameron, RNR
Sub-Lieut J.T. Lorimer, RNVR
Sub-Lieut R.H. Kendall, RNVR
E. Goddard C/MX. 89069 ERA 4
Lieut B.C.G. Place, DSC, RN
Sub-Lieut R. Aitken, RNVR

At the same time, through the Prisoner of War Code Organisation, we have got the start of the story. It reads as follows: 'Tirpitz' story, Series A; *X-6*, stick flooded, got through inner anti-torpedo net by boat gate.'

This dovetails in with the report received not long ago from a Norwegian merchant ship who said that in the early morning of 22nd September she sighted the dome of a midget submarine passing through the gate in *Tirpitz*'s anti-torpedo net, following in the wake of a cargo boat. It means, of course, that in spite of having his periscope out of action Cameron was undeterred and went through this small gate in the immediate face of the enemy, trimmed down, conning his boat through the scuttles of the dome; and he must have waited to dive until he was immediately on top of *Tirpitz*. This is one of the most daring things I have ever heard of and just true to Cameron's form.

I hope now that we shall gradually get the whole story through the Prisoner of War Code Organisation.

Other statements in the 2nd February report must have come from the Norwegian underground or moles in the German Navy, since they referred to events that happened after Cameron and Place were taken to prisoner of war camps.

Of Henty-Creer, the report of 2nd February says:

The information so far available is insufficient to show what part *X-5* took in the attack. Wreckage, presumably from this craft, was discovered by divers either on the day or the day after the attack, about one mile to seaward of *Tirpitz*'s berth, about half-way between *Tirpitz* and the entrance to Kaafjord. Some of the wreckage from this craft was also flung to the surface. No bodies or personal gear have been found and there is no knowledge of any survivors from *X-5*. *X-5* may therefore already have attacked and laid her charges and have been on the way out when depth-charged and destroyed, or she may have been waiting to attack at the next attacking period after 0900.

At the end of the report is a further reference to Henty-Creer: 'It is very much regretted that insufficient evidence is available to assess the part played by Lieutenant Henty-Creer: and the crew of *X-5*, but, from the position in which their craft was found, it is clear that they, too, showed courage of the highest order in penetrating the fleet anchorage and that they lived up to the highest traditions of the Service.'

(The report is incorrect in saying their craft was found. The Germans have never identified any wreckage as coming from *X-5*, and as we have seen earlier, underwater searches in 1974 and 1975 failed to discover any wreckage from *X-5*).

These then were the circumstances in which Henty-Creer's Victoria Cross was put on the back burner. That it has stayed there reflects little credit on the Royal Navy.

It could never be said that the Navy were given a chance to forget about Henty-Creer. His mother wielded no mean pen. She was a member of the Society of Women Writers and knew how to put a case with vigour and venom. She did not know that her son had been recommended for the Victoria Cross and that the recommendation had been approved and then withheld. She died in 1981 still not knowing.

After the awards were announced, she wrote to Rear-Admiral Barry, saying:

After your kind letters about Henty, I find it impossible to believe that his part in the *Tirpitz* exploit should have been so lightly assessed that his name appears under a 'mention' in *The Times*.

Those three boats took equal risks and had an equal part to play in the attack and even if it were possible to say what explosion maimed *Tirpitz*, the honours should surely have been equally divided, as were all the hazards over a long and terrible period. Cameron, Henty-Creer and Place shared in the exploit from beginning to end and I can only suspect some very queer influences and cross-currents have been allowed to cloud the issue if that inadequate mention in despatches is your final word. I feel sure you have heard from Captain Ingram how willingly and with what zeal my son submitted himself to every experiment, and I know you realise that no decorations have been so hardly earned nor men asked to go through such prolonged hell as he and his fellow adventurers on and before the exploit.

I have noted in various naval lists how everyone who had any part in the planning of the attack and all those who participated in any way, as well as those who were merely on the fringe of the affair, have been suitably decorated. No-one would question the rightness of those awards, but no-one will fail to ask why Henty-Creer, as a midget commander who had been presumed to have died in the face of the enemy in what you yourself have described in a letter to me as the bravest deed in history, should not only have been denied his rightful honour but cruelly passed over as expendable.

It is obvious that only two Victoria Crosses were allotted for the task and Captain Phillips confirmed this but that such a policy could be carried out in such an exceptional exploit is deeply shocking. That ruling might be applicable to conventional naval attacks when by custom so many medals are allotted to each ship but cannot be appropriate to a unique and experimental action such as this, when all were volunteers and the Royal Navy were represented by one man, Godfrey Place.

Had your son been in Henty-Creer's shoes, I feel sure you would have felt as I do and I write to ask that the subject be reviewed and the dead given equal honours with the living. Alive or dead, he did not do less than Cameron and Place.

Rear Admiral Barry replied by hand on 15th August 1944:

Thank you for your letter of 8th August. I am here (in Hampshire) on sick leave, having been taken ill with some slight heart trouble while on a trip abroad.

The facts of the case are these. There is positive evidence that Cameron and Place completed their attacks and caused all the damage. There is no (underlined) evidence that Henty-Creer did, although we know he did all he could possibly do. But it is only (underlined) on positive deeds that is it possible to give the highest award and so I fear it is really impossible in your son's case. Had he been alive there is no doubt he would have had a higher award than a 'mention' but by the rules that govern the various decorations, only (underlined) a VC or a 'mention' can be awarded posthumously. You must be alive to receive any of the other decorations that would apply.

So you see, their Lordships had no other choice than to award your son a posthumous 'mention'. As you know, I could not possibly have more admiration for your son than I have and I would have given a lot to have seen him given a higher decoration, but you will see from the frank description of the case I have given that there was no alternative. These are the facts of the case which will and must stand. You know how I feel for you in your great loss.

Rear Admiral Barry was right in saying there was no alternative award that could have been given to Henty-Creer, even though he may have been wrong in saying he could not have been awarded the Victoria Cross. The rules for the award for the VC state quite clearly that it is the only battle distinction that can be awarded after death. Nearly half of the 87 Victoria Crosses awarded during the 1939-45 war were posthumous. Queen Victoria instituted the award in a warrant dated 29th January 1856, which stipulates that all members of the services are on an equal footing for eligibility. Neither rank, nor long service, nor wounds, nor any other circumstance were to be the basis for the award.

The one criterion was to be 'the merit of conspicuous bravery.' The medal itself bears the simple inscription 'For Valour.' Nowhere is success in an operation mentioned as a criterion.

Henty-Creer obviously had 'the merit of conspicuous bravery' on 5th November 1943, when the First Lord of the Admiralty had agreed to him being awarded the VC and if all three submarine commanders had been killed, all three would have been awarded posthumous Victoria Crosses. But two survived. The one who was killed did not get the VC but the two who survived did. Rear Admiral Barry's memorandum of 8th November 1943 states in paragraph 125 (see page 210): '... some must have penetrated inside the anti-torpedo nets ...' This memorandum was written three days after the First Lord of the Admiralty had approved the award of the Victoria Cross to all three commanders. Since Rear Admiral Barry did not say all must have penetrated the anti-torpedo nets, the clear inference is that entry into Kaafjord was sufficient to justify the award of a VC. This would be reasonable enough, because to enter Kaafjord meant having crossed the minefield at the entrance to Altenfjord, run the gauntlet of patrol boats in Altenfjord and penetrated the anti-submarine nets at the mouth of Kaafjord.

The decision to withold Henty-Creer's VC while awarding it to both Cameron and Place was made on 2nd February 1944, after Cameron and Place smuggled messages back giving an account of what they had done. The honesty of the reports they sent back is not in dispute. Certainly they knew where they had placed their own mines. They knew, too, that there had been explosions under or near *Tirpitz* at 0812. They also knew that Henty-Creer had surfaced at 0843 and been fired on. But they did not know and could not possibly have known whether Henty-Creer had placed his mines under *Tirpitz*. There is evidence that the Navy assumed that Henty-Creer had not in fact placed his mines under *Tirpitz*. In a letter to Mrs Henty-Creer dated 25th June 1945, in response to yet another letter urging justice for her son, Rear Admiral Barry's successor, Rear Admiral Creasy, stated:

The return of Lieutenants Cameron and Place from captivity in Germany brought us the first positive account of the X-craft attack on *Tirpitz* and it is from Lieutenant Cameron's account that we obtained our first news of the fate of your son's X-craft. By his story, he was on deck on board *Tirpitz* when your son's ship was sighted closing to attack. *Tirpitz* opened fire and he believed that the craft suffered a direct hit and then disappeared.

That is all that is known at present. From this evidence there is good reason to believe that your son and his crew were killed outright in their gallant attempt to close the enemy. Enquiries are, however, still being pursued and I have little doubt that we shall obtain more information from German sources in due course.

The use of the phrases 'closing to attack' and 'attempt to close the enemy' indicates quite clearly that Cameron assumed Henty-Creer had not made his attack when he surfaced at 0843. This assumption was not justified by the information available to either Cameron or Place. Neither of them could possibly have known whether Henty-Creer was closing to attack or trying to escape. It is understandable that in the dramatic circumstances of 0843 Cameron could make a false assumption, possibly based on the course X-5 seemed to be taking when she surfaced. She was on *Tirpitz*'s starboard beam, on a parallel but opposite heading. The course, however, is of no significance as the boat was obviously out of control – it would not have surfaced otherwise. But Cameron's assumption seems to have stuck and been accepted at least by Rear Admiral Creasy and possibly the entire Navy.

But what if, contrary to all the evidence, Henty-Creer was in fact closing to the attack? It is significant that Cameron thought so highly of him that he assumed he was closing to attack. Would that not have been an even braver feat than Cameron's or Place's? Here was a man closing to attack against the greatest odds imaginable – a tiny, fragile 35-ton craft pitted against the world's greatest 43,000-ton battleship. Here was a man still closing to attack when he knew full well that the Germans had been alerted and would take the most desperate measures to protect their most powerful battleship. Could anything be braver? Could anything warrant the Victoria Cross more than that?

Rear Admiral Creasy's letter states that enquiries were still to be pursued, but if they were, the Admiralty has made an excellent job of concealing it, for there is no reference to it in any of the Admiralty files now open to public scrutiny. The German sources available to the Admiralty immediately after the war would have been at least as informative as those available now – more so since a greater number of eye-witnesses and members of the *Tirpitz*'s crew could then have been interviewed. The Admiralty took possession of *Tirpitz*'s log – there is a large stamp on the front cover of the log stating exactly that. The log was presumably scrutinised by Admiralty experts. It seems extraordinary that they did not notice the technical clues contained in the log and in the damage reports – that the bolts securing the turbines had been torn off and not sheared off, and that the turrets had fallen back on their ball bearings, indicating that the explosive force had come from directly underneath, which in turn indicated that somebody other than Place or Cameron had laid mines directly under the ship, since their mines were laid on the port side of the ship.

It seems extraordinary, too, that the Royal Navy did not send divers down to find wreckage from X-5 or to see whether any mines were still lying in the sea-bed of Kaafjord. Admittedly, all thoughts were on getting back to peacetime living after Japan surrendered. But those circumstances did not absolve the Navy from its obligation – indeed its undertaking – to probe the X-5 mystery. There was a commitment to solve it, contained in Rear Admiral Barry's memorandum of 2nd February 1944, in which he stated that in the case of Henty-Creer, recommendation concerning the award of the Victoria Cross would be submitted 'at such time as a decision as to his ultimate fate has been taken'. No decision has ever been taken. No effort to establish his ultimate fate has been made by the Navy.

This was no routine wartime operation, carried out by ordinary servicemen. It was unique in the proud thousand-year history of the Royal Navy. It was carried out by men who were not ordinary mortals. They were a special breed, all volunteers, all pioneers willing to be guinea-pigs in the hazardous and exacting task of developing a new weapon, all willing to put it to the ultimate test in the most perilous circumstances.

Six of the twelve men who took part in the final attack lost their lives. All three submarine commanders were recommended for the highest possible award for valour. Their bravery was equal, but their luck was not. Two survived and received the Victoria Cross. The third did not, because more evidence was needed.

The evidence has been there all the time.

Appendix A

Admiralty Reports on Operation Source

FROM...CAPTAIN (S) TWELFTH SUBMARINE FLOTILLA, H.M.S. VARBEL.

DATE...6th October 1943.   No.3074/413.

TO...ADMIRAL (SUBMARINES), NORTHWAYS, LONDON, N.W.3.

The following report covers the passage of "X.5" from Port H.H.Z. to the vicinity of ALTEN FIORD.

2. *Crew*: The passage crew consisted of: Lieutenant J.V. TERRY-LLOYD, S.A.N.F.; Leading Seaman B. ELEMENT, C/JX.159787; Stoker N. GARRITTY, C/KX.132683.

3. *Brief Summary*: The passage in tow of H.M. Submarine "THRASHER" took place without major incident and the operational crew transferred to "X.5" near position YY during the night of 19th-20th September (Day D-1). During the night of 15th-16th September, whilst on passage in calm weather, the operational Commanding Officer and E.R.A. visited the craft by means of the rubber dinghy to carry out an inspection and to remedy a leak in the hydroplane gland, returning to "THRASHER" on completion.

4. *Weather*: Weather was good up to 17th September (D-3) when it became rough. On 18th September it blew a gale and bad weather continued until the afternoon of 19th September (D-1) when it became calm. On the night of 19th September it was very calm with a long low swell.

5. *Towing Hawser*: The towing hawser was completely satisfactory throughout the tow. When slipping, however, the Hezlet Rod jambed in "X.5"'s bull-ring and two of the operational crew had to go on to the casing and hammer it free.

6. *Telephone Communication*: Telephone communication between "X.5" and "THRASHER" remained excellent until 18th September (D-2) when it became very faint. Communication failed at 2000 that evening. The cause of failure was probably due to a defective telephone (and spare phone) in "X.5", but this is not certain.

7. *Method of Communication with Telephones out of Action*:
    A.   *Submerged*: (i) A "surfacing course for the day" was arranged. When "THRASHER" turned to this course it implied that "X.5" had freedom to surface.

(ii) "THRASHER" used S.U.E.'s to order "X.5" to surface.

The above arrangements proved entirely satisfactory.

B.   *On the surface*: V/S communication by Heatier lamp was satisfactory provided that "X.5" had an officer on the casing.

8. *Trim and Control*: During the first part of the passage, when "THRASHER" was proceeding on the surface, "X.5" had the following Trim:

Fore Trim	400 lbs.
Compensating Tank	1800 lbs.
After Trim	500 lbs.

When "THRASHER" commenced her passage dived (0400 on 13th September) "X.5" adjusted her Trim as follows:

Fore Trim	400 lbs.
Compensating Tank	800 lbs.
After Trim	500 lbs.

Thereafter "X.5" maintained the same Trim, flooding Q. tank and holding the craft down on the hydroplanes whenever "THRASHER" was on the surface.

9. With Trim as above no difficulty was experienced in controlling "X.5". Some difficulty was experienced in getting a good Trim when "THRASHER" commenced her submerged passage, and whilst doing so "X.5" sank slowly to 120 feet. This was the only occasion on which she went below 100 feet.

10. *Change of Crews*: The change-over of crews was carried out in good weather on the night of 19th-20th September near position YY. The drill was carried out exactly as practised and no difficulty of any sort was experienced. The operational crew took a supply of fresh bread and a little rum with them in the dinghy.

11. *Habitability*: The longest dive carried out was nine hours.

The normal drill carried out on passage was to surface for ventilation and to run the engine for ten minutes three times during the 24 hours, plus one period nightly of two hours spent in charging. Thus the normal period between ventilating was six hours.

No oxygen or Protosorb was used and no inconvenience was experienced.

Sweating of the hull was considerable, but excessive dampness was eliminated by the Watchkeeper constantly wiping over the hull within his reach and by having a thorough wipe down every two hours.

12. *Watchkeeping Routine*: The crew kept two hour watches throughout the passage, except when the craft was on the surface when the whole crew remained closed up. This was found to be satisfactory.

13. *Compass Equipment*: The Brown's Gyro Compass and repeater worked satisfactorily.

The Automatic Helsman was not used.

The Direction Indicator was not used.

The Magnetic Compass behaved satisfactorily and was raised and checked on each occasion of surfacing. D.G. current was not switched on.

14. *Log*: The Log was not used.

15. *Periscopes*: Periscopes were satisfactory.

A 20 volt lighting lamp on a wandering lead was used as a Drying Lamp and kept switched on in the Attack. Periscope well throughout the passage.

16. *Side Charges*: No trouble was experienced with the side charges, which had been set to Two Hours before leaving harbour.

17. *Hull Defects*:

(i) *Hydroplane Gland*. This developed a bad leak at 1950 on 15th September and packing with grease did not effect a satisfactory cure. As the weather was calm the craft E.R.A. was ferried over from "THRESHER" in the rubber dinghy and remedied the defect in one hour. The operational Commanding Officer took this opportunity to visit "X.5'" and inspect the craft.

(ii) Both periscope glands and the Towing Clench pad-piece leaked slightly throughout the passage.

18. *Mechanical Defects*: The Heads developed an undetermined defect on 18th September (D-2). This defect was still extant when the operational crew took over, but the E.R.A. stated that he could deal with it without difficulty.

19. *Electrical Defects*: Insulation on the periscope hoisting motor became low on passage and a slight earth developed on the loads due to damp. The circuit and motor were dried out by means of the footwarmer and there were no electrical defects extant when the Operational Crew took over.

20. *Victualling*:

A. *Food*. The quantity of food carried was greatly in excess of requirements.

B. *Fresh Water*. The consumption of Fresh water was amazingly low, totalling only 6 gallons for the whole of the nine day passage. Consumption could have been less, but for the last three days of the passage fresh water was being used for cooking in lieu of salt water in order to try and get rid of it!

21. *Operational Crew*:

(i) *Final Instructions*. The final instructions passed to the Operational Crew were "Target Plan 4! Scharnhorst may be exercising, in which case all "X" craft are to attack Tirpitz."

(ii) *Plan of Attack*. Lieutenant Henty-Creer's plan of attack was to spend the night of D+2 in BRATHOLM ISLANDS and to attack at first light on D+2. He intended to try and dive under the Torpedo Nets from the southward.

After attacking Lieutenant Henty-Creer intended to wait half way down KAA FIORD in order to avoid being too close to SCHARNHORST and TIRPITZ.

(iii) *Slipping*. "X.5" was slipped at 2000 on D day (20th September) one mile 310° from position S A.

(iv) *Morale*. The Operational Crew were in the highest spirits when taking over "X.5".

222 The Mystery of X-5

22. *Maintenance*: A list of Maintenance Routine carried out on passage is attached (Appendix No. 1) This list of routines was rigidly adhered to.

23. *Ratings of Passage Crew*: Lieutenant Terry-Lloyd reported most enthusiastically on the behavior and efficiency of his crew and stated that if he ever undertook another passage he would wish to have the same crew.

24. *Remarks on the Passage and Performance of the Crew*:

There is no doubt that Lieutenant Terry-Lloyd and his crew acquitted themselves admirably. The craft was unquestionably turned over to the Operational Crew in almost perfect condition and this was largely due to the strict carrying out of Maintenance Routine. To carry out the 24 and 48 hour routines during the latter portion of the passage must have called for an appreciable effort and the condition in which the craft was turned over reflects very great credit on Lieutenant Terry-Lloyd and his crew.

25. A patrol report from "THRASHER" has not yet been received, but from a verbal interview at Kames Bay, it appears that "X.5" was slipped in the right place at the correct time and speed on passage was 10 knots. When the "X" craft and operational crew proceeded to the attack, the "X" craft was in very good mechanical form and the crew in the best of spirits. With the exception of one incident, namely the hydroplane gland, the passage was made "according to the book."

From...ADMIRAL (SUBMARINES), Northways, London, N.W.3.

Date...2nd February, 1944.   No. 192/SIL04351.

To...SECRETARY OF THE ADMIRALTY
      (Copy to:
         Commander-in-Chief Home Fleet).

With reference to my No. 2347/SIL04351 of 8th November 1943 be pleased to lay before the Lords Commissioners of the Admiralty the following further report on operations by X craft against the German Main Units (Operation SOURCE).

2. From information supplied by the Director of Naval Intelligence, it is now possible to reconstruct the attacks carried out by His Majesty's midget submarines on the battleship TIRPITZ on 22nd September 1943, and to make some assessment of the damage sustained by this ship as the result of the attacks.

3. Three X craft, X.5 (Lieutenant H. HENTY-CREER, R.N.V.R.), X.6 (Lieutenant D. CAMERON, R.N.R.), and X.7 (Lieutenant B.C.G. PLACE, D.S.C., R.N.), failed to return as a result of the operation, and, while it was known that one or more of these craft succeeded in carrying out a successful attack on TIRPITZ, at the time of my previous report no information was available as to which of the craft had succeeded in this

daring attack, nor were there details of how it was accomplished.

4. It was the intention of each of the three commanding officers, all of whom had TIRPITZ as their target, to close the entrance to KAAFIORD at first light on the morning of the 22nd September, having fully charged up their batteries during the night. Having negotiated the A/S net at the entrance to KAAFIORD they would then attack TIRPITZ by passing under the A/T nets surrounding her, drop their charges set to detonate at approximately 0830 G.M.T., and then retire to seaward, hoping to be well clear of the fiord by the time of the explosion.

5. P.R.U. photographs had shown that the close A/T nets around TIRPITZ consisted of three lines of nets. The flotation indicated that the nets were for anti torpedo protection, and it was considered unlikely that they would reach the bottom in the depth of water, twenty fathoms. In fact it was estimated they would only extend downward about fifty feet.

6. From the information received, the following is a reconstruction of the movements of these three X craft in their attacks, as far as is known at present.

X.6 (Lieutenant D. CAMERON, R.N.R.)

7. At some time unknown the periscope of X.6 became flooded. The Commanding Officer was therefore completely "blind" with no means of conning his craft when dived.

Having negotiated the A/S net at the entrance to KAAFIORD and entered the fleet anchorage, Lieutenant CAMERON, with a complete disregard for danger, proceeded on the surface in broad daylight astern of a small coaster through the boat gate entrance in the nets, situated only two hundred yards away from TIRPITZ.

After passing safely through the entrance on the surface, X.6 dived, and steering straight for TIRPITZ, proceeded to attack.

8. X.6 had, however, been sighted from TIRPITZ off the port bow, as Lieutenant CAMERON must have realised that he would be. The time of sighting is reported as 0800 G.M.T. The alarm was raised, and hand grenades thrown at him from the deck of TIRPITZ, and a pinnace started to drop depth charges.

9. Lieutenant CAMERON continued to carry out his attack, and on passing under the bridge of TIRPITZ, he probably released one charge. Having passed under the ship, X.6 failed to turn to starboard in time, and ran into the nets on the starboard side of TIRPITZ before he could carry out the second run of the attack.

Finding himself foul of the nets CAMERON was obliged to go astern to clear himself, and in so doing went astern into TIRPITZ.

10. Lieutenant CAMERON, realising that he had been sighted, released his second charge, and surfaced his ship almost alongside the TIRPITZ. CAMERON then saw all his crew safely out of the craft before scuttling her.

Lieutenant CAMERON and the crew of X.6 (Sub Lieutenant J.T. LORIMER, R.N.V.R., Sub Lieutenant R.H. KENDALL, R.N.V.R.,

E.R.A.4 E. GODDARD, C/MX.89069) were picked up and taken on board, the time being then approximately 0805.

X.7 (Lieutenant B.C.G. PLACE, D.S.C., R.N.)
11. In the meantime X.7 had also attacked.

Proceeding according to plan, X.7 penetrated safely past the A/S nets at the entrance to the fiord, and Lieutenant PLACE decided to attack by passing under the close A/T nets.

Here he met unexpected difficulties, for instead of the expected gap under the nets he found that they extended to 120 feet, which, with a depth of water of only twenty fathoms, meant that the nets were almost, if not quite, down to the bottom.

Lieutenant PLACE was not to be deterred, and at the third attempt he managed to worm X.7 along the bottom under the nets to carry out a successful attack, dropping one charge under the funnel and one under the after turret.

12. In negotiating the A/T nets he was able to ascertain its details which were fine wire 4" mesh – a most formidable type of A/T net.

13. Having completed the attack undetected, PLACE was then faced with the difficulty of getting through under the nets again to make his escape. To add to his difficulties the tide was by then ebbing, which meant that the nets would be even nearer to the bottom than before.

Once again X.7 found herself foul of the nets; and as they were only 170 feet from TIRPITZ and from the line on which the charges had been laid, and with the time for the explosion drawing nearer every minute, the feelings of those on board while they were struggling to extricate themselves may well be imagined.

As it was, X.7 cleared the nets with only a few minutes to spare, as at 0830, when the explosion took place, X.7 was only some 400 yards to seaward of the nets.

Even at this distance the force of the explosion so damaged X.7 that she was put out of action, and Lieutenant PLACE decided to remain on the bottom for the next hour and await events.

Around about 0930, when depth charges were being dropped indiscriminately about the fiord, although they did no damage to the craft, Lieutenant PLACE realised that owing to damage sustained nothing further could be done and that the operation was by now compromised. He therefore decided to surface the craft to give his crew the chance of escaping.

X.7 was brought to the surface, but was immediately hotly engaged by gunfire and sunk. PLACE was left swimming when she sank, and Lieutenant AITKEN, the 3rd Officer, escaped by using D.S.E.A.

Of the other two members of the crew nothing is known, nor, apparently, have their bodies been discovered.

X.5 (Lieutenant H. HENTY-CREER, R.N.V.R.)
14. The information so far available is insufficient to show what part X.5 took in the attack.

Wreckage, presumably from this craft, was discovered by divers either on the day of or the day after the attack, about one mile to seaward of TIRPITZ' berth, about halfway between TIRPITZ and the entrance to KAAFIORD. Some of the wreckage from this craft was also flung to the surface.

No bodies or personal gear have been found, and there is no knowledge of any survivors from X.5.

15. X.5 may therefore already have attacked and laid her charges and have been on the way out when depth-charged and destroyed, or she may have been waiting to attack at the next attacking period after 0900.

The Explosion

16. At 0830 a huge explosion took place, and TIRPITZ was heaved five or six feet out of the water before settling down again. The explosion extended from amidships to aft, and a large column of water was flung into the air on the port side. The explosion appeared to be caused by two or more simultaneous detonations.

Members of the ship's company on deck aft were hurled into the air, and several casualties resulted. The ship took on an immediate list to port of about five degrees; this was later adjusted by trimming. All the ship's lights failed temporarily, but lighting was soon restored. Oil fuel started to leak out from amidships.

17. Panic seems to have reigned for a short time immediately following the explosion.

More than 100 casualties were caused by panic firing, and destroyers and small craft went into action up and down the fiord.

18. Meanwhile, the survivors from X.6 were being questioned by officers from the Admiral's staff.

Prior to the explosion it is reported that the crew of X.6 were seen looking anxiously at their watches.

They were joined about an hour after the explosion by Lieutenants PLACE and AITKEN from X.7.

All of them were well treated and given hot coffee and schnapps.

Everyone on board TIRPITZ expressed great admiration of their bravery.

Salvage of craft.

19. X.7 was salvaged eight days after the attack, being recovered from a position some 400 yards off the starboard bow of TIRPITZ, outside the nets. She was taken in tow and beached in KAAFIORD. The whole of her bow was missing, probably caused either by the gunfire or depth charges.

Although divers made a thorough search, no signs of X.6 could be found inside the A/T nets, and it is presumed that she was totally destroyed by the explosion, which must have taken place very close to where she was scuttled.

The wreckage of, presumably, X.5 was found, as previously stated, about a mile to seaward from TIRPITZ, but there was insufficient of the craft left to make salvage worth while.

Damage to TIRPITZ

20. The explosive charges (of which at least two detonated, the others possibly being destroyed by their close proximity to each other) badly buckled and possibly holed the hull in two places, causing flooding and loss of oil fuel.

The harbour boiler and turbo generator rooms were affected, with consequent effect on the lighting system and forward turret machinery.

Damage aft was also caused, and one report states that all four turrets were damaged, the guns put out of alignment, and that the shaft tunnel was stove in in parts.

A further report assesses the damage as follows:
"The upper bridge is awry and the guns aft rendered useless. On the after deck, especially, there are large dents and bulges. The engine room area was particularly badly damaged."
The fact that a large proportion of the 50-60 victims among the crew, who were later buried on Norwegian soil, were engineers, stokers, etc., seems to confirm this last statement.

21. Several hundreds of workmen have been transported to ALTENFIORD to effect temporary repairs with the aid of repair ships which have been seen alongside, and there is a repair hut on deck, and welding is in progress. On 10th January 1944 a 100 ft. raft with superstructure had been towed alongside, apparently for divers.

22. It would appear conclusive that TIRPITZ has sustained considerable damage to the hull, machinery and armament as a result of the attack. Temporary repairs are still being carried out in KAAFIORD which it is estimated will not be completed for a further one or two months, and the ship cannot be made effective for prolonged operations without docking at a German port.

23. With the full story of this very gallant attack now unfolded, my admiration for Lieutenant D. CAMERON and Lieutenant PLACE and their crews is beyond words. I take special note of the complete disregard for danger in the immediate vicinity of the enemy shown by Lieutenant CAMERON in taking X.6 through the net defences in broad daylight on the surface with the full knowledge that he must be sighted, and the cool and calculated way in which he carried out his attack and then ensured the safety of his crew.

Lieutenant PLACE, undaunted by encountering unexpected obstacles, carried on with cool determination to worm X.7 under the nets under the very eyes of those on board TIRPITZ to carry out his successful attack. Then, when again caught in the nets and with the time drawing close for the explosion to take place, rather than bring his craft to the surface and so compromise the operation and thereby jeopardise the chances of other craft who might be attacking, he proceeded coolly to extricate his craft and remained submerged after the explosion, although fully aware of the danger, for sufficient time to ensure that other craft who might be attacking were clear of the area.

The acts of these two officers speak for themselves. They can seldom have been surpassed in the history of the Royal Navy. The proceedings of the two Commanding Officers would have been of no avail had they not been supported by the undaunted spirit of their crews.

24. It is very much regretted that insufficient evidence is available to assess the part played by Lieutenant HENTY CREER and the crew of X.5, but, from the position in which their craft was found, it is clear that they, too, showed courage of the highest order in penetrating the fleet anchorage, and that they lived up to the highest traditions of the Service.

25. The foregoing is compiled from intelligence, which has been received from Director of Naval Intelligence.

(Sd.) C.B. BARRY
Rear Admiral.

The above documents and those in Appendix B are Crown Copyright and are reproduced by kind permission of the Public Record Office. Appendix A is PRO Ref Adm 199/888 57451; Appendix B Adm 199/888 57104.

APPENDIX B

Recommendations for Honours and Awards – Operation Source

From...ADMIRAL (SUBMARINES)
Northways, London, N.W.3

Date...15th October, 1943. No. 2185/SM.04351.

To...SECRETARY OF THE ADMIRALTY.

Sufficient information is now available to assess as successful, the operation culminating in the attack on TIRPITZ in KAAFIORD on 2nd September, 1943.

2. A summary of the operation has been sent direct to the Admiralty. Full reports are in course of preparation and when these are completed a comprehensive list of officers and men recommended for recognition will be forwarded.

3. In the meantime I desire to submit for very early and special recognition, the three missing Commanding Officers of 'X' craft, and Forms X are attached accordingly.

4. There is no doubt in my mind that these three craft pressed home their attack to the full. In doing so they not only accepted all the dangers inherent in such vessels but they faced also every possible hazard which human ingenuity could devise for the protection in harbour of vitally important fleets units.

5. The courage and utter contempt for danger, and the qualities of inspiring leadership under these conditions of hardship and extreme hazard displayed by these officers are emphasised in the fact that none of them returned from their successful enterprise.

6. I consider that they all three fully merit the award of the highest decoration and I trust that the award of a Victoria Cross in each case will not be considered inappropriate.

Rear Admiral.

FORM X Ship etc. *H.M. SUBMARINE "X—5"* Date *14th OCTOBER 1943*

Recommendation for Decoration or Mention in Despatches

Full Surname .... *HENTY-CREER* ....

Full Christian names .... *HENTY* ....

Rank or Rating *TEMP/LIEUT.* Official No ....
(state whether R.N.,
R.N.R., R.N.V.R. .. *RNVR* . and Port Division ....
R.N.P.S., R.A.N., etc.

Whether already decorated .... *NO* ....
(Give particulars and date of
publication of award). ....

Whether already mentioned in .... *NO* ....
Despatches. (Give date of
publication of award). ....

Whether previously recommended. .... *NO* ....

If so, give particulars. ....

Whether now recommended for award of Decoration. .... *YES* ....

   or Mention in Despatches ....

Whether recommendation is for Immediate .... *YES* ....

Operational or Periodic Award .... *OPERATIONAL* ....

Description of Services for which
Officer or Man is recommended.

Lieutenant HENTY-CREER, R.N.V.R. was the Comanding Officer of His Majesty's Submarine "X.5", when she delivered an attack on the German Battleship TIRPITZ in KAAFIORD on 22nd September, 1943.

The attack necessitated penetrating the enemy's mine-fields, net defences, warning posts and gun positions. These were of an unknown extent, but must have been on a scale proportionate to the protection of the enemy's main units in one of his well established bases.

Cold blooded coolness, determination and gallantry of the first order were essentials if this exceptionally hazardous attack was to be successful. It was also an outstandingly fine feat of leadership, required the highest degree of skill in handling the submarine, and was performed by an oficer who was for the first time in command of one of his Majesty's Submarines.

I consider no award too high to recognise the outstanding bravery of this very gallant young leader in a successful, pioneering and extremely hazardous operation.

BANKS
20.9.43.   [Signed] CAPTAIN (S).
xxxxx xxxxxxx xxxxxxxx

Remarks of Commander-in-Chief etc.

I fully concur in this recommendation. The attack carried out by this officer called for that cold, calculating and deliberate courage which is the highest of all forms of physical bravery.

C.B. Barry
Admiral (Submarines)

H. & A. 1028/43.

At their request, Captain Roper, Chief Staff Officer, Submarines, came to see the Honours and Awards Committee and later sent them the attached extract from the preliminary report on Operation "Source" in which X5, X6, and X7 carried out an attack on the TIRPITZ in Kaafjord.
2. In the light of the report, citations and Rear Admiral (Submarine)'s very strong recommendation, the Committee consider that the award of the Victoria Cross to the Commanding Officers of all three of these craft would be fully justified.
3. The following awards are therefore submitted:

Victoria Cross.

Lieutenant Basil Charles Godfrey Place, D.S.C., R.N.
Lieutenant Donald Cameron, R.N.R.
Temporary Lieutenant Henty Henty-Creer, R.N.V.R.

(Signed) VICE-ADMIRAL
CHAIRMAN, HONOURS AND AWARDS COMMITTEE.
21st October, 1943.

[Handwritten addenda in order of appearance]
I have discussed these proposals with Admiral —, the D.D.N.I. and the C.O.s. to F0.S. and am convinced that the gallantry displayed by these three officers, merits the award of the Victoria Cross. [initialled, 26/10]

1st Lord
I suggest you might like to send for D.N.I. concerning this.

Fully concur with 2nd Sea Lord. Propose to approve. [initialled, 4/11]

Concur. [initialled, A.V.A., 5/XI]

FURTHER RECOMMENDATIONS FOR HONOURS AND AWARDS – OPERATION SOURCE

From...ADMIRAL (SUBMARINES), Northways, London, N.W.3.

Date...2nd February, 1944.   No. SM.055/6.

To...NAVAL SECRETARY TO FIRST LORD.

With reference to my 2185/SW.04351 of 15th October, 1943, addressed to the Secretary of the Admiralty, further information is now available on the successful attack carried out on TIRPITZ in KAAFIORD on 22nd September, 1943. A copy of my further report on this action is attached (192/SM.04351 of 2nd February, 1944.).

2. It is now known that of the three commanding officers missing from this operation, Lieutenant D. CAMERON, R.N.R., and Lieutenant B.C.G. PLACE, D.S.C., R.N., are prisoners of war in enemy hands. Lieutenant H. HENTY-CREER is still missing.

3. It is therefore desired to re-submit the names of Lieutenant CAMERON and Lieutenant PLACE for the award of the Victoria Cross in the light of the attached report. Copies of the original forms X are enclosed.

4. A recommendation with regard to Lieutenant HENTY-CREER will be submitted at such time as a decision as to his ultimate fate is taken.

5. A suggested citation is attached. It is suggested that this should be shown to Director of Naval Intelligence before publication.

6. I suggest that the awards to the two commanding officers and their crews be published simultaneously.

C.B. Barry
Rear Admiral.

Appendix C
Forebears of H. Henty-Creer

JOHN AND ROBERTO DE			
HENTYE	c	1327	All of
WALTER HENTY	c	1379	Wivelsfield,
THOMAS HENTY	c	1524	Sussex
JOHN HENTY	-	Susan	
of Burwash 1620-1729			
JOHN HENTY	-	Sarah Crossingham	
		Of Littlehampton	
		1689-1750	
WILLIAM HENTY	-	Jane Olliver	
of Littlehampton		of Kingston	
1731-1796			
THOMAS HENTY	-	Frances Elizabeth Hopkins	
of West Tarring and			
Field Place, Worthing			
1775-1839			
STEPHEN GEORGE HENTY	-	Jane Pace of Swan River	
of Portland, Australia		(a cousin for Captain Cook)	
RICHMOND HENRY	-	Agnes Reid	
of Portland, Australia		(Grand-daughter of Sir Edwin	
		Sandys)	
ERNEST GEORGE HENTY	-	Katherine Cobham (a descendant	
		of the medieval Cobhams, one of	
		whom was married to Humphrey	
		Duke of Gloucester, brother of	
		Henry V	
EULALIE HENTY	-	Reginald Creer (a descendant of	
		Lord Ferrers who married Mary	
		Plantagenet daughter of John of	
		Gaunt	
DEIRDRE, HENTY, PAMELA	-	Pamela Married Lt. Col. Gerard	
		Mellor	

NOTE:
Eleanor Cobham and Humphrey Duke of Gloucester had a palace called Placienta, which in later years became the Royal Naval College Greenwich where in due course young Henty was to attend classes.

Bibliography

Above Us The Waves, by C.E.T. Warren and James Benson (Harrap, 1953)

Sink the Tirpitz, by Leonce Peillard (Jonathan Cape, 1965, English translation)

The Tirpitz, by David Woodward (Wiliam Kimber, 1953)

Against all Odds, by Thomas Gallagher (Macdonald, 1971)

Menace, by Ludovic Kennedy, (Sidgewick and Jackson, 1979)

Index